IN DEFENCE OF PHILANT

IN DEFENCE OF PHILANTHROPY

BETH BREEZE

agenda
publishing

To my parents, Sue and John Egan, for showing me the importance of living a generous life

First published in 2021 by Agenda Publishing

Agenda Publishing Limited
The Core
Bath Lane
Newcastle Helix
Newcastle upon Tyne
NE4 5TF
www.agendapub.com

ISBN 978-1-78821-260-1 (hardcover)
ISBN 978-1-78821-261-8 (paperback)

British Library Cataloguing-in-Publication Data
A catalogue record for this book is available from the British Library

Typeset by Newgen Publishing UK
Printed and bound in the UK by 4edge Limited, UK

CONTENTS

ACKNOWLEDGEMENTS

To all my students, past and present, for their thoughtful views which often challenged me, and helped refine my position. Particular thanks to Jayne Lacny for drawing my attention to the effigy-burning incident mentioned in Chapter 2.

To my colleagues in the emerging field of philanthropic studies, especially Ali Body, Calum Carmichael, Elizabeth Dale, Angie Eikenberry, Chris Einolf, Jurgen Grotz, Tobias Jung, Michael Moody, Susan Phillips, Wendy Scaife, Krystian Seibert, Gen Shaker, Ben Soskis and Pamala Wiepking. Many of us disagree with each other about all manner of things, and this book is what I have taken away from my conversations with them rather than any reflection of their opinions. But our shared belief in the need for a better, more nuanced understanding of philanthropy makes my job a joy. I feel particularly lucky to have met and learned from some of the longstanding names in my field such as Helmut Anheier, Dwight Burlingame, Hugh Cunningham, Peter Halfpenny, Jenny Harrow, John Mohan, Colin Rochester and Adrian Sargeant. I strive to be as generous with my time and as supportive of the next generation of philanthropy scholars as they have been to me.

To the many people who work in the philanthropy sector who have taken the time to share their insights over the years, especially David Carrington, Philippa Charles, Amanda Delew, Dan Fluskey, Gloria Jollymore, Charles Keidan, Bridget Kohner, Theresa Lloyd, Louise Morris, Paul Ramsbottom, Jeff Shears, Paul Streets, Marc Whitmore and Karl Wilding. Particular thanks to Rhodri Davies for years of inspiration in his work encouraging philanthropy through the Charities Aid Foundation, and for drawing my attention to the Venerable Bede example and the John Boyle O'Reilly poem.

To my colleagues at the University of Kent: Ben Baumber Geiger, Heejung Chung and Tina Haux who provided encouragement and "get on with its" in equal measure. And to all my friends who are essential at the best of times and even more so when writing a book during lockdown. Special shout outs to Pam Allen, Jacqueline Cassidy, Lucy Hayward, Jane Milton, Caroline Shield, Catherine Stihler, Terese Weiss, Jennifer Weston and Liz Wilson.

ACKNOWLEDGEMENTS

A number of people kindly took the time to read the draft manuscript and offer incredibly helpful comments: Calum, Chris, Rhodri, Michael and Theresa I will long be in your debt, and of course any remaining errors are mine alone.

Finally thank you to my husband Michael and our children Beren and Merrie who have yet again put up with mum being an inattentive grump for longer than is reasonable.

INTRODUCTION: THE NEED FOR A DEFENCE OF PHILANTHROPY

This book begins with a story about a philanthropist, some prostitutes and a proposition involving massage. It also begins with a warning not to jump to conclusions.

The philanthropist David Gold asked Shelagh O'Connor, director of the New Horizon Youth Centre in the King's Cross area of London, "What's the one thing you most want to do but you think no one will ever be willing to fund?" New Horizon was founded in 1967 to work with young people involved in substance misuse and, like all organizations dealing with social problems, its mission has evolved over time in response to the changing needs of the people it serves: 16–24 year-olds with no one else to turn to. By the turn of the millennium, when this conversation took place, the centre's staff had noticed a sharp rise in vulnerable young women on their patch being drawn into sex work, many of them fresh off the train at King's Cross station. The centre's daily programme of free meals, bathing facilities and help with education, employment and self-development was freely available to these young women but they did not come through the door. "What I'd like to offer", said Shelagh, "is something to make them feel good about themselves, to remind them of their self-worth and potential. With more self-esteem they might decide to seek help and choose a different future, but there's to be no strings attached – no pressure to attend our programme in return." And so David agreed to fund free reflexology, aromatherapy and massage sessions for these young women, many of whom – as wise Shelagh predicted – rediscovered their confidence and desire to move on, with the help of the centre's more traditional youth services.

Another big donor whose giving style challenges common assumptions about philanthropic aims and motivations is Dame Stephanie Shirley, known as "Steve", a name she started using when her attempts to succeed in the male-dominated world of computer programming were stymied by people refusing to take meetings with a woman. Her company, Xansa, peaked at over £2 billion sometime after she retired in 1993. In common with many wealthy people, she has amassed a large private art collection. When the time came to find a new home for her £3 million collection of contemporary art, craft and design the obvious choice would have been to donate it to a prestigious art gallery in London in return for the elite association and immortality offered by a naming opportunity on the gallery walls (a practice referred to by some as the "graffiti of the rich"). But instead of promoting her taste and name in front of fellow members of the elite, Dame Stephanie always had in mind a quite different milieu. Between 1998 and 2012 she donated a collection for the enjoyment of patients receiving treatment in National Health Service hospitals, and for the children and young adults with severe autism attending the residential Priors Court school in the small market town of Thatcham, 50 miles west of London. The residential school, founded in 1998 with a £30 million donation from Steve's eponymous Shirley Foundation, operates on the premise that a welcoming and uplifting environment is essential to help residents meet their full potential. Filling the buildings with striking art and dotting the grounds with eye-catching sculptures is consistent with evidence-based approaches to meeting the needs of young people with complex needs, even if it inconveniently contradicts sweeping assertions about how rich donors are meant to behave in terms of flaunting their wealth and taste in front of others.

A third example of non-self-aggrandizing philanthropy illustrates how a relatively small sum of money can have an enormously positive outcome. British-born Peter Lampl amassed a large enough fortune in New York through management consultancy and private equity to be able to retire in his mid-forties. Soon after returning to the UK, intending to focus on his golf game, disaster struck the small Scottish town of Dunblane when a man in legal possession of a small arsenal of guns walked into the primary school and killed 16 small children and their teacher. Hearing that bereaved parents were organizing an effort to ban private ownership of handguns, Lampl offered to underwrite the costs of the campaign. Within months the legislation was passed, and thankfully there has never been a school shooting in the UK since. One of the founders of the Gun Control Network, Gill Marshall-Andrews, explains:

> Peter Lampl had seen me on the television talking about the need for gun control. He got in touch and invited us to his house where he gave us our first ever financial donation of £5,000. It was a statement of support that he was behind us, which was just as important as the money. Since then, we have received core funding from other supporters but Peter was the first, the kickstarter, the enabler who got something started and helped us to leverage in more money. I think that's a very important kind of philanthropist. Once the issue had gone off the radar his help was just as important. Peter has been a very good friend to the Gun Control Network for many years. We know we can always go to him for support if we really need it.

The experience also changed Lampl, whose golf handicap never did improve: "It changed my life too, as the amazing success of the campaign encouraged me to devote myself to philanthropy."

This book is written for those who have never met, or heard of, philanthropists such as David Gold, Steve Shirley and Peter Lampl, and who are becoming increasingly suspicious that big giving is at best a ruse, and at worst does more harm than good. Criticism of philanthropy and philanthropists is not new, but it has become increasingly vocal and is now a mainstream position that has so far encountered little pushback. The purpose of this book is to offer an alternative take. In the following pages we will meet many donors who are quietly and effectively using their resources to make things better for other people, who share Gold's explanation of why they give, "It's just about being a reasonable human being", who relate to Dame Stephanie's comment, "I like to have something worthwhile to get up for each morning" and who got into giving, as did Lampl, by simply "asking how I could help".

But my intention is not to throw more anecdata at a topic already mired in personal observations masquerading as facts. I have no wish to join an unproductive game of philanthropy tennis where I volley back the name of a "good" rich donor in response to an egregious case of philanthropic bad behaviour. Each example knocked back over the net simply illustrates that, like any aspect of social life and human action, philanthropy can be done well or badly in terms of intentions, actions and outcomes. There is little to be gained by a reductive debate that either sentimentalizes or demonizes philanthropy, other than promoting pseudo-proof of pre-existing opinions. What is needed is a more nuanced understanding of what philanthropy is, what role it plays in contemporary society and why it is therefore worth defending and even – not always, but more often than detractors would allow – worth celebrating.

Nuance is not easy to convey when debates are routinely fought and won on character-restricted social media platforms. As you have picked up this book, you are clearly willing to engage with an extended discussion but here is the nutshell, 19-word version of my argument: hyper-criticism of philanthropy underestimates the complexity of its target and carries the significant risk of curtailing the philanthropic impulse.

The need for a defence of philanthropy

I began writing this book after becoming increasingly concerned by the mainstreaming of attacks on "big giving" that were being lapped up by a receptive public and risked undermining the legitimacy of all kinds of philanthropy which includes smaller and bigger monetary gifts. I think the anti-philanthropy arguments need a response to avoid deterring future donors, demoralizing those currently funding and working in philanthropy and – most crucially –harming beneficiaries if the result is less funding for the nonprofits they rely on. Almost all of us benefit in some way from the work of organizations that need philanthropic gifts of all sizes to fund activity that benefits everyone, such as stronger communities, a cleaner environment, medical advances and new knowledge. But the highest price for a world with less philanthropy would be paid by those facing the toughest life circumstance, who fall through whatever public sector safety net exists, cannot purchase necessities in the market and are most reliant on the kindness of strangers.

I was also prompted to write this book because having worked in, and studied, philanthropy all of my adult life, I did not recognize critics' blanket depictions of big givers and I objected to the attribution of mendacious motives, especially in the absence of any rigorous empirical study of the donor community. I was exasperated by the focus on analysis over solutions in the most well-known critiques. Perhaps most pettily, but nonetheless true, I feel my blood pressure rise each time critics present their arguments as novel insights for a world that is unwittingly engaged in a self-destructive love affair with wealthy donors. There is little to be said, either in favour or against philanthropy, that has not already been said numerous times before. The lack of novelty in articulating concerns about philanthropy does not mean they are not worth saying, but the big reveal is redundant. It is obviously true that there is scope for structural and individual improvement in the design, implementation and outcomes of philanthropic action. It is also the case that the importance of philanthropic action for individual, social and environmental well-being means these positions are worth restating and re-examining. I have no quarrel with useful critique, even those that involve retreading worn paths, if it leads to new knowledge, better practice and social improvement. The challenge in saying something useful about philanthropy is to navigate well clear of both repetitive carping and mindless cheerleading.

Somewhat to my – pleasant – surprise, the route I took to formulate this defence of philanthropy covers much shared ground with those who initially seemed to be on a different path. Perhaps that should not have been a surprise – anyone who dedicates their time to thinking and writing about philanthropy is demonstrating a commitment and care for that activity that is probably shared with fellow travellers. So let me say from the outset that I agree with much of what is being said by those who have chosen to emphasize the known problems of philanthropy. These are largely undeniable, longstanding and worth attention. But the question I am tackling comes from a different angle: do the problematic aspects of philanthropy make it an illegitimate or an improvable activity? If the former (as suggested by hyper-critics), what is the plan to fill the gap left by the withdrawal of private initiatives for the public good? If the latter (which I hold), how can we more carefully draw attention to the paradoxes and problems with philanthropy in a manner that avoids harming, however unintentionally, the overall greater good?

My interest in understanding philanthropy

Having pre-empted my conclusion, let me jump back to the beginning. My introduction to big philanthropy was as a 16-year-old beneficiary. After a working-class childhood in the north of England, I took an overnight leap into the world of privilege and cosmopolitanism when I was awarded a scholarship, funded by Maurice Laing of the British construction dynasty, to attend the United World College of the Atlantic, an internationalist boarding school perched on the side of a cliff in South Wales. A few years later, private giving from the St Andrews Society of Philadelphia enabled me to spend the junior year of college at the University of Pennsylvania in the United States. After I'd been working in the charity sector for a few years, a bursary funded by the high street retailer Marks & Spencer paid half the fees for my postgraduate degree at the London School of Economics. Receiving so much support from different types of philanthropy – from an individual major donor, a group of ex-pats and a corporate donor – has made me grateful and also curious about why and how private money is used for the benefit of unknown others. Answers started to emerge while studying gift-giving within a first degree in social anthropology, and voluntary sector studies at master's level; then ten years in practice as a fundraiser and charity manager brought theory to life and eventually prompted a move into academia so that I could focus on understanding the meaning, purpose and practice of philanthropy.

The empirical basis for this book

My curiosity to understand the part of society that lies beyond government and the market – philanthropically funded goods and services provided by individuals and nonprofit organizations that variously challenge, complement and cooperate with those better-known sectors – has continued unabated. Over the past 15 years I have conducted a large number of studies focused on the world of philanthropy, including many different types of donors, the organizations and individuals they fund, those who mediate and support these relationships, and – crucially – the end beneficiaries. I have interviewed over 100 major donors, many of whom have made single gifts worth £1 million or more, and have interacted with significant philanthropists on four continents. I have conducted multiple studies of people donating at all monetary levels, including those who choose to give alone and collectively, anonymously and publicly. I have studied those who ask for charitable gifts as both professional and voluntary fundraisers, as well as those responsible for managing and leading nonprofit organizations, those working to support and advise donors and those running the umbrella bodies (known as "peak bodies" in some countries) that organize, regulate and advocate for the philanthropy sector. I have conducted research with individuals and organizations in receipt of philanthropic funding to better understand their perspective and reflections on the merits and problems of philanthropy. I have analysed media coverage of philanthropy and philanthropists, and have also commissioned major surveys to measure public opinion and attitudes on a range of issues relating to charity and philanthropy. This body of evidence – covering data from interviews, focus groups, large surveys and secondary data analysis – provides the empirical basis for this book.

Criticism and generalized cynicism affect both askers and givers

My extensive experience of meeting the array of people who populate the philanthropy sector has also spurred the writing of this book because the need for a defence of philanthropy has become more and more apparent during my research career. Many fundraisers, whose job is to raise the money to keep good causes in business, are increasingly telling me that the largest challenge they face is not a lack of donors with the capacity or willingness to give, nor that old chestnut "compassion fatigue", but rather the constant running down of wealthy givers that they feel deters potential donors from sticking their head above the philanthropic parapet. This is confirmed by colleagues who work as philanthropy advisers, one of whom told me: "The mindless media sledging of the wealthy and the successful is the biggest single deterrent to increased giving." Many major donors have shared with me their exasperation at how they are perceived and treated in public discourse, with one saying: "You need to accept from the outset that whatever you do will be rubbished … If you are giving money away people will think you are doing it for self-aggrandisement" (quoted in Breeze & Lloyd 2013: 158). My analysis of media coverage shows these concerns are grounded in experience because major philanthropic announcements routinely generate cynical reactions in print, broadcast and social media.

The normalization of attacks on big donors, the belief that this is making the onerous task of fundraising even more difficult, and the growing sense among philanthropists that they are more likely to get shot down in flames rather than ride high on public approval, all combined to strengthen my desire to investigate and understand this phenomenon. While my research is focused on the UK, this is clearly a broader phenomenon. The head of a major US foundation, while visiting the UK in early 2020, told us that "the discourse has become toxic", and US philanthropy expert Phil Buchanan argues that giving among the biggest donors worldwide may fall as their charitable efforts are increasingly caricatured as self-protective ruses (Buchanan 2019b). The real-world impact of the problematizing of philanthropy is also noted by George McCully, founder of the US-based Catalogue of Philanthropy initiative that seeks to promote and encourage private giving: "A major inhibiting factor on charitable giving is that the donating public doesn't know or understand the first thing about philanthropy, and they tend to regard it with scepticism because what they do know, from the media, and ultimately the profession itself (including scholars) has been generally negative" (McCully 2012: 14).

As I make clear throughout this book, I am not against greater scholarly attention being paid to the role, purpose and outcomes of philanthropy. How could I be when that is my job as a philanthropy academic? But I firmly believe that useful critique is not the same as generalized cynicism: the former can make philanthropy more effective, the latter risks eroding cultural norms about helping others and creating a perverse incentive to hoard rather than share wealth.

A justification of the role, purpose and value of philanthropy in society

Having watched this situation develop throughout my career, and having realized that simply griping about it with like-minded colleagues was not the most productive use of breath, I found inspiration in the work of the political theorist Bernard Crick. Crick describes his masterly book *In Defence of Politics* as an attempt "to justify politics in plain words by saying what it is" in a way that avoided "the capacity of academics to over-complicate things". Replacing the word "politics" with "philanthropy" in the following extract from Crick, summarizes my own intentions: "[This is] simply an attempt, inspired by seeing a fairly obvious impatience with politics in the new nations of the world, and provoked by a personal dislike of exhortation and mere cant about 'the ideals of freedom', to describe what in fact are the minimum benefits of politics as an activity" (Crick 2000: 2).

"Impatience" and "mere cant" may sound like irritations that one ought to be able to rise above, but I believe the current wave of hyper-criticism of philanthropy cannot be safely ignored without putting the viability of many good causes at risk, for the simple reason that donors and doers are co-dependent. Doers need funding and big donors can only make things happen by funding people and organizations who share their goals. Despite the concept of philanthropy bringing to mind large piles of money, philanthropic success requires far more than deep pockets – it relies on the right combination of money, action and know-how, as explained by Thomas Tierney and Joel Fleishman in their book *Give Smart*: "For the most part, donors' results depend on the performance of the nonprofits they support. Great giving is not accomplished in a vacuum … very little can be accomplished by individuals acting on their own, even when those individuals are extraordinarily wealthy. The grander your ambitions, the more certain it is that success will require working with and through a broad range of other players" (Tierney & Fleishman 2011: 15).

Despite the reality that donors and nonprofit actors need each other, philanthropists are usually discussed as if they exist in splendid isolation with the agency to make things happen – for good or bad – without the involvement or collaboration of anyone else. Yet, as Trevor Pears, a leading UK philanthropist, told me: "We are *part* of the sector, not *apart* from the sector. I'm interested in going on a journey with those we fund. I wish there could be less 'them and us' language, because what's happening is we are coming together to make something happen."

This sentiment is echoed by many other major UK donors. To take two examples from either end of the generational spectrum, Fran Perrin, a member of the fifth generation of the philanthropic Sainsbury family, says, "I'm always very clear that the ideas and the change don't come from me – I'm just fortunate enough to support some extraordinary individuals and projects", while self-made almost-centenarian Jack Petchey, who has given away over £100 million to causes supporting children and young people, told me: "I often say it's like a dance, and we need a partner!" If one-half of a quick step or waltz is repeatedly told their presence is problematic, they may well decide to leave the floor and the dance cannot continue. The mutual interdependency in philanthropy is equally crucial – we cannot knock donors without also affecting those they fund. If we choose to damage the reputation of philanthropy then we need to accept that this might impede the flow of funds to good causes.

The problematic consequence of damaging the reputation of philanthropy

Why does hyper-criticism of philanthropy affect fundraising success? The status and reputation of philanthropy matter because fundraisers rely on private giving being generally perceived as a commendable, admired act. The body of knowledge on the drivers of philanthropy finds that people give because they are in pursuit of a positive reputation or psychological benefits (such as feeling good about oneself), have a desire to be altruistic or to implement prosocial values, have a belief that gifts will make a positive difference, and calculate that the costs of giving are outweighed by the benefits (Bekkers & Wiepking 2011). Generalized attacks on philanthropy, and the insistence that donors should be critiqued and never cheered, undermine these drivers of philanthropic giving. The demand side of nonprofit economics is also damaged when philanthropy is viewed with suspicion because those seeking funding for good causes have little else to give supporters other than thanks and praise. Charity law forbids any substantive benefits for donors, including interference in the political process, so fundraisers must rely on the power of intangible extrinsic and intrinsic motivations, such as public recognition and cultivating the "warm glow" and "helpers' high" that drives much other-oriented behaviour (Andreoni 1990; Luks 1988).

Unlike strategies available in the other sectors, where governments are funded by compulsory tax payments and markets function because paying customers have needs and wants, charity fundraisers can only *ask* for gifts. That fundraising "ask" includes a promise – usually implicit – of social approval, enhanced reputation and personal fulfilment from making something good happen. The critics of philanthropy call that promise into question, and therefore make successful fundraising harder. As Louise Morris, a major donor fundraising specialist, told me:

> I worry that incessant criticism of big donations will affect charities' ability to raise money. Major donor fundraising only works when it has the backing of the whole organization and when fundraisers are motivated to ask for those large gifts. When colleagues and trustees hear these criticisms and echo them internally, that makes it much more difficult for their fundraising staff to have the confidence and drive to raise the money to keep the organization going.

Fundraising success relies on many factors and it is not possible to isolate the effect of attacks on philanthropy, but we do not normally expect negative feedback to encourage a behaviour, quite the opposite. The problematic consequences of knocking big donors feel real for charities and nonprofit organizations, which cannot run on goodwill alone. Even without the aggravating factors of recessions and a global pandemic, most exist in a fragile state lacking secure, long-term core funding that is memorably described as the "nonprofit starvation cycle" (Gregory & Howard 2009). This fragility is longstanding but is being exacerbated by critiques of philanthropy that have reached new heights in terms of scale and volume, with a troubling lack of potential solutions on offer.

Three critiques of philanthropy

There are different types of criticisms of philanthropy doing the rounds which share some features in common such as an assumption that philanthropy has been overcelebrated and avoided censure to date, and concern about nefarious philanthropic motivations and the existence of benefits gained by donors that require urgent exposure to an unwitting public. Yet historic studies highlight that suspicion of the motives of philanthropists has been evident for many centuries, and that donors have long stood accused (fairly or not) of being motivated by factors such as "love of power, ostentation, and vanity" along with a desire to save their own soul and to spite their descendants (Cunningham 2020: 141).

All critiques of philanthropy are obviously not the same, and there are overlaps in the critiques that I identify and discuss in this book, but it is possible to identify three sets of fundamental criticisms which together create an existential challenge to the fundamental legitimacy and propriety of philanthropy. The first set of critiques is focused on the "how" of philanthropy, asking whether its existence and current methods, especially the in perpetuity foundation form, entrench unequal power structures, exacerbate inequality and undermine the democratic principle of political equality at the ballot box and subsequent law-making. In essence this critique is concerned that giving is undemocratic. The second set of critiques is largely focused on the "what" of philanthropy, questioning whether the causes chosen and prioritized by donors are the "correct" ones, the basis on which philanthropic spending should be allocated and how "better" giving decision can be made. In essence this set of critiques is concerned that giving is misdirected. The third set of critiques concerns populist denunciations of big giving. As with populism in general, these arguments provide simple explanations for complex phenomena. They are almost exclusively focused on the "why" of philanthropy – scrutinizing the motivations of donors and the benefits that may be gained, as well as making ad hominem attacks on individual philanthropists. In essence this set of critiques holds that giving is really taking in disguise.

These three types of critique that form the focus of this book which I call, respectively, the "academic", "insider" and "populist" critiques, have been in currency for a very long time but have never before landed so successfully. I am interested in why that is. Why are we so receptive to hyper-criticism of philanthropy now? There is nothing new about pointing out problems with major individual and institutional giving, nor have the specific charges laid at philanthropy's door evolved significantly over time. The very fact that critics believe themselves to be saying something novel is enough to arouse sociological interest in their assumptions and motivations.

When and why did hyper-criticism of philanthropy emerge?

The New York correspondent for *The Times* penned an article in which he noted: "This donation is believed to be the largest single sum ever given for a philanthropic purpose. One looks almost in vain, however, for an expression of enthusiasm or gratitude in the newspapers." While these words could apply to any recent major philanthropic pledge, they were written in 1907 (*Times* 1907) in reaction to John D. Rockefeller's gift of $32 million to the General Education Board which, among other positive outcomes, funded schools for African American children and helped eradicate hookworm in the southern states. When Rockefeller and his fellow turn-of-the-last-century titan, Andrew Carnegie, first proposed establishing enduring charitable trusts, a congressional committee described the idea as "a menace to the future political and economic welfare of the nation", and a decade later, in 1917, Rockefeller wrote to his father that, "I feel more and more that to increase the funds of the foundation is not going to meet with general popular approval" (Karl & Katz 1987: 13). As these examples show, philanthropists have attracted popular criticism for as long as they have impinged on the public consciousness, and big donors have long been well aware of this fact. Nonprofit staff and volunteers share this longstanding awareness – the "insider critique" articulated from within the realm of voluntary action has been vocal since at least the mid-nineteenth century, and academic critiques have existed since philanthropy became a serious focus of study in the 1970s. But the widespread reach and acceptance of hyper-criticism of big donors is a relatively recent phenomenon. Three well-received books published between 2015 and 2018 enumerated many serious problems with "big philanthropy" and resonated with a public that had become increasingly suspicious of the motivations and actions of elites. Their arguments are encapsulated in their titles: *No Such Thing as a Free Gift: The Gates Foundation and the Price of Philanthropy* by Linsey McGoey (2015); *Just Giving: Why Philanthropy Is Failing Democracy and How It Can Do Better* by Rob Reich (2018); and *Winners Take All: The Elite Charade of Changing the World* by Anand Giridharadas (2018).

The mainstreaming of anti-philanthropy sentiment was cemented in January 2019, when the Dutch historian Rutger Bregman told those gathered for the World Economic Forum in Davos to "Stop talking about stupid philanthropy schemes … we should be talking about taxes, taxes, taxes." These words were uttered in relation to a question about what corporations should do to prevent a social backlash, but Bregman's incisive intervention struck a global chord relating to *all* private giving and fuelled the assertion that philanthropy per se is emblematic of, or even a cause of, unjustified inequalities, rather than a force for good that is capable of easing inequality as, it became apparent, the public and policymakers expect. Despite there being no historical precedent or legal obligation for philanthropy to be solely directed at this one goal, and despite decades of much better-funded government action also failing to halt the tide of growing inequality, philanthropy's reputation has largely foundered as a result of being tried and found wanting on this charge.

The successful landing of hyper-criticism

The emergence and successful "landing" of hyper-criticism of philanthropy at the start of the twenty-first century needs to be placed in a wider societal context, much of it flowing from the fallout of the banking crisis in 2008: an understandable concern at growing inequality in society, widespread distrust of elites and experts, and polarized politics. The rising tide of populism, which offers simple answers to complex issues, makes the problematic framing of philanthropy seem like common sense by obscuring subtle but significant differences in the problems of wealth accumulation and wealth distribution, and elides the distinction between meeting fiscal responsibilities (i.e. paying compulsory tax) and the "social responsibilities of wealth" (i.e. making voluntary donations). Populists understand philanthropy as simply a fig leaf to cover the iniquities of an affluent, global elite, or a plaything that can be used to fund vanity projects such as buildings bearing donors' names. Critics also often oppose tax relief on charitable donations by casting it as an indefensible public subsidy for private passions, rather than a successful "nudge" to encourage generosity over yacht-buying.

Counterposing private generosity with state-organized welfare is a common tactic of those who find large-scale giving problematic, yet it is a false opposition. It is perfectly possible to support high levels of progressive taxation and the urgent need to close tax loopholes, while also advocating for the merits of widespread, effective philanthropy. There is also no basis for conflating concerns about the wealthy being taxed too lightly with beliefs that philanthropy occurs to distract observers from noticing, or caring about, the amount of tax paid by rich donors. The case for higher taxation of the rich has been made repeatedly by many of today's most high-profile donors, including Bill Gates and Warren Buffett, and set out in an open letter published in the summer of 2020 requesting a "permanent tax increase" signed by 83 millionaires, many of whom are also well known as donors (Millionaires for Humanity 2020). In the US a movement of "Patriotic Millionaires" goes beyond calls for a fairer tax system to demand a guaranteed living wage for all, affordable housing and equitable access to higher education. Such interventions confound simplistic assumptions that all the rich are tax-dodging plutocrats with no concern for their fellow citizens and future generations. This belief ought also to be undermined by the huge growth in charitable trusts and foundations which help avoid the problem of dynastic wealth inequality, diverting money that would otherwise have become part of an intergenerational transfer of wealth. Yet the perception of philanthropy as inherently problematic has increasingly taken hold nonetheless.

The need for scrutiny and constructive critiques

None of the foregoing is incompatible with also stating that scrutiny and constructive critique are welcomed by all who care about the health and sustainability of the nonprofit sector. Critiques of philanthropy can helpfully reveal the nature of our shared expectations for philanthropic action and the values that surround it, highlight assumptions about the "proper role" for philanthropy in contemporary society and raise important questions about power, transparency, inclusion and obligation (Moody & Breeze 2016: 172).

A key feature of philanthropy is that it involves private, voluntary action that has tangible consequences in the public sphere. Decisions made behind donors' front doors affect unknown people living in our neighbourhood, country or even the other side of the world. This juxtaposition of private interests with public needs means it is important to make informed calls about the trade-offs involved in allowing private influence to fund public goods (Frumkin 2006: 3). The need for scrutiny and accountability is especially acute when the philanthropic act involves significant donations that seek to influence how society is run and administered, for example to change a law or advance an issue up the legislative agenda. Democratic societies operate on the basis that decisions are made at the ballot box with all eligible adults enjoying an equal say, regardless of the size of their personal bank account or family fortune. As US-based philanthropy researcher Ben Soskis notes, "given the power that private philanthropy can wield over public policy, a spirited, fully-informed public debate over the scope, scale and nature of that influence is a democratic necessity" (Soskis 2014).

Yet the word "can" in that sentence is instructive. Philanthropists can, but do not always and by no means often, seek to gain influence over public policy. Philanthropy comes in a huge variety of forms, of which policy-oriented philanthropy is only one – arguably niche – interest. There has been a slippage from noting that in *some* instances philanthropy can be a way of wielding power, which is obviously true, to the statement that "*all* philanthropy is power", which is at best an odd exaggeration given the reality of how much philanthropic funding is spent on mundane and prosaic goods and services as detailed in this book.

How the Covid-19 pandemic highlights the need for careful consideration of criticism

While the need to offer a critique of the critics has been necessary for some time, the global pandemic of 2020–21 has brought that need into even sharper relief. The first of the recent cluster of academic critiques of contemporary philanthropy was written by the UK-based Canadian academic Linsey McGoey, offering a thoughtful analysis of "the price of philanthropy", by which is meant the benefits gained by big donors in return for their largesse. Less helpfully, McGoey's book includes a denunciation of the Bill and Melinda Gates Foundation for its choice of funding research into communicable health issues, rather than chronic and non-communicable diseases, approvingly citing a former director at the World Health Organization whose words now ring extremely hollow: "It's a no-brainer that the major problem in the future is not infectious diseases" (cited in McGoey 2015: 224). The same year that book was published, Bill Gates gave his now-renowned TED talk in which he accurately forecast that an infectious pandemic would bring the world to a standstill. Fortunately Gates put his money where his crystal ball was and contributed $100 million to help establish the Coalition for Epidemic Preparedness Innovation in 2017, a global alliance of public, private and philanthropic funding to develop vaccines and improve collective responses to newly emerging infectious diseases, which has proved presciently useful in ensuring a speedy respond to find cures and vaccines for the global Covid-19 pandemic of 2020–21.

Having accused Gates of "misjudging where the world's largest health burden lies" (McGoey 2015: 224), it seems reasonable to ask when and how critics might acknowledge the power of their words and their potential for making misjudgements which nonetheless linger and damage the reputation of philanthropy. This miscalculation regarding the likelihood and impact of a pandemic is a good reminder of the need for humility on all sides as it is clearly not just big donors who sometimes make the wrong calls. It also seems timely to remind ourselves of the positive value of philanthropy and how its potential might best be realized.

The positive potential of philanthropy

I have written this book because I believe the current wave of pessimism about the role and potential of private giving is a reactionary and damaging development that is overstating the nature of the threat and understating the positive benefits of philanthropy. Simply noting that philanthropy can be a force for good – which seems unarguable if, for example, you are the parent of one of the millions of children whose lives have been saved by philanthropic funding of vaccination programmes and disease eradication efforts – is to invite accusations of being a naïve apologist for the rich. Yet some of those leading the charge to improve philanthropic practice, such as Darren Walker at the Ford Foundation, also readily acknowledge its benefits: "much of the work of philanthropy has been undeniably beneficial: Millions of people worldwide have been lifted out of poverty, protected from terrible diseases, provided with social and economic opportunity, and given access to new tools and resources with which to improve their lives" (Walker 2020: 3).

I am obviously not suggesting that nothing ever goes wrong in the process and practice of philanthropic giving, but there is a logical flaw in leaping from noting the existence of human fallibility in private giving to presenting philanthropy as inherently problematic. Like politics, philanthropy is "a messy, mundane, inconclusive, tangled business" (Crick 2000: 54–5), but to make the unarguable point that philanthropy *can* be problematic is not the same things as implying – or stating outright – that philanthropy *is* inherently problematic at all times, and in all places.

Concerns about philanthropy are not new, but the argument of this book is that criticism is now at an unprecedented level, and its amplification by moral grandstanding on social media risks undermining the whole enterprise of philanthropy, rather than correcting specific problematic cases. It is also worrying that these critiques tend to be focused on a handful of elite philanthropists, but get generalized to become critiques of all philanthropy. This situation threatens the supply of funding for nonprofit activity whose operations cannot run on goodwill alone. Those attacking philanthropy should be careful what they wish for, and may accidentally or intentionally bring about. We have taken the resilience of private generosity for granted and assumed that the philanthropic impulse can withstand substantial attack with minimal pushback. Yet there are costs of criticism and a need to be responsible in the tenor of critiques to avoid the perverse outcome of discouraging donors and making it harder for intermediaries such as fundraisers to cultivate generous societies.

That is why this introductory chapter began with three examples of praiseworthy private giving, and why other positive contributions of philanthropy are highlighted throughout this book. Conceding that some good can, and has, come from private donors enables us to move away from the suggestion that philanthropy is a fundamentally illegitimate activity, and to focus instead on its improvability. Things can always be done better, but it is a classic mistake to let perfection be the enemy of good, and the price of that mistake will be felt most acutely by those who rely most on private giving. Hyper-criticism of big donors risks causing more harm than those it claims to be exposing, which is why this defence of philanthropy is so sorely needed.

The next chapter provides more detail on the purpose of philanthropy and shows how private giving benefits countless individuals and communities across time and place, and strengthens global civil society by encouraging activities that challenge, complement and collaborate with government and market action.

1

WHAT IS PHILANTHROPY?

In the twenty-first century the idea of "philanthropy" and the word "philanthropist" typically bring to mind images of rich white men, who either inherited
their fortune or made it in a business such as finance or information technology.
They are unlikely to be associated with a diminutive female country music icon
from a "dirt poor" background. Yet Dolly Parton's philanthropy made headlines
across the world in late 2020 when her $1 million donation helped fund the devel-
opment of the Moderna vaccine, one of the early viable solutions to the global
Covid-19 pandemic that turned the world upside down in 2020. How did the
talent behind songs such as "Jolene" and "9 to 5" come to play a role in funding a
pivotal epidemiological breakthrough? As this book explains, most philanthropy
starts with a personal connection, an autobiographical stroke of fate – for better
or worse – that, given the right combination of generosity, sympathetic stewardship by the recipient organization and cultural approval by wider society, results
in private actions that promote the public good. The serendipitous incident in
this case was a minor car crash in Nashville in 2013 which led Parton to check
into the Vanderbilt University Medical Center where she met physician Dr Naji
Abumrad. Despite knowing nothing about each other's careers, the two clicked
and enjoyed talking about current affairs and science. When Dr Abumrad, who
works at the university's Institute for Infection, Immunology and Inflammation
later told Parton that his lab was making "exciting advances" in the early stages
of the search for a cure for Covid-19, the million dollar gift was made to honour
her friend and, in Parton's words, "to help" and "do good". This research eventually received nearly $1 billion in federal funding and was the second poten-
tial vaccine to demonstrate high levels of efficacy. Reflecting on the impact of
Parton's donation, Dr Abumrad said: "Her work made it possible to expedite
the science behind the testing. Without a doubt in my mind, her funding made
the research toward the vaccine go ten times faster than it would be without it"
(quoted in Bella 2020).

Parton described feeling "very honoured and proud" to have given money to research into one of the most promising Covid-19 vaccines, noting the collaborative nature of the success: "I'm sure many millions of dollars from many people went into that [research fund] but I felt so proud to have been part of that little seed money that will hopefully grow into something great and help to heal this world" (quoted in Snapes 2020). Parton is correct that big gifts from noted individuals like herself are typically joined by many smaller amounts from a mass of anonymous individuals, with the combined value of the latter far outweighing the total value of major donations. The word "philanthropy" may bring to mind famous names and faces such as Andrew Carnegie or Bill Gates but it is not, and never has been, the preserve of the rich.

"Philanthropy" is a tricky word to pronounce and even trickier to define, but broadly means the practice of private, voluntary efforts to help unknown others and to benefit wider society. Its provenance is simple enough – "philo" meaning "love of" and "anthropos" meaning "humankind" – but there is nothing straightforward about how it is understood, practised, interpreted and discussed. Philanthropy has been in existence for at least 2,500 years and continues to be a common feature in many societies today. It is a dynamic concept and practice that varies over time and place in terms of who gives, the amounts given, the methods of giving and the chosen causes. Despite being a complex, contested, diversified and ideologically loaded concept, it often only hits the public radar in an anaemic form that is stripped of complexity and nuance, and packaged in a way that reflects dominant preconceptions about wealth, celebrity and big money.

The story of Dolly Parton and the Covid-19 vaccine has everything that mass and social media could hope for: a quirky, topical story involving a famous person and a large sum of money. In many ways it was a typical radar-hitting example of philanthropy making it into the headlines. But the story behind how the gift came about, Parton's obvious delight at its impact and her acknowledgement of the role of other donors and the recipient scientists who did "something great" with the money, means it also offers a broader insight into the role and nature of philanthropy in contemporary society: the importance of social networks connecting those who have money with those who can put that money to good use, a desire to express gratitude for help received, an exciting opportunity and an aspiration to make something good happen.

Parton's donation grew from her friendship with Dr Abumrad, boosted the recipient scientists, leveraged broader support and potentially helped end a lethal pandemic. This is philanthropy in action: what's not to like about it? Plenty, as this book explains and discusses in detail.

Before explaining and illustrating the problematizing of philanthropy and its consequences for encouraging generosity, this chapter is focused on explaining what philanthropy is, why the philanthropically funded sector exists and how it differs from the purpose and functioning of the other two main sectors in society: government and business. Philanthropy is shown to be a complex and contested phenomenon that needs to be understood in context, often causes confusion, yet is crucial for both individual and societal welfare. We begin with three examples that help illustrate the varied historical and contemporary roles of philanthropy.

The roles and impacts of philanthropy across time

Bert, the chimney sweep friend of Mary Poppins, was brought to life on the big screen by Dick Van Dyke who portrayed him as having a chirpy "chim chim cher-ee" life, in the words of the Oscar-winning song. Yet "grim child misery" would have been a more accurate lyric, as the sweeping of chimneys was filthy, painful, life-limiting and life-threatening work undertaken by children as young as four. For four centuries this form of child labour was not just tolerated but positively encouraged by government, which shifted the burden of care for orphans and children living in workhouses by apprenticing them to adult sweeps. Tiny, half naked children were forced to climb into narrow, hot flues where they often got stuck in the cramped spaces, were suffocated by falling soot and died in situ. The survivors experienced stunted growth, deformed spines and limbs, burns, loss of sight, respiratory disease and chimney sweeps' carcinoma, the first identified occupational cancer which was caused by soot irritating the child's skin. This abuse was finally ended in 1875 when the Chimney Sweepers Act was passed after decades of effort by the philanthropically funded Society for Superseding the Necessity of Climbing Boys, founded in 1803 with funding from an anonymous donor who paid for campaigning, private inspectors to observe sweeps in action, and also a £200 prize for the inventor of the best sweeping machine to demonstrate that the practice was unnecessary as well as inhumane (Gray 1908: 11–12; Davies 2015: 93–4).

Nearly 150 years later, in 2018, the grand opening of a new car park providing over 1,000 free parking spaces for staff, patients and visitors took place at the Aberdeen Royal Infirmary. The full cost of £10.7 million was covered by local businessman Sir Ian Wood. This gift was prompted by his wife, Lady Helen (after whom the car park is named), whose friends and relatives had told her of their anxiety and distress at being unable to find parking when attending appointments or visiting loved ones. Success in easing stress was confirmed by a woman visiting a relative who explained, "Words can't do justice to what it means to have one less thing to worry about when making hospital visits. A car park may not be the most auspicious of buildings but in terms of fulfilling a daily, hourly need, it is second to none" (Wood Foundation 2019).

The first statue in the UK to memorialize a named black woman, Mary Seacole, was erected in London in 2016 on the banks of the Thames directly opposite the House of Commons. The cost of commissioning and installing the work honouring the Jamaican-born Crimean War nurse who cared for British soldiers, was covered by a campaign that raised £500,000, including contributions from rich individuals and corporations. Eminent health practitioner and campaigner Professor Dame Elizabeth Anionwu reflected on

> The joy of having this wonderful, wonderful monument in the grounds of St Thomas' hospital, overlooking the Houses of Parliament. Mary is striding forth and it's as though she's keeping an eye on those politicians! It's wonderful whatever background you are. But can you imagine how important it is for groups of individuals who don't always feel accepted? … My granddaughter can see a statue of a woman that looks like her in terms of skin colour and it's just wonderful.

The ending of child chimney sweeps, a new car park for a Scottish hospital and a historic statue that has renewed resonance in the time of the Black Lives Matter movement are three very different examples, illustrating the diversity of motivations, acts and outcomes that are collectively classified as "philanthropy". Philanthropy is ubiquitous and universal but it is not uniform (Payton & Moody 2008). It is not easy to pin down because it is a dynamic, contextual concept that changes across time and place, and because different people can have quite different views on what philanthropy can and should do.

For example, from our twenty-first-century perspective, the philanthropic achievement of helping to end child labour in the chimney sweep trade appears inadequate because the material and emotional needs of the orphans and workhouse children, such as safe housing, an education and supportive family life, were still unlikely to be met. In Scotland today, alongside those who are pleased about the new, free hospital car park there will be others who do not agree that rich oil tycoons should have anything to do with funding and building facilities connected to the National Health Service. And the appearance of one statue in London of a named black woman will be welcomed by some and interpreted by others as an inadequate response that risks giving the appearance of change while leaving institutionalized racism intact.

These three examples highlight that philanthropy is a product of its time, is shaped by existing arrangements within wider society and is appraised through the eye of the beholder. In short, there is no straightforward, objective answer to the question "what is philanthropy?", rather there are multiple, changing, competing subjective opinions on its role and purpose.

The ongoing contested terrain of philanthropy

Whatever examples of philanthropic actions had been chosen to open this chapter, there would be legitimate views offering different perspectives and opinions on the rights and wrongs of those actions. To take three more examples:

- Food banks are supported by those who feel compelled to help neighbours that are struggling to feed their families, and criticized by those who believe that they normalize and exacerbate food poverty by deflecting the need for structural change in terms of austerity and welfare policies (Garthwaite 2016).
- Granting wishes to terminally ill children, such as visits to Disneyland or meeting their favourite celebrity, is supported by those who believe it brings joy and hope to the child and their family, and is attacked by others who believe it is wasteful because the same amount of money could pay for cheap life-saving interventions in poorer countries (Singer 2015: 6).
- Philanthropic funding of cultural activities such as excellence in, and access to, the arts, literature, theatre and film, strikes some people as an elitist diversion from more worthy causes while others claim that a decent human life requires access to cultural goods (Pevnick 2016).

To briefly mention three more examples of the highly contested terrain inhabited by philanthropy: both pro-choice and pro-life advocates benefit from philanthropic support for their positions, as do those in favour and against hunting live animals, and those promoting religiosity and secularism. It would be possible to fill this entire book with examples of how one person's idea of a gift is viewed by another as poisonous. This is perhaps less surprising when we learn that the Greek and Old Germanic roots of the word "gift" refer to poison (Smith 2006: 15). Such differences in viewpoints are not resolvable by analysing empirical evidence or by recourse to philosophical reasoning, because these are ultimately ideological and personally held positions.

We might think we know what we – and everyone else – are talking about when we say the word "philanthropy" but our contemporary vocabulary struggles to accommodate the understandings and assumptions of those who practised and wrote about philanthropy in the past (Sulek 2010a, 2010b), as well as those who emphasize how it manifests differently around the world today. For example, the contemporary role of philanthropy in relation to funding health, education and welfare services clearly differs between countries that have advanced welfare states and those that do not.

We can try to guard against the straw man arguments that frequently recur in discussions of philanthropy by resisting the temptation to define philanthropy in a way that suggests it has a constant, agreed-upon character and objective, and by paying more attention to the history of philanthropy, which underlines both consistent themes in relation to the mixed motivation of donors and the dual benefits created for benefactors and beneficiaries, and how it develops over time as a result of being embedded in changing political, economic and social contexts.

A diversity of causes and contexts

What can we learn from examples of how philanthropy has been practised, understood and interpreted across time and place?

Evidence of philanthropic activity exists from the earliest known civilizations and – with local variation – is found in every known society. We can easily point to longstanding evidence of philanthropic activity, from the enormous – and enormously expensive – cathedrals built across northern Europe during the Middle Ages, to the 2,500 libraries built across the world in the late nineteenth and early twentieth century by Scottish American philanthropist Andrew Carnegie, to the recent expansion of food banks across many countries affected by austerity policies and the Covid-19 crisis. But it is much more difficult to provide a precise and widely accepted definition of either "philanthropy" or "philanthropist".

The word "philanthropy" was first used in the fifth century BCE, in the Greek tragedy *Prometheus Bound* in which Prometheus incurs the perpetual wrath of the gods by giving the gifts of fire and optimism to humans. So the first meaning of the word, and hence its Greek roots, refers to gifts from the gods to humans. Its usage spread in the Greco-Roman world of classical antiquity to apply to earth-bound rulers who treated their subjects well, and then broadened further to encompass wealthy citizens who were considered generous in their disposition as well as in relation to concrete gifts (Cunningham 2016: 43).

Almsgiving and religious donations have a long history. The Judeo-Christian traditions involve clear charitable obligations with exhortations to generosity in both the Old and New Testaments, as does the Islamic faith in which *zakat* (obligatory almsgiving) is one of the five pillars, and adherents are also encouraged to make voluntary and personal gifts known as *sadaqah* (Singer 2008). Despite the apparent continuity from pagan benevolence, to Jewish, Christian and Muslim charity, to modern philanthropy, the vocabulary and meanings to which they refer – including how much to give, who ought to be helped, by what means and with what consequence for the giver – have not remained constant over time (Andrews 1950: 31).

Changes in who is called a "philanthropist"

The first British person to be labelled as a philanthropist was John Howard, who gained renown in the late eighteenth century for helping debtors and prisoners, dedicating his life and ultimately sacrificing his health to help them, although not through providing any financial assistance (Rodgers 1949; Davies 2015; Cunningham 2020). Today Howard would be described as an activist focused on prison reform, because the word "philanthropy" has become synonymous with donating large sums of money. When I asked a representative sample of the British public to define "philanthropist" in three words, three of the ten most popular responses were: wealthy, rich and money (Breeze 2020). Meanwhile, non-wealthy people who make charitable donations are typically referred to as "donors" rather than "philanthropists".

Changes in philanthropy causes and beneficiaries over time

Preferred causes and beneficiaries change over time to reflect social norms and perceptions of the most urgent social problems. Climate change and racial justice are prevailing concerns at the start of the twenty-first century just as, for example, it was popular to build public baths in ancient Rome, to help poor maids to marry in the fifteenth century, to pay ransoms for people captured by pirates in the sixteenth century and to make contributions to rebuild London and Lisbon after they were affected by fire and earthquakes in, respectively, 1666 and 1755 (Jordan 1959; Owen 1964).

New forms of urban poverty created by the Industrial Revolution, such as unemployment and slum dwellings, spurred a philanthropic response in the shape of housing and health care for the poor, as well as education and vocational institutions, while the Age of Reform also saw donors' enthusiasm for science, the arts and municipal philanthropy, which involved providing parks, public baths, town halls, libraries, museums and art galleries for local populations (Cunningham 2020: 152).

The mid-twentieth-century creation of welfare states in many developed countries meant that governments took over many of the functions of philanthropy, including the funding and running of hospitals and schools and the provision of a wide array of welfare services. When these new institutions were created, UK public opinion overwhelmingly predicted they would make philanthropy superfluous (Kendall & Knapp 1996). However, private philanthropy did not disappear as a result of increased public spending. New causes emerged that attracted philanthropic support, including the civil rights movement, environmentalism and equalities campaigns.

A useful typology of the roles that philanthropy plays in contemporary societies is offered by Rob Payton and Michael Moody, who view philanthropy as "moral action" by which people advance their subjective vision of the public good. This translates into five roles: providing services to meet needs that government and the market cannot or will not deliver; advocating for reforms; preserving and expressing cultural traditions; building community; and funding social innovation. There is also a sixth, "private" role of meeting the psychic and social needs of donors who wish to shape the world around them, transforming their self-image and how they hope to be perceived by others. This framework is useful in highlighting the wide variety of activities that comes under the umbrella of philanthropy, and underlining the norm of mixed motives – that donors advance their own goals at the same time as trying to make a positive impact (by their definition) on the wider world.

Philanthropic motivation over time

Comprehensive surveys of the history of philanthropy attest to changes in interpretations of donor motivation over time. Yet mixed motives – including the simultaneous pursuit of a range of both private and public benefits – are shown to be historically typical. Historian David Owen observes a complex blend of religious, humanitarian and private motives across four centuries of philanthropy, and notes it is "dangerous and absurd" to seek reductionist classifications of the charitable impulse because "human behaviour rarely exhibits such helpful singleness of motive" (Owen 1964: 36), and observes a complex blend of religious, humanitarian and private motives across four centuries of philanthropy. Prosocial motivations, including compassionate responses to human suffering and a desire to improve communities and wider societies, sit alongside at least four types of private motives identified in historical studies: salvation, social control, social mobility and self-construction by the wealthy.

Salvation. Historically, philanthropy has often been understood as a strategy to secure salvation in the afterlife, described variously as "the purchase of paradise" (Rosenthal 1972), a "hedge against hell" (Davis 1996: 17) and "a fire-escape to heaven for the rich" (Whitaker 1974a: 44). Common belief in the reality of heaven and hell meant it was widely understood that when donors founded almshouses or endowed a hospital they "were built for the glory of God and the soul of the founder" (Rosenthal 1972: 57).

Social control. The use of philanthropic gestures to protect the rich from riots and avert social unrest is identified as a factor behind a range of philanthropic acts, from funding entertainments to keep the mass of the poor population in "good temper" in ancient Rome, to appealing for donations to found Harvard University in the 1640s by encouraging donors to "Educate and save ourselves and our families and our money from mobs" (cited in Whitaker 1974a: 53). From the seventeenth century, as agrarian societies rapidly industrialized and large numbers of urban poor emerged, philanthropy became viewed as "a means of keeping the populace, if not contented, at least reasonably submissive" (Owen 1964: 97). In this interpretation, which continues to be supported today, philanthropy enables the worst consequences of economic modernization to be diminished without the economic leaders relinquishing control over society.

Social mobility. Philanthropy during the Victorian era is often depicted as a key mechanism behind social mobility, providing an opportunity for "new money" to buy the status required to be integrated into the elite by exchanging money for social capital. Prominent eighteenth-century philanthropic ventures capitalized on the increasingly symbiotic relationship between philanthropy and elite culture (Lloyd 2002: 29). For example, supporters of the Foundling Hospital in London included the artist William Hogarth, whose paintings hung on the institution's walls, and the composer George Frederick Handel, who raised funds with annual performances of his composition *Messiah*. The association with such prominent supporters meant the Foundling Hospital became, "a popular rendezvous for London society [because it combined] ... that rare trinity, Art, Charity and Fashion; to be able on the same occasion to visit the orphans, discuss a modern picture and parade the latest costume" (Rodgers 1949: 34).

Self-construction by the wealthy. More recent studies highlight that philanthropy's role is also linked to dynamics of self-construction of the wealthy, giving donors a sense of identity and meaning such that philanthropy is a means for turning "riches" into a "richer life" (Schervish 1994a; Odendahl 1990; Ostrower 1995; Breeze & Lloyd 2013). This alchemy occurs by the simultaneous presence of public and private functions which generate both outer-and inner-directed benefits (Frumkin 2006: 11–18; Payton & Moody 2008). Paul Schervish argues that everyone – rich or otherwise – creates a story with themselves at its centre, yet normative expectations of wealth holders mean they are obliged to formulate more elaborate self-justifications about the direction their lives have taken. He therefore concludes that philanthropy is part of the efforts under-taken by rich people to write their "moral biographies", by which he means the "narrative procedures they [use to] explain how it is possible for them to be rich and good at the same time" (Schervish 1994a: 167).

This brief review highlights how the concept of philanthropy has changed over time, both in what it applies to and how it is understood by observers. There is also continuity in the combination of prosocial intentions and private benefits that accrue to donors, which are neither new, nor newly observed, phenomena.

The logic of philanthropy, the collective action problem and the impossibility of free gifts

To understand the distinctive role and purpose of philanthropy, it is helpful to compare how it relates to the other two sectors of society: government and business. Where government involves public action in pursuit of public benefits, and business involves private action in pursuit of private benefits, philanthropy involves the distinctive combination of private action in pursuit of public benefits. This succinct seven-word summary conceals an iceberg of complexity:

- "Private action" can include that of individuals, families, informal groups of friends and colleagues and more formally constituted giving circles, as well as institutional givers such as philanthropic foundations and corporate donors.
- Being "in pursuit of" can be implemented by giving money, time, expertise or other resources, through very informal, fleeting acts or highly institutionalized and permanent processes, and where the thought process behind the act ranges from careless to meticulous.
- And "public benefits" involve subjective decisions on the part of the private actors as to which social and environmental goals they feel most capable of pursuing, and which are the most worthwhile to pursue.

This complexity means that in the philanthropy sector neither inputs nor desired outcomes are clear cut, the processes by which resources are provided range widely and change rapidly, everyone is a stakeholder and consensus is impossible.

A further complicating factor is the absence of either compulsion or compelling self-interest to generate the funding stream for philanthropy. Government compels individuals to pay tax in order to provide public benefits for all. Businesses provide direct benefits to those who choose to pay for goods and services. But philanthropy lacks both the stick and the carrot: there is no compulsion to contribute, and no way to exclude "free riders" who do not contribute from enjoying the benefits, be it medical advances, a cleaner environment, public art or a world with less preventable deaths. This is why "collective action problems" are prevalent in the philanthropy sector, meaning the problem of how to get self-interested individuals to participate in achieving common goals when those individuals can benefit regardless of whether or not they made a contribution (Olson 1965).

The two main strategies for overcoming collective action problems are coercion and incentives. Governments choose coercion by making payment of taxes compulsory, whereas both business and philanthropy rely on incentivizing, respectively, consumers and donors. The positive inducements in for-profit settings are obvious because customers directly benefit from their expenditure, and may also be motivated by negative inducements to avoid social sanctions, such as teenagers needing the "right" label trainers or aspirational adults joining the "right" private members' club or choosing the "right" kind of wine. The use of incentives for donors in nonprofit settings is far more complex because, by legal requirement, there must be some public benefit and because observers are increasingly critical of the presence of any type of donor benefit, regardless of how intangible or trivial they are. Even feeling a "warm glow", or receiving expressions of gratitude and praise after making a gift, are enough for some to call into question the authenticity of philanthropic acts and the sincerity of donors' intent. Unprompted and unrewarded generosity is more culturally valued, yet normative expectations of "free gifts" are problematic in both theory and practice. Decades of anthropological and sociological research have established that gift-giving always involves a return of some sort because reciprocity is one of the rare universal norms. The paradox of the gift – that in giving we receive – means that philanthropy involves an intractable and irresolvable contradiction: the most viable lever to overcome free riding is to encourage and incentivize those with the capacity to give, yet that encouragement and inducement falls foul of normative expectations held by both observers and the donors themselves.

Furthermore, as discussed further in Chapter 6, free riding is only half the problem. Research also identifies widespread sanctions or "antisocial punishments" for those viewed as "over-contributing" because their actions establish undesirable behaviour standards and threaten the self-image of others by comparison (Herrmann *et al.* 2008; Irwin & Horne 2013; Pleasant & Barclay 2018). Acting "too generously" can be off-putting and unappealing, leading to contempt for, and rejection of, generous individuals (Parks & Stone 2010; Tasimi *et al.* 2015) as expressed through "do-gooder derogation" which results in the suppression of prosocial behaviours (Minson & Monin 2012). The main defence against free riding is social sanctions for non-contributors, such that individuals find it more costly to be shamed for being uncooperative than to stump up, however unwillingly. But as yet there is little understanding of the mechanisms of do-gooder derogation, yet alone a viable plan to overcome them, beyond fundraisers taking on a larger burden of donor stewardship and gratitude work in an attempt to offset antisocial punishments (Breeze 2017).

Solving the free rider problem (that people can benefit without contributing) is a longstanding concern for those charged with keeping philanthropically funded activity solvent. Reducing hostility to donors and pushing back against do-gooder derogation is a further battle front for nonprofit leaders who are typically already stretched too thin keeping their organizations solvent and delivering their missions effectively and efficiently. This is why the perspective of beneficiaries, fundraisers and charity leaders recurs across this book – a defence of philanthropy is not an abstract enterprise, it is a necessity for those facing the reality of both the free rider problem and do-gooder derogation. It is hard enough to fund a sector in the absence of compulsion or compelling self-interest, and that challenge is compounded when aspersions are cast on the legitimacy of philanthropy, the efficacy of philanthropic acts and the motivations of philanthropists.

Explanations for the existence of the contemporary philanthropy sector

Given the more straightforward funding mechanisms enjoyed by government and business, why does a sector that contains such easily exploitable flaws as free riding and do-gooder derogation exist at all? Some explanations for the existence of the contemporary philanthropy sector point to failings by the other sectors to adequately supply certain goods and services.

"Market failure" occurs when profit cannot be made in the market because "customers" are unable to pay (such as people in need of soup kitchens or disaster relief), because the good or service cannot be restricted to paying customers (such as public art or cleaning up the oceans which are examples of non-rivalrous and non-excludable goods) or because information asymmetries make providers' motivation and lack of incentives to cut corners a key concern (such as organizations that run services for vulnerable or voiceless clients like a homeless shelter or an animal rescue service) (Hansmann 1986, 1987).

"Government failure" (also known as public goods theory) occurs when there is insufficient popular demand to give government a mandate to step in as provider, either because it is a minority interest or a concern that does not appeal to the typical voter (such as a new social problem, a rare disease or a niche cultural taste), or because the demand is expressed by "unpopular" or marginalized groups (such as providing arts activities to prisoners, or support for asylum seekers or people with addictions) (Weisbrod 1986, 1988).

An alternative, more positive approach than these two "failure theories" for explaining the existence of the philanthropy sector focuses on the comparative advantages of a voluntary response. Philanthropic action may be preferable in situations where the beneficiaries are financially disadvantaged (too poor to pay), personally disadvantaged (unable to take control or make decisions), societally disadvantaged (are members of stigmatized groups) or experiencing community disadvantage (living in geographical areas neglected by both the private sector and the state) (Billis & Glennerster 1998). There are also some circumstances in which the nature of the service being provided is intimately connected to shared social and emotional experiences, and is therefore best provided by people with first-hand knowledge and a desire to help that lacks a profit motive (Ben-Ner 2002: 7). For example, if someone was feeling suicidal or seeking support after sexual assault or a bereavement, they would arguably prefer to be helped by an empathetic volunteer or nonprofit employee, rather than a civil servant or a representative of a profit-making body.

The presence of philanthropy is interpreted by many as signifying failure on the part of government to adequately provide for its citizens, and there are certainly many examples – especially under austerity policies – where this is a reasonable analysis. Some donors who step in to plug gaps do so unwillingly, sharing the view that government should "do its job" and that the role of private donors is to put "the icing on the cake" (Breeze & Lloyd 2013: 97). But this brief tour of theoretical explanations for the existence of nonprofit action shows that philanthropic provision is sometimes the only, better or preferred option for supplying some goods and services.

The philanthropy paradox: greater public support for philanthropy than for philanthropists

Confusion about the role and desirability of philanthropy is common, and is related to its complexity, changeability and contestation. In debates about philanthropy, people are not always talking about the same thing. Some are concerned about how philanthropy was conducted in the past and the ongoing consequences of those practices, some are focused on present inadequacies, while others have in mind the unrealized potential of philanthropy in the future. Each of these sets of concerns plays a more or less dominant role in, respectively, the academic, populist and insider critiques that are the focus of later chapters. The relevant point here is that mistakenly viewing "philanthropy" as a uniform and unvarying phenomenon means that very different issues and concerns get folded into the same debates. This causes confusion that is often left unpacked.

A public attitude survey that I conducted in 2019 found that the British public feels far more positively about philanthropy (the things that are funded) than it does about philanthropists (those doing the funding). As one cannot exist without the other, the gap in approval gives us an insight into public confusion about how philanthropically funded goods and services come into existence. While most people (84 per cent) believe that philanthropic donations help make things better for other people and society, only 69 per cent agree that philanthropists are good for society with only a bare majority (53 per cent) of the lower-income group concurring. Concern about the motivations of philanthropists is evident in the finding that, across the population, a minority (47 per cent) trust donors to do what is right with their donations. How can it be that people feel far more positively about the fruits of philanthropy than about those who fund it? An expert observer of the US philanthropy scene, David Callahan, confirms that the public in his country also do not understand much about how philanthropy works despite having a high regard for the charitable sector that it funds (Parnell & Callahan 2017). There are no simple explanations of how people can separate the philanthropic act from the philanthropic actor, other than to note that this illustrates the ongoing confusing place of philanthropy in public life and discussions.

Longstanding mixed motives and the problem of generalizing about philanthropy

This brief review has shown that not only is philanthropic activity evident throughout human history, but also that concerns raised today about the practice and the donors are largely familiar. Many critics suggest there is something distinctively and newly problematic about philanthropy in the twenty-first century that needs to be called out and rectified: that today's philanthropists, especially the biggest donors, have distorted a previously disinterested practice and have remoulded philanthropy so that it primarily serves their own interests. Yet the proposition that a selfless practice has become selfish in the hands of today's super-rich is not supported by the historical evidence.

In addition to emphasizing the longstanding presence of mixed motives driving philanthropic acts, and the unavoidable duality of their impact on both donors and the wider world, this review also underlines the trap of offering simplistic conceptualizations and interpretations for such a complex and multi-faceted aspect of human life and behaviour. Mark Twain's wise counsel that "All generalizations, including this one, are false" is usefully applied to philanthropy, especially in conjunction with Machiavelli's observation that "We are more apt to be mistaken in our generalizations than in our particular observations." The problem of generalization has been noted by others whose scholarly work seeks to counter blanket criticisms of philanthropy, concisely expressed by Ilana Silber's insistence that when thinking about philanthropy "there is need to introduce sub-categories, nuances and distinctions as well as a dose of historical and cultural variability" (Silber 2001: 3).

Referring to "philanthropy" as one homogenous entity, and assuming there is something coherent and consistent that is available for analysis, lies at the root of many disagreements between those who lean towards more positive or negative interpretations of philanthropy. As noted in the Introduction, if we respond to examples of poor philanthropic behaviour and outcomes with more hopeful illustrations, or vice versa, we will be stuck in a very long and unsatisfying game of philanthropy tennis. What is needed instead is recognition that private giving is complex, contested, often confusing and not compatible with simple explanations. To stick with the same letter of the alphabet, Ralf Dahrendorf's phrase about the "creative chaos of charity" (as discussed in Prochaska 2002) is useful to keep in mind when trying to impose order and exactitude on the multifarious array of philanthropic activity. As Karl Zinsmeister explained in his response to common criticisms of philanthropy that culminate in calls to contain what philanthropy can and should be, "Part of what makes philanthropy powerful and beautiful is its riotous variety. Allowing donors to follow their passions has proven, over generations, to be an effective way of inspiring powerful commitments and getting big results. Cramped definitions of philanthropy that limit donors to approved areas would suffocate many valuable social inventions" (Zinsmeister 2016).

The reason to be acutely aware of "cramping" or "suffocating" the philanthropic impulse is because the final lesson of history is that philanthropy is (yet another "c"): crucial, which of course is what makes the overall practice worth defending.

Philanthropy's greatest achievements

My last job in the philanthropy sector before moving into academia was a role at the Institute for Philanthropy in London, which sought to increase effective philanthropy through research, advocacy and donor education. During my time there, I led a project called – rather grandiosely – UK Philanthropy's Greatest Achievements, for which I surveyed the opinion of sector colleagues and donors associated with the institute, asking them to nominate and vote for the most outstanding historic and contemporary achievements that had been secured with the help of philanthropic support. The results highlight how crucial philanthropy has been across time, and continues to be today.

Historic greatest achievements

The largest area of pre-1900 philanthropic achievement concerns the provision of a wide range of social and health services, paid for and provided by philanthropists long before the government took responsibility for the welfare of its citizens. In addition to the well-known tradition of the rich giving alms or poor relief direct to the needy, this achievement covers the formal provision of services such as providing housing for the poor, almshouses for older people and care for orphaned and abandoned children, as well as building hospitals and covering health care fees for those unable to pay. The philanthropic roots of a range of public services were also highlighted, including the ambulance service, probation service, social workers and institutions caring for those injured fighting for their country. Finally within this category are the philanthropically funded research efforts which mapped out the existence and scale of need, analysed the roots of poverty and provided the evidence which helped to create the foundations on which the British welfare state was eventually built.

The single most frequently cited historic achievement was the philanthropic effort of those involved in financing and running the campaign to end the slave trade in the UK. The Society for the Abolition of the Slave Trade was founded in 1787 by Granville Sharp and Thomas Clarkson, and the political leadership provided by William Wilberforce is widely remembered and admired. But many thousands of individual philanthropic women and men joined the campaign, ran local groups, raised funds, distributed pamphlets and worked collectively for decades to secure the successful passage of the 1807 Abolition of the Slave Trade Act and the 1833 Slavery Abolition Act. This included prominent industrialists such as the pottery manufacturer Josiah Wedgwood, whose company produced cameos for brooches and snuff boxes depicting enslaved people with the evocative words "Am I Not a Man and a Brother?" to help raise public awareness of, and support for, the anti-slave trade movement (Gray 1905: 195).

The third most admired historic philanthropic achievement was the widespread provision of education and leisure opportunities. A range of schools was founded to cater for the needs of poor children who had to work to help support themselves and their family for most of the week, including ragged schools, charity schools and Sunday schools. The ongoing needs of the working adult population to learn and gain new skills has been consistently funded by philanthropic contributions. One of the best-known philanthropic efforts of this type is the mass provision of public libraries funded by Andrew Carnegie, which brought educational opportunities and a love of literature to ordinary people. Also in this category are the philanthropic efforts that ensured ordinary people had access to the countryside, public parks, sporting facilities and significant buildings such as town halls and art galleries.

Modern greatest achievements

The most frequently cited modern achievement was the philanthropic response to famine and poverty in developing countries. While international aid and development are often the focus of critical scholarship, usefully highlighting many issues in relation to neocolonialism and the consequences of exacerbating North–South power imbalances and exploitation (for example as discussed by Moyo 2010), the British public continue to be enthusiastic supporters of providing disaster relief and funding long-term development projects. Examples include promoting fair trade, providing microfinance, funding healthcare infrastructure and supporting the Jubilee Debt Campaign which resulted in billions of pounds of unjust and unpayable debt held by the poorest countries being cancelled at the millennium.

The second theme identified in modern philanthropic achievements is health research and pioneering health services. Three very different and significant examples include the establishment and funding of hospices to provide dignified and pain-controlled environments for the dying, the philanthropic response to the AIDS epidemic which provided preventative education and support for those infected before government got involved, and the enormous scientific enterprise that resulted in the mapping of the human genome in which the Wellcome Trust, a UK-based organization that is the one of the world's largest philanthropic foundations, was a major partner. Since this survey was conducted, philanthropy has helped achieve another significant feat in the health field: the virtual eradication of polio. In the 1980s a thousand children each day were paralysed by polio. Now, after 2.5 billion children have been vaccinated, with funding provided by many big and small donors, including $3 billion from the Bill and Melinda Gates Foundation, the type 2 and type 3 wild polio viruses have been declared eradicated, and only a handful of cases of type 1 persist (Global Polio Eradication Initiative n.d.). Philanthropic contributions have also successfully helped tackle other diseases, for example 13 philanthropically funded nonprofit partners (channelling contributions from both mass giving and very wealthy individuals) support the Global Fund, founded in 2002 to accelerate the end of AIDS, Tuberculosis and Malaria in over a hundred countries. By 2020 this funding partnership, which, like many philanthropic efforts, works collaboratively with governments, private sector and nonprofit organizations, has saved the lives of 38 million people (Gates & Gates 2020).

The third area of modern philanthropic achievement identified is the continuing use of philanthropically funded campaigning to bring about significant social change. Examples include the campaigns that secured the right of women to vote, the banning of handguns in the UK after the Dunblane massacre (as discussed in the Introduction), the ban on the production and use of landmines and other explosive remnants of war, and campaigns resulting in equalities legislation such as equalization of the age of consent and same-sex marriages. Philanthropists also support campaigns tackling intractable and as yet unresolved issues, such as homelessness, domestic violence and modern slavery, funding the compilation of evidence and helping to build a consensus that action can and should be taken. Many campaigns are aimed at government, either to change the law or provide additional funding. When critics state that there would be no need for philanthropy if only people and companies paid more tax, it is worth noting that the government would not use the money it collects to lobby itself. Significant social change that requires the passage or amendment of legislation comes about as a result of private individuals making demands on the government and holding it to account. Democracy crucially ensures that every adult has a voice at the ballot box, and philanthropy equally crucially enables voices to be heard in-between elections. Chapter 3 looks closely at concerns that the philanthropic funding of campaigns is problematic and skewed in favour of elite interests. While this is clearly a possible outcome, and appears to be of special concern in the US, it is nonetheless also the case that many philanthropically funded campaigns have helped created a safer society and greater equality for groups that had been treated unequally by the state.

Reflections on philanthropic achievements and how they relate to critics' concerns

It is undoubtedly true that philanthropy alone cannot claim credit for the entirety of all the achievements described above, but the contribution of philanthropic funding is frequently overlooked, and is worth highlighting in the context of growing attacks on the role and purpose of privately funded initiatives. Money is an essential element in creating social change and bringing about social justice, yet all too often those who voluntarily provide such funds are at best ignored and at worst vilified.

The examples provided throughout this chapter, from "superseding" child chimney sweeps, to eradicating polio, to sequencing the human genome (which also, not incidentally, ensured the "recipe book of life" stays in the public domain rather than being available for private profit), all help to support the view that philanthropy is worth defending.

Conclusion

This chapter has looked in depth at the role and nature of philanthropy to demonstrate the huge diversity of activity across time and place, that sits beneath the banner of "philanthropy". I began by noting that philanthropy is a tricky word to pronounce and define: it is not a word that trips off the tongue easily, or is always immediately understood by those who hear it, which is why I have sometimes been asked why I study stamp collecting for a living.

Like many fellow scholars, my favoured way of pinning down this complex, contextual, contested and confusing concept is to lean on the definition that philanthropy is "voluntary action for the public good" (Payton & Moody 2008). The beauty of this definition is not only its simplicity and brevity, but also the fact that it opens up, rather than closes down, the sphere of philanthropy to include everything that donors believe to be worthwhile. It also helps to avoid making the debate more complicated than necessary. No one is in charge of philanthropy – even the legislation that sets out what qualifies for charitable status and tax breaks is extremely inclusive and allows room for most concerns and preferences to be inside the very big tent of philanthropy. Arguably, problems arise mostly because of overly officious bouncers on the door of that tent, who prefer a much narrower definition in line with their view of the role and purpose of philanthropy, as is discussed when we turn to the critiques in Chapters 3, 4 and 5.

This chapter has also underlined that philanthropy is a dynamic, ever-changing concept that is a product of its time and circumstances. Private giving for the public good is part of every culture and society, yet it looks different – and is viewed differently – according to the local context. Philanthropy exists in dynamic interaction with the state, the market and norms in the domestic spheres, which themselves are always changing. The cultural and historical context in which people live also profoundly shapes their understanding of what needs to be done and how (Payton & Moody 2008: 95; Ilchman *et al.* 1998). So philanthropy is both a universal norm and context dependent as a product of its time.

This is why I agree with Paul Ylvisaker's comment that "Philanthropy is not easy to generalize about ... There can't be a more esoteric human activity, nor one more extraordinarily diverse" (Ylvisaker 2008: 460). Yet one generalization can be made, which is why philanthropy is worth defending: in the round – not every specific act or every individual donor, but overall – philanthropy makes a crucial contribution to society. As the achievements described above illustrate, a lot of critical work only gets done – and funded – because of philanthropy. Private action for the public good is only one part of a much wider, ongoing and probably unfinishable debate about how best to meet individual and social needs. But however governments and the market are reorganized, we cannot – and should not – stop people who feel the need "to do something", be it express solidarity or offer more practical assistance, when they encounter existing and new needs.

This may seem an uncontroversial position, but as Chapter 2 shows, those seeking "to do something" have long come under attack as a result.

2

IS PHILANTHROPY REALLY UNDER ATTACK?

Southsea Common is a large open space next to Portsmouth seafront on the south coast of the UK. Today it is a safe place to picnic, fly a kite or enjoy the beach volleyball court, but one bonfire night near the end of the nineteenth century it was the site where an energetic female philanthropist, Sarah Robinson, was burnt in effigy for being "The Best Hated Woman in Portsmouth" (Black 2015: 47). What did Sarah do to provoke others to set her image on fire in a symbolic act of violence? She used her own money, including selling her possessions, and fundraised for decades to establish and run the Soldier's Institute for Portsmouth, which pioneered a new ethic of care for military employees, providing hospitality for soldiers and their families in need of accommodation, education and entertainment, as well as a place of worship in line with her commitment to evangelical Christianity. Her efforts were opposed by those who did not appreciate female meddling in military culture, and disliked her decision to offer an alcohol-free welcome to those she felt might otherwise have fallen prey to the squalor and drinking culture then prevalent in the town. Despite being disabled by a spinal condition, Robinson faced continuous verbal and physical abuse – "I could not go out in a cab without dirt being thrown on me; our windows were broken, doormats stolen; disgusting anonymous letters sent" (Robinson 1892: 158) – and was the butt of a mocking music hall song before her likeness was burnt. She described herself as being able to withstand public and media abuse but noted that such criticism can deter donors because "others are not so 'thick skinned', and this kind of thing prevented ladies joining me" (Robinson 1892: 158).

Over a century later, philanthropists continue to be "burnt" and have dirt thrown at them, although the site has moved from grassy seafronts to social media. In the first decades of the twenty-first century big donors have attracted public censure for giving too much and too little, for giving publicly and giving secretly, for giving at home when need is greater overseas and for giving overseas and therefore not caring about needs at home. As in the past, many attacks are ad hominem, aimed at the person's character or presumed motives rather than their acts or expressed views.

In the summer of 2020 the link between philanthropists and effigies continued when Bill Gates, described as "the voodoo doll of Covid conspiracies" (Wakefield 2020), stood accused of having created the coronavirus pandemic in order to profit from selling vaccines and enabling global surveillance (Wakabayashi *et al.* 2020). Research conducted at the University of Cambridge found that 21 per cent of a representative sample of the UK population agreed to some extent with the statement that "Bill Gates has created the [Covid-19] virus in order to reduce the world population", of whom 3 per cent "agree completely" that he created the virus (Freeman *et al.* 2020: 6), while a similar proportion of Americans believe that Gates wishes to use a mass vaccination campaign to implant microchips to track people with a digital ID (Sanders 2020). Conspiracy theories are known to be a form of coping strategy in unsettling times, with the choice of scapegoat dependent on pre-existing cultural attitudes and fears about certain groups, usually defined by religious beliefs or ethnicities. In the case of the Covid-19 conspiracy theories they reveal widespread concerns about "powerful philanthropists" (Harambam 2020). What makes this choice of scapegoat all the more galling is that no private donor has spent more on fighting diseases than Bill Gates, including contributing $1.75 billion to find treatment and a vaccine for coronavirus during 2020 (Gates & Gates 2021).

Moving from the fantastical to the fictional, but staying in the realm of global villains, the James Bond film franchise successfully capitalized on the public's fear that philanthropists are wolves in sheep's clothing, especially high-profile businessmen with wolfish smiles and zeitgeist philanthropic postures. Near the start of Bond's 22nd big-screen outing, in *Quantum of Solace*, Daniel Craig's superspy is in the MI6 building being briefed about his next assignment by M's chief of staff who explains that "Dominic Greene's been doing a lot of philanthropic work, buying up large tracts of land for ecological preserves". After 007 has pursued his target at glamorous fundraising events around the world, requiring numerous car, boat and plane chases, Bond confronts Greene in the Bolivian desert where his cover as an environmental philanthropist is literally blown up. The Tierra Project is not, as claimed, an eco-park focused on reforestation and environmental science but rather an audacious attempt, in league with a newly installed dictator, to control Bolivia's water supply so that the population can be exploited and terrorized. Greene's fictional deception reflects a common current interpretation of philanthropists – that their superficial stance as social and environmental warriors conceals a desire to preserve and benefit from an economic system that is responsible for the very harms they pretend to care about. Unlike most Bond villains, Greene has no physical deformity, blending easily into the world of glamorous philanthropic parties in order to empha-size the hidden evils in society, as articulated by Bond's ally, retired spy René Mathis: "I guess when one's young, it seems very easy to distinguish between right and wrong. But as one gets older, it becomes more difficult. The villains and the heroes get all mixed up."

Why is it so plausible for a philanthropist to turn out to be a James Bond villain? What is the context that makes it feasible for a fifth of the population to agree that Bill Gates has some culpability for, or seeks to benefit from, Covid-19? What fears have been fomented about philanthropists that make them fodder for effigy burning, conspiracy theorists and Hollywood baddies? This chapter documents how attacks on philanthropy have been commonplace over at least the past 300 years, showing that aspersions have been cast on philanthropists by voices from across society including the media, popular culture, political leaders and public intellectuals.

Philanthropists have not enjoyed ceaseless praise to date

Enduring and widespread disquiet about the motivations, actions and implications of private philanthropic action undermines claims made in contem-porary critiques that philanthropy has enjoyed a free ride in public opinion to date, and is well overdue some critical scrutiny. Critics say that philanthropy has been considered "a paradigmatic form of virtuous behavior", that philanthropists have long been showered with "ceaseless praise" (Reich 2018: 14, 7), that private donors have successfully "silenced their critics" (McGoey 2015: 28) and that most people long believed philanthropic foundations to be "on the side of the angels" (as quoted in Tompkins-Stange 2016: 7). The experiences of Sarah Robinson and Bill Gates, and many more described below, demonstrate that people using their own resources to help others are used to being on the receiving end of intem-perate reactions and personal attacks, and could be forgiven for not recognizing the suggestion that philanthropy is overdue a critical turn.

Criticism of philanthropists varies across cultural contexts

The degree to which philanthropy is praised or criticized is in part a function of context and location. Those standing on US soil in the early twenty-first cen-tury might understandably have felt that big donors could do no wrong. In 2005 the "Persons of the Year" featured on the front cover of *Time* magazine were philanthropists Bill and Melinda Gates and the Irish pop singer and social activist Bono. The Gateses were commended for having "spent the year giving more money away faster than anyone ever has" with a focus on improving global health, and the U2 frontman's efforts, including organizing that year's Live 8 concerts, were hailed for successfully lobbying world leaders to double international aid and cancel $40 billion of debt of the poorest nations" (*Time* 2005).

Six months later, in June 2006, the Gateses were in the news again, along with their friend Warren Buffett, holding a press conference in the appropriately evocative setting of the Carnegie library in New York to announce Buffett's decision to commit almost all of his wealth – $31 billion at that time – to the Bill and Melinda Gates Foundation. Rather than set up his own eponymous "Warren Buffett Foundation" the Omaha investor explained that he thought the Gateses were doing a good job and that it made more sense to collaborate. This merging of the Gateses' and Buffett's philanthropic fortunes involved historically unprecedented amounts of philanthropy, and demonstrated a lack of ego on the part of the newest member of the triad. What was the media and public reaction? It depended which side of the Atlantic you were on.

In America, the media coverage was primarily positive. Some offered only a "one handed clap" and drew concerning parallels with nineteenth-century big giving (Nasaw 2006), but many other American journalists used words like "laudable", "astonishing gift" and "a refreshing move". Even the usually sober *Economist* (US edition) drew parallels with cheesy Hollywood moments, reporting that: "It was an extraordinary sight. The world's two richest men hugged each other as a room full of New York's great and good cheered … In cinema, such a scene would have seemed implausible."

Meanwhile, on the other side of the Atlantic the media told a rather different story. UK journalists wrote: "some perspective is called for" and "all that fuss … left me more than a little bemused". One of the most perplexing media reports began with this sentence: "When the world's second-richest man gives most of his money to the world's richest man we do well to count our spoons". If you are not familiar with the idiomatic expression of "counting your spoons", it comes from Samuel Johnson writing in the eighteenth century about the need to ensure nothing is stolen by suspicious house guests. This expression was later developed by Ralph Waldo Emerson to warn against being deceived by those falsely seeking to make a good impression rather than simply steal the silverware, as Emerson wrote: "The louder he talked of his honour, the faster we counted our spoons."

The use of those words in media coverage, and the clear allusion to suspicious intent on the part of Buffett and the Gateses, highlights the reputational problem faced by philanthropists. Big donors are depicted as intrinsically dodgy and there is not much they can do about it: the more willing they are to talk about their giving – to go public and invite the cameras and journalists in – the more antipathy they generate, despite simultaneous criticism of a lack of transparency by those giving below the radar. Perhaps it could be argued that a brief period of unreflective celebration of philanthropy occurred within the US during the first few years of the twenty-first century, but that was most certainly not the case outside of that country or for very long within it. A few years after that Hollywood moment in New York's Carnegie library, critical views about the role and impact of elite donors became commonplace, and caricatured representations "that were once considered the realm of conspiracy theory" became (or, I would suggest, reverted to) the "mainstream" (Tompkins-Stange 2016: 8).

In order to demonstrate that if any overly celebratory stance towards philanthropy ever existed, it was partial and extremely fleeting, the following sections illustrate the longstanding, mainstream and often repetitive nature of attacks on big givers and big giving over the past 300 years and more.

The longstanding nature of attacks on philanthropy

There is no basis for claims that philanthropists have enjoyed unmitigated applause and approval until twenty-first-century critics finally turned their attention to the issue. To take two examples from past millennia, the biblical injunction against seeking praise for almsgiving, "when you give to the needy, do let not your left hand know what your right hand is doing" (Matthew 6:3), has entered popular parlance and continues to be referenced to admonish donors who give publicly. The early eighth-century writings of the medieval monk and scholar known as the Venerable Bede note the injustice of gifts to the poor being made from wealth derived from the exploitation of those who then stood in need of charity. Mockery of the self-serving motives of donors can be enjoyed as far back as the sixteenth century when Henry Brinklow noted in *Lamentations of a Christian* (published in 1545) that "The rich are said to have left the blind and lame unhelped except it were on Sundays", a critique of Christian charity echoed four decades later in Philip Stubbes' acerbic comment in his pamphlet "The Anatomie of Abuses" (published in 1583) that "people thought themselves halfway to heaven as a reward for giving away an old coat" (both quotes cited in Gray 1905: 23).

Attacks on philanthropy in the eighteenth and nineteenth centuries

The high level of philanthropic activity in the eighteenth and nineteenth centuries has been well documented (Cunningham 2016; Davies 2015; Owen 1964; Prochaska 1990) and its quantities might be assumed to indicate general approval and enthusiasm for such action. But anxieties about the existence and implication of private initiatives in the public sphere were prevalent, as articulated by British politician Charles Greville in 1844: "We are just now overrun with philanthropy, and God knows where it will stop, or whither it will lead us" (cited in Owen 1964: 89).

An early example of the nature of concerns about philanthropic motivation comes in the form of a poem, "The Fable of the Bees", written in the early 1700s by Dutch-born philosopher Bernard Mandeville. Foreshadowing a central feature of contemporary critiques, the poem highlights the self-interest that propels much seemingly other-oriented action in these satirical lines: "Thousands give Money to Beggars from the same motive as they pay their Corn-Cutter, to walk easy ... Pride and Vanity have built more Hospitals than all the Virtues together" (Mandeville 1714).

In the 1730s, English poet Alexander Pope offered further reflection on the sincerity of religious giving in Epistle III of his "Moral Essays" when he wrote: "Who builds a church to God, and not to Fame, Will never mark the marble with his Name." A later eighteenth-century English poet, George Dyer, reiterated the central concern of cloaks of virtue, "The philanthropy that attends public charities is frequently selfishness in disguise", and articulated a point that recurs in discussions of the relationship between philanthropy and social justice: "There would be less occasion to erect so many temples to Charity, if we erected more to justice" (both quotes cited in Cunningham 2020: 87).

An anecdote from the eighteenth century demonstrates the existence of enduring assumptions regarding the lack of sincere and spontaneous generosity among wealthy people: "The Bishop of Salisbury entertained both Mrs Trimmer, who set up schools for poor children, and Hannah More, who fundraised from the rich. The Bishop noted that 'one undertook to reform all the poor and the other all the rich' and he congratulated Mrs Trimmer on having the more hopeful subjects" (Rodgers 1949: 156).

The historian Hugh Cunningham argues that during the eighteenth century, philanthropy became a feature of public life and discourse, replacing "benevolence" as the accepted shorthand for describing good works (Cunningham 2020: 34–5). Cunningham's historic study of the reputation of philanthropy demonstrates that during the eighteenth and nineteenth centuries the concept and practice enjoyed many positive connotations, being understood as an aspirational virtue and encouraged by all major religions, as well as being promoted in many fictional narratives and articles in national newspapers and popular magazines, which encouraged and confirmed philanthropic norms in their readership. However, Cunningham also shows that these positive depictions of philanthropy were concurrently challenged by a wide range of voices including religious leaders, politicians and journalists who variously criticized philanthropy for being unpatriotic, demoralizing and "effeminate". Universal love of humankind and sending funds to help people overseas was felt to be at odds with the nationalistic sentiment needed to support and fund frequent wars, and offensive to those focused on solving local problems such as child labour and domestic poverty. Yet charitable support for the vulnerable – whether at home or abroad – was also viewed as incompatible with the precepts of political economy because it fostered dependency and demoralized recipients, which undermined the workings of the market. The involvement of women in philanthropic work and the "softheartedness" displayed by philanthropists laid them open to accusations of being "unmanly" or "self-perfuming coxcombs" according to *The Times* in 1841 (cited in Cunningham 2020: 117).

Attacks on philanthropy in the nineteenth century

One of many nineteenth-century writers to highlight concerns and anxieties about philanthropy was Ralph Waldo Emerson with his précis of a common explanation for big donations: "Take egotism out, and you would castrate the benefactors." More expansive ruminations on the practices and qualities of philanthropy appeared in the most heralded fiction published in that century, including the novels of Charles Dickens in which he frequently examined and satirized the philanthropic impulse. His caricatures of philanthropists include the foolish Mrs Jellyby in *Bleak House*, who neglects the welfare of her own dirty and dishevelled children while preoccupied with providing assistance to the Borrioboola-Gha in Africa.

A detailed analysis of representations of philanthropy in British and American nineteenth-century fiction, covering Nathanial Hawthorne, George Eliot and William Dean Howells as well as Dickens, shows how these authors reflect on the nature of philanthropy's contribution to wider social, political and economic relations, which was a matter of widespread debate and "anxiety" (Christianson 2007: 12). Some depictions could move beyond binary options of showing philanthropy in a positive or negative light and provide more subtle examples of better and worse philanthropic practice, but a contemporary is quoted in *The Times* in 1884 as saying that: "Novelists generally make their philanthropists fools" (F. B. Money-Coutts, cited in Cunningham 2020: 148). Philanthropists fared little better in the hands of poets and playwrights, as exemplified in Oscar Wilde's 1895 play *An Ideal Husband*, in which Mrs Cheveley complains that "Philanthropy seems to have become simply the refuge of people who wish to annoy their fellow creatures."

Such sentiment was not confined to fiction. A study of media coverage of philanthropy and philanthropists in the 1830s and 1840s finds an array of pejorative adjectives attached to the idea and person of philanthropy, including: "morbid", "puffing", "pseudo", "uninformed", "inconsiderate", "ignorant", "mistaken", "spurious", "so-called", "false", "mealy-mouthed", "misplaced", "pinchbeck", "sham", "blundering" and "misapplied" (Cunningham 2020: 135). According to the author of that study, the critics of philanthropy made more noise than its friends, and the result of this sustained criticism in both factual and fictional publications meant that by the middle of the nineteenth century, philanthropy "carried baggage that it would be difficult to shed" (Cunningham 2020: 126, 130).

In the second half of the nineteenth century, scathing comments about private giving include an article in an 1859 edition of the *Saturday Review* which stated: "No one expects that a person principally occupied in philanthropy will be very wise, very sympathetic, or very large-minded" (cited in Cunningham 2020: 141); and Anthony Trollope's observation in *North America*, published in 1862: "I have sometimes thought that there is no being so venomous, so blood-thirsty, as a professed philanthropist." A more even-handed comment was made by British journalist Walter Bagehot in 1872 when he wondered "whether the benevolence of mankind does most good or harm. Great good, no doubt, philanthropy does, but then it also does great evil." But in the following decades, when Andrew Carnegie's philanthropy emerged, such equitable consideration was lacking. Political leaders condemned him for giving away money they viewed as not rightfully belonging to him, an attack supported by prominent churchmen, including Bishop Hugh Price Hughes, who described Carnegie as "an anti-Christian phenomenon, a social monstrosity, and a grave political peril" (Nasaw 2016). The notion of illegitimacy recurs some years later when the Scots-born steel magnate and his peers are described by Labor leader Eugene V. Debs as "the philanthropic pirates of the Carnegie class" (Krass 2002: 422).

At the end of the nineteenth century a satirical account of the lives of the upper class, written by proto-sociologist Thorstein Veblen, depicts philanthropy as an attempt by rich people to flaunt wealth and win public esteem through actions of "conspicuous consumption" and "honorific waste". Veblen's reference to the widely held assumption that rich donors are motivated by self-interest is clear, and worth quoting at length:

> It is a matter of sufficient notoriety to have become a commonplace jest that extraneous motives are commonly present among the incentives to this class of work [charity] – motives of a self-regarding kind, and especially the motive of an invidious distinction. To such an extent is this true, that many ostensible works of disinterested public spirit are no doubt initiated and carried on with a view primarily to the enhanced repute, or even to the pecuniary gain, of their promoters ... [The invidious motive] would hold true especially with respect to such works as lend distinction to their doer through large and conspicuous expenditure; as, for example, the foundation of a university or of a

public library or museum ... These serve to authenticate the pecuniary reputability of their members, as well as gratefully to keep them in mind of their superior status by pointing the contrast between themselves and the lower-lying humanity in whom the work of amelioration is to be wrought.   (Veblen 1994 [1899]: 208)

Attacks on philanthropy in the twentieth century

The twentieth century began with another satirical takedown of wealth and wealthy donors. In 1901, Irish playwright and eventual Nobel Prize winner George Bernard Shaw's *Socialism for Millionaires* addressed the "sorrow" and "plight" of those having "more money than you can possibly spend on yourself". Describing almsgiving as a "mischief to society", his acerbic pen wrote: "Most of the money given by rich people in charity is made up of conscience money, 'ransom', political bribery and bids for titles ... a millionaire does not really care whether his money does good or not, provided he finds his conscience eased and his social status improved ... the mere disbursement of large sums of money must be counted as a distinctly suspicious circumstance in estimating public character" (Shaw 1901: 14–15).

Eight years later, the English writer G. K. Chesterton developed the same theme in a newspaper article originally headlined "Gifts of the millionaires" which became retitled as "Whitewashing the philanthropist", emphasizing both the focus and subject of his critique:

Philanthropy, as far as I can see, is rapidly becoming the recognizable mark of a wicked man. We have often sneered at the superstition and cowardice of the medieval barons who thought that giving lands to the Church would wipe out the memory of their raids or robberies; but modern capitalists seem to have exactly the same notion; with this not unimportant addition, that in the case of the capitalists the memory of the robberies is really wiped out. This, after all, seems to be the chief difference between the monks who took land and gave pardons and the charity organizers who take money and give praise: the difference is that the monks wrote down in their books and chronicles, "Received three hundred acres from a bad baron"; whereas the modern experts and editors record the three hundred acres and call him a good baron.

(Chesterton 1909)

The "bad baron" that Chesterton specifically had in mind was Standard Oil tycoon John D. Rockefeller, who in 1909 was seeking congressional approval to establish a permanent endowed philanthropic foundation of then-historic proportions. The plan encountered trenchant opposition from senior political, labour and religious leaders, including from the sitting president William Taft and his immediate predecessor Theodore Roosevelt, who said: "no amount of charity in spending such fortunes can compensate in any way for the misconduct in acquiring them". The Rockefeller Foundation was eventually given approval by the New York state legislature in 1913 but not before this episode had revealed the extent and depth of concern across society about wealthy donors and their philanthropic plans.

A year later, in 1914, popular antagonism to the term "philanthropist" was underlined by the publication of *The Ragged Trousered Philanthropist*, a best-selling fictionalized account of Irish author Robert Tressell's experience as a house painter in the south of England, whose labour created disproportionate rewards for his bosses and meant the badly clothed worker was more deserving of the soubriquet. Tressell's classic story, described by fellow social critic George Orwell as "a book everyone should read", continues to be adapted for television and stage performances, and its title has been incorporated into popular culture as a pejorative reference point for understanding philanthropy in contemporary Britain. Other early twentieth-century voices that amplified a critical take on philanthropy include the first of John Galsworthy's *Forsyte Saga*, in which a wealthy London family is described as being "supporters of such charitable institutions as might be beneficial to their sick domestics", and an editorial in *The Times* in 1914 which stated: "Philanthropist is about as much a term of abuse as of praise; indeed, it has been said that, if ever there is a revolution in England, the first blood let will be that of the philanthropists" (cited in Cunningham 2020: 177).

In countries where revolutions did occur in this century, the reputation of philanthropy did not fare well. According to the 1950 edition of the *Soviet Concise Dictionary of Foreign Words*, "philanthropy" is "A means the bourgeoisie use to deceive workers and disguise the parasitism and its exploiter's face by rendering hypocritical aid to the poor in order to distract the latter from class struggle", while in Maoist China organized charity was denounced as a "sugar coated bullet", the means by which elites attempt to prevent class struggle by placating the labouring class (Jeffreys 2016). The argument that philanthropy is a superficial appeasement causing the postponement of fundamental reform originated in totalitarian regimes to justify the prohibition of voluntary action, and now enjoys support across Western capitalist regimes from the likes of populist writers such as Anand Giridharadas (2018a) and his enthusiastic social media followers.

Publications in the second half of the twentieth century captured popular ambiguity about the merits and expectations of philanthropy. A social history of philanthropy in America noted: "The word philanthropy and the idea it carries with it arouses mixed emotions... We expect rich men to be generous with their wealth and criticize them when they are not; but when they make benefaction, we question their motives, deplore the methods by which they obtained their abundance and wonder whether their gifts will not do more harm than good" (Bremner 1960: 2).

In the UK sentiment about philanthropy was less equivocal. Leading 1970s Labour Party politician Richard Crossman noted that many of his political colleagues felt that philanthropy was "an odious expression of social oligarchy and churchy bourgeois attitudes", and "do-gooding a word as dirty as philanthropy" (cited in Prochaska 2014: 5). In the same decade a comprehensive study of UK charities offered a definition of "philanthropist" that presages many themes found in twenty-first century critiques: "[A philanthropist is] fuzzy minded, self-indulgent, too preoccupied with his own emotional satisfactions... He is a capitalist, interested in perpetuating his own privileged status by maintaining an inequitable system as cheaply as he can: stealing the hog and giving the feet for alms" (Nightingale 1973: 111–12).

In the same decade a study of philanthropic foundations highlighted the ongoing dilemma faced by institutional philanthropy, rooted in broader popular discontent, noting that donors "must feel that whatever they do is going to attract criticism" because: "They are accused, simultaneously and seriatim, of manipulative liberalism; or trying to play God; of being too staid; too crackpot; too pink; too conformist; too subversive; and too indistinguishable from secret intelligence agencies. Writers as different as Dickens, Ian Fleming, the Webbs, Dwight Macdonald and Sinclair Lewis ... have lampooned them" (Whitaker 1974a: 20).

By the end of the twentieth century the American historian Gertrude Himmelfarb, writing about perceptions of philanthropy in contemporary society, highlighted issues of donor power, efficacy and self-serving motives that lie, respectively, at the heart of what I call the contemporary academic, insider and populist critiques:

> the charge now is that philanthropy is all too often a self-serving exercise on the part of philanthropists at the expense of those whom they are ostensibly helping. Philanthropy stands condemned, not only as ineffectual, but as hypocritical and self-aggrandizing. In place of "the love of mankind", philanthropy is now identified with the love of self. It is seen as an occasion for social climbing, for joining committees and attending charity balls in the company of the rich and famous. Or as an opportunity to cultivate business and professional associations. Or as a way of enhancing one's self-esteem and self-approbation by basking in the esteem and approbation of others. Or as a method of

exercising power over those in no position to challenge it. Or as a means (a relatively painless means) of atoning for a sense of guilt, perhaps for riches unethically acquired. Or as a passport to heaven, a record of good works and virtues to offset bad works and vices. Or (the most recent addition to this bill of indictment) as a form of "voyeurism".

(Himmelfarb 1995: 160)

Attacks on philanthropy in the twenty-first century

In the present century, commentary on philanthropy continues to be entangled with concerns about the existence and morality of wealth accumulation and growing inequality. In 2019, when I asked a representative sample of the British public to define a philanthropist in three words, among the negative words that came to the public's mind were: bad, cheat, condescending, crafty, crap, cunning, cynical, deceptive, deluded, demanding, egotist, erratic, evasive, exaggerates, failure, greedy, guilty, hubris, idiot, insensitive, liar, naïve, opinionated, out-of-touch, ruthless, self-centred, self-obsessed, self-promoting, self-serving, tax avoider, tax dodger, too much wealth, undemocratic and untrustworthy (Breeze 2020). These public attitudes are in line with adjectives that the UK print media uses to present big givers: austere, couture-clad, Dickensian, high-rolling, philandering, ruthless, so-called, status-seeking and tax ruse (Breeze 2011).

Those public attitudes are shaped and reinforced by wider commentary on philanthropy. A study of Britain's "super-rich" in the twenty-first century claims that their charitable activity is driven by a desire to impress, rather than by altruism, making philanthropy "the rich person's equivalent of a peacock's tail" because its goal is to make the donor appear more attractive and help them to win the approval and admiration of others (Lansley 2006: 175). Echoing Lansley, leading social commentators Polly Toynbee and David Walker also question the sincerity of contemporary philanthropic acts. A chapter in their exposé of "Unjust" Britain, entitled "Philanthropy is no excuse", describes charitable giving by the rich as "mere ostentation", a "passport to the in-crowd" and "another way of exerting power and control", while philanthropy is "a way to fame and extra fortune ... the ultimate door-opening lifestyle accessory", devoid of any genuine interest in those they profess to help (Toynbee & Walker 2008: 174, 177). These themes recur in media coverage, for example a piece on the Ark Gala Ball, which raised over £100 million between 2002 to 2012 for children's health and education charities, is depicted as an "appalling spectacle" – a "vulgar" gathering of the "obscenely rich". At a time when philanthropy was supposedly enjoying uncritical praise, the author of that article – in line with her newspaper's editorial stance and readership's outlook – proclaims, "I object to high-net-worth philanthropy in principle" (Williams 2011). A decade later, when reporting on MacKenzie Scott's historic philanthropic announcement, another UK journalist felt impelled to make a similar declaration: "I count myself a philanthropy sceptic" (Moore 2020).

More celebratory accounts of capitalism also acknowledge the ongoing philanthropy problematic. In Irish business guru Charles Handy's profiles of *The New Philanthropists* – so-called because they are younger, self-made, cosmopolitan and outcome-oriented donors – many interviewees resist calling themselves "a philanthropist" because of a "feeling it still carries overtones of Victorian noblesse oblige, of paternalistic and interfering do-gooding" (Handy 2006: 9).

Despite some unreflective US press comment at the turn of the century noted above, concern about rich donors is not absent in twenty-first-century media coverage, as illustrated by two pairs of articles in leading national newspapers in the US and UK. The *Washington Post* ran an article with the headline, "The hidden dangers of million-dollar donations" (Rogers 2012), and published a response to MacKenzie Scott's norm-changing gifts of 2020 that noted: "When we hear of massive donations from the super-rich, we should consider it less a sign of goodwill and more an indication of a system that is far out of whack" (Villanueva 2020).

In the UK, *The Guardian* published two "long reads", both with antagonistic headlines: "The trouble with charitable billionaires" (Rhodes & Bloom 2018) and "How philanthropy benefits the super-rich" (Vallely 2020).

Philanthropy in contemporary popular culture

Philanthropic activity is also regularly satirized in popular culture. A number of sitcoms have featured plots revolving around philanthropic acts, such as the painful unfurling of an unrealizable commitment made by Steve Carell's character in *The Office* to pay college tuition for underprivileged students ("Scott's Tots", series 6, episode 12), running jokes about mismanagement at the Sweetums Foundation and the indignities of negotiating naming rights for donors in *Parks and Recreation* (Schiller 2015), and a toe-curling episode of *Curb Your Enthusiasm* in which Larry rails at the faux humility and "fake philanthropy" of a not so anonymous donor (series 6, episode 2).

Big-screen portrayals are also riven with plots and characterization that problematize big giving. "Hollywood never gets it right when it sets out to depict philanthropy. Donors are shown as meddlesome bumblers, wealthy scoundrels, or superheroes able to work wonders with a simple check" (Lenkowsky 2012). The new millennium began in Hollywood with the film *Pay It Forward*, starring A-listers whose on-screen young son pays the ultimate price for trying to encourage chains of generosity. The belief that no good deed should go unpunished is a familiar theme in big-screen depictions of philanthropy, as is the portrayal of philanthropists "as well-meaning but boring ... whose efforts often wind up being self-serving or harmful" (Lenkowsky 2009). This trope dates back to at least the 1950s when the CBS television series *The Millionaire* featured a philanthropist named John Beresford Tipton whose anonymous million dollar gifts often left the recipients no better off than they were previously. The disembodied depiction of this benefactor, who only appeared as a voice giving instructions to his assistant and an arm signing the cheques, reflects the belief that big giving happens in the shadows with no meaningful relationship between givers and recipients. By 2009, when another American TV network, NBC, broadcast *The Philanthropist*, the donor was in full view, but had another trope-ridden backstory as a billionaire playboy whose efforts were unimpeded by the prosaic bureaucratic concerns facing real-life humanitarians seeking to do good on the African continent. Unlike real contemporary philanthropists, who must collaborate with the machinery of global governance and work through local partnerships to effect change, NBC's twenty-first-century philanthropist is an action man who survives the jungle and seduces the charity's medical director while delivering cholera vaccines in rural Nigeria. The philanthropist as a James Bond-style hero may seem like some progress is being made in popular culture depictions of philanthropy, but it perpetuates an unhelpful example of the white saviour complex and an unrealistic idea of how big giving accomplishes change through "muscular charity", which could harm rather than help its reputation because "exaggerating what philanthropy, especially of the more personalized kind, can accomplish is risky, potentially leading to a backlash built upon frustrated expectations" (Lenkowsky 2009).

For the most part, philanthropy on the big screen is used as a convenient plot device (typically the twist that an apparent goodie is a baddie in disguise) rather than as a central topic that can carry a movie in its own right, which is surprising given the extraordinary stories and larger than life characters that populate the history of philanthropy (Davies 2016).

One notable recent development concerns the role of philanthropy *behind* the camera. In 2004 eBay founder Jeff Skoll founded Participant Media to make films that "inspire audiences to engage in positive social change" (Participant n.d.). Participant has so far released over a hundred feature and documentary films including Al Gore's *An Inconvenient Truth*, which played a key role in alerting the public to the dangers of global warming, and two winners of the Oscar for Best Picture: *Green Book* (in 2018) and *Spotlight* (in 2015). Whether the movie-going public is aware that some films have an agenda beyond box office receipts, and how kindly they would feel about their date night with popcorn being a successful outcome of a philanthropic plan, is debatable. But the idea of harnessing the power of storytelling through films as a tool for philanthropy is certainly an intriguing one (Davies 2016).

Meanwhile, depictions that delegitimize the philanthropic impulse continue to be broadcast and gain attention on social media. In the Netflix comedy *Patriot Act*, broadcast in late 2019, Hasan Minhaj takes aim at the wealthiest philanthropists in an episode entitled "Why Billionaires Won't Save Us", claiming, to vigorous approval from the studio audience, that huge donations are made because "the rich don't want us coming after them with pitchforks". The audience was receptive to that line because they had been exposed to plenty of similar material from factual, fictional and popular sources. As noted in the Introduction, the mainstreaming of anti-philanthropy sentiment was cemented at the start of that year, in January 2019, when comments at the World Economic Forum gathering in Davos by the Dutch historian Rutger Bregman went viral: "Stop talking about stupid philanthropy schemes, we should be talking about taxes, taxes, taxes." Bregman also memorably described Davos as being like a firefighters' conference where attendees were not allowed to speak about water. That links to another memorable sound bite from a populist critic, discussed further in Chapter 5, that "Arsonists make the best firefighters" (Giridharadas 2018a: 129), by which is meant that rich people start fires then show up as the firefighters to reap the glory of solving a problem they caused. Giridharadas' book promotion led to a slew of critical headlines, including "Meet the 'change agents' who are enabling inequality" (Stiglitz 2018) and "Inside the self-serving world of wealthy do-gooders" (Higgins 2018).

The following year a major philanthropic story hit the headlines after Notre Dame Cathedral in Paris burnt down in the early hours of 15 April 2019. By daybreak, as the fire still smouldered, half a billion euros had been raised in donations from high-profile French business people and their families to help pay for its reconstruction. The speed with which such an enormous sum could be raised kicked off a global discussion about the rights and wrongs of that philanthropic reaction, largely focused on whether a building, however culturally significant, should be prioritized over the needs of the poor in Paris and beyond. Far less attention was paid to the manner in which those mega donations were reported in the media, and what that tells us about the reputation of philanthropy. A week after the fire an article appeared on the BBC News website containing a sentence that caught my eye as I read it at the crack of dawn: "France's mega-rich have *trumped* up huge sums to restore the gothic architecture" (Cuddy & Boelpaep 2019, emphasis added). The phrase "trumped up" means "fabricated" or "invented as an excuse" – something that is "trumped up" is not true. This seemed a curious phrase for a reputable global news network to use. Regardless of opinions on whether Bernard Arnault, the Bettencourt-Meyers family and the Pinault family should have given, respectively, €200 million, €200 million and €100 million, those donations were not made up, invented or fabricated. But "trumped up" was the phrase that came to the journalist's mind, and it got past the subeditor. Later that day I went back online to look at the same story again, by which time the wording had been amended. The new version, which is still online now, says: "France's mega-rich have *stumped* up huge sums to restore the gothic architecture". The truthfulness of the gifts was no longer under question but is the phrase "stumped up" – which means to have paid a sum of money unwillingly or reluctantly, to pay when one does not want to – much better? In the first version of this news story the philanthropy was fabricated, and in the second version it was made unwillingly, despite there being no evidence to support either scenario. What this insight into journalistic writing and subediting shows is that when it comes to philanthropy, especially on a very large scale, people are primed to smell a rat.

A final example takes us from rodents to amphibians. After completing the first draft of this chapter, I sank onto the sofa to watch a movie with my kids. Their choice was the 2011 movie reboot of the Muppets in which the anarchic puppets reunite to try and raise $10 million to save the Muppet Theatre from being demolished. Who is the scheming, archetypical baddie with a maniacal laugh pretending to have a sympathetic interest in preserving the building, and yet fully intending to tear it down to drill for oil? As Kermit explains: it is "oil baron Tex Richman, the wealthy philanthropist". Of course he is. It 'aint easy being mean, without also bashing philanthropy.

Summary of concerns raised about philanthropy: continuity and change

While criticism of philanthropy has clearly been a constant over time, its content has undergone some changes. The dominant concern in the earliest criticisms exemplified above was that rich donors were using philanthropy as a shortcut to heaven, inaccessible to those without the wealth to enhance their chances of making a good impression at the pearly gates. As belief in the realities of heaven and hell declined, and as the percentage of philanthropists making their fortunes in industry began to eclipse those who had inherited their wealth, criticisms of big donors refocused on concerns about how philanthropy was being used by "new money" and "robber barons" to elevate their standing by burnishing their earthly reputation and accessing elite networks. The latest iteration of concerns about philanthropy encompasses and extends both the previous "vanity cloaked in virtue" and "self-advancement" arguments, with a hyper-critical twist that philanthropy is not just a symptom but the enabler of the problematic that it seeks to conceal, and from which donors benefit.

A further development in the twenty-first century is that many contemporary critics believe themselves to be making novel observations, noticing concealed truths that have not so far been identified and that demand to be revealed. There is clearly a contextual aspect to the depth and strength of attacks on philanthropy, with some countries such as the US enjoying a more positive perspective on philanthropy than, for example, the UK. But generalized comments about philanthropists enjoying "ceaseless praise" and their critics being silenced suggests an ahistorical perspective when over a century earlier, Thorstein Veblen's satirical takedown of rich donors began by noting that concerns about philanthropy were "a matter of sufficient notoriety to have become a commonplace jest".

Criticizing the "do-goodism" of the wealthy is clearly historically typical, normative and an old sport (Alexander 2019; Lenkowsky 2020). Yet critics curiously view themselves as being daringly counter-cultural for suggesting that philanthropy is problematic and that philanthropists are "not all they seem". Yet once potshots and wisecracks about "wealthy philanthropists" pop up on sitcoms and are voiced by Kermit the Frog, to state that there is something dodgy about rich donors is clearly a mainstream, rather than a subversive, stance.

This review of examples from across four centuries supports the conclusion of a comprehensive historic analysis that "Philanthropy's reputation was never secure" (Cunningham 2020: 202). These charges come from all quarters of the public sphere, are rarely met head on with rebuttals and exist in conjunction with an increasingly voluminous academic critique, which is the focus of Chapter 3. The resulting contemporary milieu is one in which donors – particularly big donors – face widespread and ingrained beliefs and assumptions about their motivations and intentions.

Conclusion

This chapter has shown that attacks on philanthropy are longstanding, with unknowable but predictably negative impacts on the philanthropic impulse and therefore on the resources available to nonprofit organizations to fund their work. The historical record shows that praise and criticism of philanthropy have coexisted for a long time, yet contemporary critics overstate the former and overlook the latter. Despite the assertion that philanthropy has thus far had a "free ride" in public opinion and is "long overdue" a critical backlash, it is clear that philanthropy and philanthropists have long held "an uncertain position in the popular and political imagination" (Brooks 2015: 38).

On the night that Sarah Robinson's effigy was paraded through the streets of Portsmouth, the "admiring mob" en route to burn her likeness were rewarded with beer from the public houses they passed (Robinson 1892: 159). Reflecting on the cumulative experience of being abused on the streets and in the local press, and being frustrated by local government and the military who tried to block her efforts to help the soldiers of Portsmouth and their families, Robinson wrote: "I then began to realize what the Institute was to cost me" (Robinson 1892: 155). Clearly the "cost" being referred to was not just the monetary value of her donations but also the high personal price she paid which, as noted at the start of this chapter, "prevented ladies joining me" (Robinson 1892: 158). Being attacked may spur some people to redouble their efforts, but it deters and takes a toll on others. The decision to avoid that personal cost, and protect loved ones from being drawn into the line of fire, can lead some to decide not to stick their head above the philanthropic parapet. The impact of philanthropy's bad reputation, owing to the broader price incurred by donors, is difficult to assess in relation to those who currently give and entirely unknowable regarding those who have not yet accumulated or inherited wealth.

While the nature of critiques has changed over time, three sets of concerns have been constant: (1) that philanthropy is undemocratic because those possessing wealth can divert it as they choose, to their preferences, with a tax break but little oversight; (2) that philanthropy is not redistributive, and people think it should be, because the causes receiving philanthropic support are not those with the greatest economic need; and (3) that philanthropists' motives are suspect – image polishing at best, self-dealing at worst. These are, respectively, the core concerns found in the academic critique, the insider critique and the populist critique, each of which is explained, illustrated and discussed in greater detail in Chapters 3–5.

3
THE ACADEMIC CRITIQUE

The death of a child is an unthinkable tragedy. A time-honoured way of coping with bereavement and trying to make something positive come from the depths of grief is to create a philanthropic legacy in memory of lost loved ones. In 1884, when Leland and Jane Stanford lost their only child, 15-year-old Leland Jr, to typhoid fever they decided to found a university in his name so that, in Leland Sr's words: "the children of California shall be our children" (Greer & Kostoff 2020: 53–4). Stanford has become one of the world's top universities, producing over 80 Nobel laureates, one president of the United States (Herbert Hoover) and some of the most noted academics engaged in the scholarly study of philanthropy. Their work is appreciated by fellow philanthropy academics and has helped our subject become one that is taken seriously across the globe. But that body of work, which often argues that philanthropy is undemocratic, an exercise in power and insufficiently concerned about inequality, reinforces the problematization of philanthropy and ironically promotes a much narrower conceptualization of private giving than that expressed in their institution's founding gift.

The academic critique of philanthropy

Academic writing on philanthropy includes descriptive, analytical and theoretical work, and covers a huge range of topics and perspectives, which collectively have advanced our understanding of the purpose and practice of private action for the public good. But three key concerns recur in this body of work that together constitute what I am calling the academic critique: that philanthropy is *not* democratic, *not* concerned about power dynamics and *not* focused on equality. The foregrounding of negatives is familiar turf for the "nonprofit sector" which, as the name indicates, is defined on the basis of what it does *not* do – it does not distribute a profit – rather than highlighting what the sector *does* do and does well. This results in the value and positive potential of philanthropically funded nonprofit action being obscured by a focus on negative characterizations.

Criticisms of philanthropy's undue influence on wider society, lack of accountability and resulting erosion of democratic principles are longstanding (Eikenberry & Mirabella 2017: 43), but are now receiving extensive attention and emphasis in contemporary scholarship, and are landing successfully with public, practitioner and policy audiences who are repeating and amplifying these concerns, which are explained in turn.

Philanthropy is undemocratic

The most straightforward version of this claim states that philanthropy is not democratic because philanthropic decision-making is undertaken by people without an electoral mandate. Philanthropists – and their employees – decide what does and does not get funded, so their personal connections to some charitable causes and organizations, and their greater interests in some issues over others, mean that the whims of rich donors drive the distribution of funding. This is not how decisions that affect the public good are supposed to be made in modern democracies. Political equality at the ballot box – one vote per eligible adult – is the chosen mechanism for reaching collective decisions that are implemented by elected representatives who remain accountable to those who put them in office, and whose power is contingent on retaining the support of the electorate. Ordinary citizens have no mechanisms to hold philanthropists to account because big donors cannot be voted out of office or put out of business. This is why Stanford scholar Rob Reich argues that "wealthy elites can cause problems for democratic politics" (Reich 2018: 64), and why his fellow institutional scholars Aaron Horvath and Walter Powell describe "big money philanthropy" as being hostile to democratically driven state provision, because philanthropically funded ideas are "imposed without public deliberation or consultation" (Horvath & Powell 2016: 121).

Philanthropic engagement with education policy in the US is a commonly cited example of philanthropy that breaches democratic tenets. Examples range from the harmful effects of school fundraising on exacerbating inequalities, because schools in richer areas can rely on greater support from wealthier parents (Reich 2005), to state- and national-level efforts to promote ideas backed by philanthropists such as school vouchers, charter schools, the common core curriculum and the $100 million of funding from Mark Zuckerberg to reform the Newark public school system. Not only are these viewed as undemocratic in the here and now, they are assumed to represent a long-term agenda to undermine democratically organized services in the future: "disruptive philanthropists are eager to scale up their alternatives in the hope that they might replace forms of public provision" (Horvath & Powell 2016: 92).

This final key aspect of concerns about the relationship between private giving and democracy states that not only does philanthropy run counter to agreed-upon ideas about how public decisions should be made and enacted, it risks eroding support for democracy itself by promoting the "superiority" of charity in providing for disadvantaged citizens (Reich 2014: 409). When public services are funded privately, this enables philanthropy to "crowd out" government action and positions plutocracy (the rule of the wealthy) as a viable alternative. The threat of supplanting governmental provision is particularly problematic when the means by which some donors became wealthy is "ill gotten" and exacerbates the very problems that require collective solutions, such as insecure and exploitative conditions for workers (McGoey 2015: 8–9). It is also problematic if philanthropy becomes the preferred method of delivering services across society, because those lacking financial resources will become dependent on the goodwill of their fellow richer citizens (Pevnick 2016), rather than provision to mitigate inequality being directed by social justice considerations.

Philanthropy is an exercise in power

The second central claim of the academic critique, that philanthropy is a form or exercise of power, has been a cornerstone of scholarly writing about private giving for decades. Over 40 years ago, Donald Fisher's analysis of the Rockefeller Foundation concluded that philanthropic funding of social science research in universities sought to maintain, rather than alter, the social order, by producing and reproducing cultural hegemony that preserved both the existing economic structure and the social inequalities inherent in that structure (Fisher 1980, 1983). This analysis of how the bourgeoisie use their wealth to maintain and expand their power in capitalist societies draws on the ideas of the Italian Marxist theorist Antonio Gramsci. Around the same time a collection of essays, focused on the activities of the Carnegie, Ford and Rockefeller Foundations, also offered a critical analysis of the sociopolitical consequences of organized philanthropy, arguing that these institutions: "have a corrosive influence on a democratic society; they represent relatively unregulated and unaccountable concentrations of power and wealth which buy talent, promote causes, and, in effect establish an agenda of what merits society's attention" (Arnove 1980: 1).

There has been minimal development in the content of this analysis in the intervening years as philanthropy continues to be understood as a form of "bourgeois hegemony" with ideological objectives that seek to defend elite interests and avoid reforms that favour the non-wealthy. In this vein, the current academic critique frames philanthropy as "a form of private power that disrupts the exercise of public power" (Bernholz *et al.* 2016: 12), with philanthropy depicted as an "unaccountable, non-transparent, donor-directed, and perpetual exercise of power ... that fits uneasily, at best, in democratic societies that enshrine the value of political equality" (Reich 2018: 7–8).

Philanthropy is described as a form of power because it is skewed towards the preferences of the rich and amplifies their existing louder voice. This interpretation is backed by US data showing the growing dominance of big donors within total philanthropic income from individuals (Rooney 2018, 2019). The problematic implications of this shift towards "top-heavy philanthropy", in which nonprofit organizations become increasingly reliant on larger donations from smaller numbers of wealthy donors, mean that "the giving sector is increasingly becoming a tax-subsidized province of the wealthy, who exercise considerable private power over the nonprofit sector and civic life as a whole" (Collins & Flannery 2020: 1).

The "power problem" also has a historic angle as critics dispute the right of long-dead donors to establish foundations that exist in perpetuity, and therefore continue to exercise power and influence over future generations. This "deadhand" or "mortmain" argument was set out almost three centuries ago, in 1757, by the French economist Anne-Robert Turgot who expressed concern that donors could "subject unborn generations to their caprice" (as cited and discussed in Clarke 1964: 498). This perspective was supported in the following century by Arthur Hobhouse, who wrote: "it seems the most extravagant of propositions to say that, because a man has been fortunate enough to enjoy a large share of this world's goods in this life, he shall therefore and for no other cause, when he must quit this life and can enjoy his goods no longer, be entitled to speak from his grave ever and dictate ever to living men how that portion of the earth's produce shall be spent" (Hobhouse 1880: 28).

Skewed patterns of giving, uneven engagement in philanthropy and the ability of some citizens to use donations to draw attention to their preferred causes, issues and solutions creates an "empowerment gap" and exacerbates civic inequality that impacts on how the public conversation is shaped: who gets heard and who drives the social agenda (Callahan 2017). This "imperilment of democracy" (Collins & Flannery 2020), through the amplification of rich donors' concerns and muting of ordinary citizens, is not viewed as accidental; rather it is understood as the result of proactive efforts by policymakers and citizens to incentivize and encourage philanthropy by the richest citizens.

State-sponsored financial inducements to donate exist in most countries around the world, despite the inability to precisely quantify what societal benefit occurs as a result of foregone tax revenue (Layton 2015). In the US, tax breaks to incentivize philanthropy are worth around $50 billion each year (CRS 2020: 9), and in the UK the cost of incentivizing donations is around £2.8 billion (HMRC 2019).[1] As donors receive a deduction based on what they would have otherwise paid in tax, those who pay higher tax rates – namely the wealthiest – receive a higher charitable deduction than those who pay lower rates, and for non-taxpayers there is no deduction at all, meaning that the "cost of giving" is highest for those too poor to pay tax. While all progressive taxation systems create the perverse outcome that philanthropy is cheapest for the wealthiest, it is aggravated in the US where the itemized charitable deduction creates particular equity concerns. In that country, the design of charity tax relief means that ordinary Americans are much less likely to be able to take advantage of the incentive, as only those who itemize their taxes, typically the highest earners, can claim tax reliefs (Piper 2019). This situation was predicted to worsen after the Republican tax reforms in the 2017 Tax Cut and Jobs Act reduced further the number of US taxpayers who will itemize their taxes and can therefore claim charity tax breaks. As the author of a historical review of the US charity deduction concludes: "As in 1917, policymakers have chosen to protect the philanthropy of a small number of very generous wealthy donors with favourable tax treatment, even as the contribution deduction will be newly unavailable to millions of more ordinary donors" (Duquette 2019).

Concerns that fiscal arrangements unfairly enhance the existing power of the rich are compounded by a lack of scrutiny that would otherwise accompany public expenditure. As the tax incentive for donors is funded from the collective tax base, that means a percentage of the value of total philanthropic funds represents public, rather than private, money – with the proportion coming from public funds being highest for those donations made by the wealthiest, higher-rate taxpayers. For example, a donor who pays a 40 per cent tax rate receives twice the public subsidy for their donations than a donor paying a 20 per cent tax rate. Therefore it is argued that philanthropic expenditure ought to be scrutinized in the same way as any other form of government spending, rather than mistakenly treated as a purely private enterprise that exists in the realm of individual moral action. To allow individual donors full autonomy to direct this spending, which would otherwise be available for allocation by democratically elected representatives, is – according to critics – to permit a state-subsidized power grab.

In addition to fiscal incentives, the rich are also targeted by their wealthy peers to increase their giving. The Giving Pledge, founded in 2010 by Bill Gates and Warren Buffett, encourages fellow billionaires to make a public commitment

---

1. While around half of UK charity tax breaks are paid to the recipient charity rather than to the donor, this uplift may be factored into the calculation by savvy givers.

to give away at least half of their wealth during their lifetimes or in their will. After a decade, by December 2020, it had 216 signatories from 24 countries and represents well over $100 billion committed to philanthropy. The Giving Pledge is described as a "textbook case" of top-heavy philanthropy in action: "What was intended to be a civic-minded initiative to encourage generosity is, instead, continuing the concentration of taxpayer-subsidized private charitable power" (Collins & Flannery 2020: 7). Although the majority of Giving Pledge signatories are based in the US, and the data supporting the concept of top-heavy philanthropy are also based on the US population, the trend of having fewer but richer donors is occurring globally, with documented evidence in the United Kingdom, Australia, the Netherlands and Canada (Rooney 2019).

The contention that philanthropy is an exercise in power is thus derived from three factors: the unequal distribution of income and wealth which is reinforced by philanthropic spending; the louder "voice" available to those able to make big donations who can decide what does and does not get funded; and the exacerbation of this power differential by tax reliefs which subsidize the personal interests of big donors and do not produce equitable outcomes. This last point leads into the final plank of the academic critique.

Philanthropy is insufficiently concerned with inequality

The third concern of the academic critique is that philanthropic activity and charity tax breaks have become a subsidy for elite private tastes, rather than being focused on tackling poverty and redressing inequality. The proposition that equalizing life chances ought to be the central – or only – goal of private giving overlaps with the insider critique, as discussed in Chapter 4, which also promotes ideas around cost-effectiveness within this focus. But the redistributive consequences of philanthropy are a longstanding feature of academic studies, and the argument that philanthropists are not sufficiently agents of social justice and greater equality has been concisely summed up in yet another pithy quote from Stanford scholar Rob Reich, who writes that "philanthropy is not often a friend of equality, can be indifferent to equality, and can even be a cause of inequality" (Reich 2018: 69).

The greater benefits for big donors described above, in relation to extending and reinforcing their dominant position within society and receiving higher tax subsidies, is exacerbated by evidence that the rich support different kinds of causes than non-rich donors, including those that facilitate and sustain elite culture such as arts organizations and universities (Odendahl 1990; Ostrower 1995). More recent surveys of philanthropic distributions support this conclusion, finding that the majority of donations are not focused on welfare provision and alleviation of basic needs, and that the lack of data tracking who benefits from charity means it can at best be described as potentially "modestly redistributive" (Reich 2005, 2013; Wolpert 2006).

This lack of focus on inequality persists despite compelling evidence that the ever-growing wealth gap is socially divisive, economically inefficient and environmentally destructive. The most recent data underline that concentrations of wealth continue to grow, despite all the recent social and economic turmoil. Globally by 2019 there were 20.8 million high-net-worth individuals (defined as having investible assets of at least $1 million, excluding primary residence, collectibles, consumables and consumer durables), of whom around 9 per cent (1.9 million people) have over $5 million and just over 1 per cent (201,000 people) have $30 million or more (Capgemini 2021: 10). Within each band, the population and wealth of all these groups has increased, and the percentage change in the financial wealth of high-net-worth individuals from 2019 to 2020 was positive in every region (from a 0.5 per cent increase in Latin America to 11.9 per cent in North America, with Africa 3.8 per cent, Asia-Pacific 8.4 per cent, Europe 4.5 per cent and Middle East 10.7 per cent) (Capgemini 2021: 7, 10). The most devastating statistic about inequality is that the world's richest eight men possess the same wealth as half the global population (Oxfam 2017: 2). Other powerful data show that since 2015 the richest 1 per cent own more wealth than the rest of the population combined (Credit Suisse 2016), and that in the US, over the last 30 years, the growth in the incomes of the bottom 50 per cent has been zero, whereas incomes of the top 1 per cent have grown 300 per cent (Piketty *et al.* 2016). While inequality has long been a concern for many people, protests against its seeming acceptance as a "natural" by-product of the way we organize our societies and economies spread across the world in 2011, starting with Occupy Wall Street in New York, whose slogan "We are the 99%" refers to the target of the protest: the 1 per cent – including rich donors – who hog wealth, property and power.

Having set out the damning concerns that philanthropy is undemocratic, that philanthropy is an exercise in power and that philanthropy is insufficiently concerned about inequality, what is the response to the academic critique?

Defending philanthropy against the academic critique

This chapter began with the story of wealthy parents who founded a university to make sense of losing their only child, to illustrate that a gift borne in grief has, in part, enabled a body of work that questions the propriety of philanthropy. My defence against this academic critique begins with two further examples of philanthropic activity, which illustrate how private action for the public good can be far removed from assumptions that have fomented this critique of philanthropy.

If you search for examples of "philanthropic success" you will probably come across a name that is not especially well known and does not otherwise often come up in discussions on philanthropy: Dr John Dorr. Born in the late nine-teenth century, Dorr was an industrial chemist living in the north-eastern United States who was troubled by the number of road traffic accidents occurring at night and in bad weather. Having a scientific frame of mind, he came up with the hypothesis that poor visibility driving conditions prompted drivers to hug the white lines painted down the middle of highways, and he proposed that painting another set of white lines on the outside edges of roads would reduce the number of deaths and serious accidents. When he persuaded highway engineers to test this idea, fatalities were significantly reduced, but the high cost of "shoulder striping", at $150 per mile, meant it took years of funding and advocacy by the Dorr Family Foundation before this idea became standard practice for safer highways (Schindler 2007b). When this philanthropic success story is recounted, the standard sign-off goes something like this: "everyone who travels on roads is indebted to John Dorr for this life-preserving discovery", which, of course, is true. But in the context of the academic critique of philanthropy, another post-script is more salient: this example demonstrates a benign interaction between philanthropy and government, where the former makes the world better without undermining or trying to "take over" the latter. We can cheer this idea without expecting the descendants of John Dorr to commit to funding and undertaking the painting of white lines on every highway for all time. This example of phil-anthropic success is also devoid of any worrying abuse of power, and does not address inequality – quite the opposite, given the demographics of car owner-ship in the early twentieth century – yet still generates obvious public benefit. So none of the key concerns expressed in the academic critique are necessarily integral to philanthropy in action.

To take another example, the critics of philanthropy based at Stanford and other universities all directly benefit from another "undemocratic" philanthropic intervention: the ability to retire with financial security and dignity. In 1905, Andrew Carnegie created the Carnegie Foundation for the Advancement of Teaching with a $10 million endowment to ensure financial independence for higher education faculty members; in 1918 this became the Teachers Insurance and Annuity Association of America, which today is the biggest provider of pensions and life insurance for educators, as well as retirees from government, medical, cultural and other nonprofit occupations. Carnegie's motivation was twofold. First, an admiration for scholars and a desire to promote their lifelong comfort and dignity, and to remedy the disparity between the great value con-ferred on society by higher education faculty and the miserly financial benefit society gave faculty in return. Second, a less high-minded, meddling motive: to provide an attractive inducement for professors past their prime to retire and free up positions for younger scholars (Schindler 2007a: 26). Pensions for professors was "at the time an unusual benefit" (Lagemann & de Forest 2007: 51) that is now entirely mainstream and funded through non-philanthropic mechanisms, just like white lines on highways.

These examples not only highlight the value of undemocratic interventions, the absence of abuse of power and the norm of non-indigent beneficiaries; they also undermine the assertion implicit in the academic critique that philanthropy and government exist as mutually exclusive alternatives: that to be in favour of private giving is therefore to be opposed to democratically organized and collectively funded provision. This may seem like a plausible scenario when studying the topic from the abstract perspective of a political philosopher or an economist, which can take the view that "the entire philanthropic world exists as an artifact of political choices – the tax and corporate code first among them" (Bernholz 2020), but it is not supported by the empirical evidence of philanthropy that long predates and exists far beyond the reach of such political constraints and economic constructs. Nor does what is known about donor motivation and intentionality support arguments put forward in the academic critique. Those involved in either providing or receiving private funding understand that philanthropy is not the same as public spending and cannot replace it (Davies 2015: 206). Philanthropists are as united as they are ever going to be on any point, as voiced by Bill Gates: "We know that philanthropy can never – and should never – take the place of governments or the private sector" (Gates & Gates 2020). What elite donors do want is "additionality"– they want to make things happen that would not otherwise have happened. Simply turning off the government tap and connecting to a philanthropic supply is neither desirable nor feasible, because even those with an ideological preference for private over public provision are faced with the reality of philanthropic insufficiency (Salamon 1987): the fact that the sums of money and timescales involved in indefinitely providing a universal public good or service are well beyond the reach of any individual donor, however wealthy they are right now.

So even a cursory reflection on philanthropy in practice illustrates that there is no necessary existence, or intentional goal, of disrupting democracy; but let us dig deeper into the claims that constitute the academic critique.

The defence against the claim that philanthropy is undemocratic

The charge of "undemocratic" is made to shut down the argument because no reasonable person would countenance, let alone encourage, something that runs counter to the egalitarian principles of modern society. However, this rhetorical bullseye belies the fact that healthy democracies require that choices be challenged, and political leaders called to account (Weale 2018). Representative democracy works through a process of ongoing conversation and consultation, and one way that elected representatives are exposed to new ideas, or are supported in making the case for currently less popular ideas, is with the support of privately funded research, advocacy and campaigns.

The gadfly defence

John Dorr's white lines and Carnegie's pensions for professors point to an important role that philanthropy plays within democratic societies – generating new ideas to improve the lives of individuals and the wider community that, once proven, can be picked up and taken over for delivery by the government or market. This innovation function of philanthropy, dubbed the "discovery rationale" by Reich (2016), finds an original defence in the writing of ancient Greek philosopher Socrates, who argued that however great and noble the state may be, it inevitably moves slowly owing to its size and therefore needs stirring into action by external pressure, like a gadfly biting a sluggish horse. The gadfly may be a moral philosopher or another type of public intellectual, and it can also manifest in other forms such as investigative journalists, campaigning activists and philanthropists. All are needed to help stimulate social improvements by identifying new and overlooked problems, promoting and popularizing alternatives to the status quo and agitating to make change happen. As an early historian of English philanthropy explained: "The strong state is impossible without its cohort of troublesome men ... Philanthropy's highest distinction is to produce a perfect agitator" (Gray 1908: 300–3, 316).

At the start of the twentieth century, the Irish writer George Bernard Shaw also offered an early version of this argument in favour of philanthropy's role, which addresses the concern that private philanthropic efforts are at odds with democratic collective action. Highlighting the role of one of the UK's oldest charities, the National Society for the Prevention of Cruelty to Children (NSPCC) established in 1884 after the philanthropic founders were inspired by similar organizations on the other side of the Atlantic, and which quickly led to the first UK legislation to protect children from abuse and neglect in 1889, Shaw explained that: "The objection to supplanting machinery does not apply to private action to set public machinery in motion [which] ... does a great deal of good ... not by supplanting the State, or competing with it, but by co-operating with it and compelling it to do its duty" (Shaw 1901: 10–11). The NSPCC continues to be one of the most significant nonprofit organizations, responsible for the largest ever public fundraising appeal to date in Britain, £274 million, including 36 donations worth £1 million or more (Pegram 2017).

One reason that philanthropy can play this "gadfly role" is precisely because of the features that most concern the academic critics – its greater freedom, flexibility and different accountability than is experienced by actors in the government and market sectors. No one is above the law, including rich donors, so philanthropists must still abide by democratically decided legislation that determines what private citizens may or may not do, and which activities are and are not entitled to charity tax breaks. But abiding by legislation is a different matter to coping with the normative pressures felt by politicians and business leaders to keep their voters and shareholders happy. This absence of short-term popularity-courting enables philanthropists to act more quickly in response to new – and newly identified – problems, and to take risks by trying out untested ideas. As Karl Zinsmeister argues in his response to common criticisms of philanthropy (published in the *Stanford Social Innovation Review*, which is a platform for both critiques and ripostes): "Philanthropy solves problems differently than government. It tends to be more inventive and experimental, quicker, nimbler, more efficient, more varied, more personalized, more interested in transformation than treatment" (Zinsmeister 2016).

The final quality mentioned by Zinsmeister, that philanthropy is "more interested in transformation than treatment", is crucial to the defence against the academic critique. It is true that in the short term philanthropic interventions are undemocratic and can aggravate inequality because they are only available in the first instance to a restricted number of people. But the failure to pick up and run with philanthropic successes and make them universally available is a failure of governments and markets (or of their voters and shareholders), not the donors whose "innovation" or "gadfly role" was intended as the start, not the end, of a process. Once private donors have borne the cost and effort of developing innovative ways to tackle new and entrenched social problems, these solutions can only be taken to scale by organizations that have much bigger resources and permanent capacity. This is precisely the pattern followed in the provision of public education and public health in the UK (and in other modern welfare states): schools and hospitals were founded and funded by private donors until there was sufficient electoral support for the value of an educated and healthy population to shift this responsibility from private hands to the apparatus of government. Similar trajectories can be mapped for provisions as diverse as libraries, public baths, cultural organizations, child welfare and social housing, demonstrating in action the point made by George Bernard Shaw, that philanthropy is justified when the donor "recognizes the fact that it is not going to reform the world, but only, at best, to persuade the world to take its ideas into consideration in reforming itself" (1901: 11). This is why many people have described philanthropy as society's "risk capital" or, to cite another useful analogy, as "society's passing gear" because "it speeds along changes that otherwise might take much longer, or might never happen at all" (Callahan 2017: 171). Private initiatives to ameliorate immediate and obvious needs can be taken over and run on a universal and equitable basis by governments because only government has the power and capacity to fund and run them in the long term through public taxation and the apparatus of the state. This remains an idealized depiction as clearly nonprofit organizations continue to be needed and useful in relation to a range of services that are ostensibly government duties, such as the provision of decent housing for all, but arguably the failings here are on the part of the state, and voters' reluctance to support higher tax and spend policies, leading to needs being plugged – often reluctantly – by philanthropy.

The crucial point here, in relation to the contention that philanthropy is undemocratic, is that private giving is episodic while society's needs are enduring. Being the world's richest, or most philanthropic, person in 1900 or 2020 does not mean you can fund the universal provision of a good or service in ten years' time, never mind for the next generation or in the next century. No donor has ever claimed that they have the desire or the capacity to provide a public service or public good on a universal basis, for all time, yet the academic critique operates on the basis that their desire to do so is a given. It also overlooks the reality that democracy can be improved by outside pressure, and unfairly contrasts an idealized version of democracy with the messy reality of philanthropy.

The distinct and legitimate role of philanthropy

Philanthropy is not part of government; it plays a useful role in relation to government and can be helpful in improving the processes of democracy and helping achieve goals that are shared by politicians, policymakers and philanthropists, but these are distinct actors, they are not synonymous. As Peter Frumkin explains: "Philanthropy has a vital role to play as an independent actor in society, acting not simply based on what government defines as public needs, but in its own autonomous way" (Frumkin 2006: 376).

It is true that philanthropists and their staff are not elected, and that they make decisions that can affect the public good, so to that extent philanthropy is undemocratic. It is also the case that many valuable aspects of democratic societies are successfully run in similarly "undemocratic" ways, without provoking the consternation heaped on philanthropy. Countless non-governmental actors enjoy undemocratic influence over others, such as business leaders, lobbyists, journalists, trade unionists, community activists, celebrities and members of private families. All must abide by the laws and regulations that are decided by democratically elected representatives, but members of a free society are otherwise entitled to live and act as they choose – including discharging their assets as they see fit. Philanthropic freedom, the right of an individual to decide what they do with their own resources, including giving them away, is warranted within a free society (Ealy 2014).

Charity tax breaks are a tiny fraction of all fiscal incentives

Many other types of expenditure are in receipt of public funds without the expectation that elected officials will oversee and approve every decision, and many other activities are incentivized through the fiscal system. In the UK there are around 1,100 tax reliefs offered by government to nudge people to do various things, from saving for a pension to starting up businesses to making charitable donations. The total cost of all of these reliefs is around £400 billion of foregone revenue, of which around half a per cent (£2 billion) is accounted for by tax reliefs to encourage charitable donations; the larger part of that relief goes directly to charities, with just £490 million being reimbursed to higher-rate taxpayers (Charity Tax Commission 2019: 15–16). The situation is similar in the US, where more than $1.3 trillion of federal tax breaks are available to encourage a range of activities that provide primarily personal benefits such as health insurance, retirement income and mortgage relief, with the $50 billion cost of incentivizing philanthropy accounting for a small fraction of this expenditure. It is unclear why tax advantages to encourage the pursuit of purely private benefits (such as buying one's own house) provoke far less concern than those offered for encouraging philanthropy, which is obliged to generate public benefits alongside any private benefits, yet only the latter is the focus of concerns about "undemocratic" subsidy and demands for greater scrutiny.

Charity tax breaks are decided by democratically elected bodies

Regardless of the merits of tax breaks for philanthropic donations, they cannot be described as undemocratic, given that all tax reliefs are the result of legislative action. Philanthropy is only tax-advantaged because democratically elected governments have decided to make it so, and such decisions are neither uniform nor universal. Each government defines which causes and what non-profit organizations are eligible, which donors can claim them, the size of the tax breaks and any further details of how they operate. These decisions vary across time and place. For example the UK government marked the millennium by offering additional incentives for donations to international aid and disaster relief organizations in the 1999–2000 financial year, and has subsequently provided uplifts for donations made through payroll giving and legacies, while the Canadian government offered enhanced reliefs for first-time donors from 2013 to 2017. Other governments, such as in Sweden and Finland, choose to offer no, or extremely minimal, fiscal incentives for donors. Citizens who are unhappy with the existence, scale or allocation of charity tax breaks can express that view at the ballot box, because the provision and nature of tax advantages is in the hands of democratically elected bodies. To most observers, the US system for processing charity tax reliefs does seem inequitable, but the solution from the outside seems obvious: level up rather than level down by making reliefs available to all taxpayers (as is the case in the UK), including non-itemizers. The proposal to limit the deduction available to itemizers to a charitable tax credit worth no more than $1,000 (Reich 2018: 133) would increase equity at the point of donations, but so too would extending the same reliefs to all taxpayers, without the accompanying concern that the result might be a drastic reduction in donations resulting in "a weaker, diminished civil society" (Parnell 2019). This would be a problematic outcome at the best of times, and certainly more so at a time when there is a need for greater, not reduced, giving.

Charity tax breaks increase giving and are helpful for the demand side of philanthropy

Why might less generous tax breaks for donors reduce giving? A review of almost 50 academic studies on the effect of tax incentives confirms that fiscal incentives have a positive effect on the amount of money that nonprofits are able to raise: "When the costs of a donation are lowered, giving increases" (Bekkers & Wiepking 2011: 932). The responsiveness of donors to charity tax relief is not, as some might assume, because tax reliefs tip non-donors into becoming donors. The maths does not support that assumption: unless the tax rate is 100 per cent it will always cost more to make a donation than to not make a donation, so those seeking to be generous at no cost to themselves will remain unmoved by tax breaks whatever their size. As one rich donor told me: "No one has ever said 'If I give £10,000 to this charity then I'll get £2,000 back'!" Tax breaks are attractive because they make donations go further, as another donor explained to me: "People dodging tax are not remotely connected to people giving money to charity. If you give £1 million to charity and you get £400,000 tax relief then you've 'lost' £600,000 of your own money. There's something magical about saying 'I'll give a million pounds' but it only costs £600,000. But at the end of the day, £1 million has gone to charity" (cited in Breeze & Lloyd 2013: 102).

On this reasoning, rich donors in the UK value tax relief because it increases the value of gifts received by charities (Breeze & Lloyd 2013: 102). Tax breaks also serve as a general encouragement, signalling social approval of philanthropy, and a nudge to those who are already inclined to give by positively affecting the timing and size of gifts (hence the focus on "year-end giving"), as well as providing those seeking funds with extra tools to use in their interactions with potential donors.

Those who study philanthropy in the abstract, away from the front line of practice, are probably unaware that tax reliefs are helpful for the demand side (asking) as well as – and perhaps more than – for the supply side (donors). Tax breaks lower the price of giving and create opportunities to begin conversations about philanthropy. For example, Scotland's first home-grown billionaire, Sir Tom Hunter, who made his fortune at the age of 37 in 1998 when he sold his company Sports Division, created The Hunter Foundation after learning from his accountants that a £10 million endowment would be significantly boosted by tax breaks. His foundation has now given away over £55 million, primarily to tackle poverty in Scotland and Africa. Hunter became a signatory of the Giving Pledge in 2015, and has set himself the personal goal of becoming the first Scot to give away £1 billion. We need to understand the role of tax reliefs in relation to the demand side as well as the supply side of philanthropy, and to calculate their value in terms of the lifetime contributions of donors who were first prompted to think big by the existence of tax reliefs.

What of the other two planks of the academic critique: that philanthropy is an exercise in power and is insufficiently concerned with inequality?

Against the claim that philanthropy is an exercise in power

It is clearly the case that people in possession of great wealth tend to have more power than those without economic resources, but it is equally clear that the subset of the wealthy who are philanthropic do not enjoy singular or unfettered power. The synonymous assertion that "philanthropy *is* power" is a gross over-statement given how much philanthropy is concerned with funding extremely prosaic and mundane goods and services, given the extent of power held by those whom big donors must work with in order to achieve their objectives, and given how much non-governmental power resides outside of the universe of philanthropists.

The first of these points is exemplified by Canadian philanthropist Willard Garfield Weston, who was born above his father's bakery in Toronto in 1898. By the time Weston died in 1978 he had grown the family business into a global food-processing and distribution company and had established, with his wife Reta, two philanthropic foundations – one in his native Canada and one in the UK where he had lived and raised nine children – which are now counted among the biggest private foundations in both countries. The UK-based Garfield Weston Foundation has assets of over £7 billion and often features on lists of the "world's biggest foundations". Weston marked its 60th anniversary in 2018 by distributing an additional £11 million to small volunteer-led charities across the UK to help improve or provide new facilities to local communities. Funding decisions approved by the trustees, all of whom are lineal descendants of the founder, confound the notion of "conspicuous contributors" supporting elite interests (Odendahl 1990). The typical grants made to celebrate Weston's diamond jubilee were for decidedly unglamorous and inclusive projects such as building accessible toilets and entranceways in village halls and Scout huts, and buying minibuses to transport vulnerable people to activities and enable the freecycling of furniture. The recipient of a project that received Weston funding to upgrade the shower room and toilets in a project serving homeless people described it as: "a sum of money that has allowed us to do something special to an area which doesn't often get much attention in buildings like ours, whereas people in their own homes invest heavily in their bathrooms. We have really taken a massive step forward in creating a home of hospitality in the heart of the city".

This reaction pleases Philippa Charles, director of the UK Foundation, who says: "We trust applicants to tell us what they need most, and we don't tie them up in restrictions or red tape. The money might be paying for better lavatories but we know the benefits include greater self-respect for those who use them, the potential to hire spaces out to generate revenue and a morale boost and affirmation for the staff and volunteers that their work makes a difference."

If the story of a globally significant grant-maker funding better bathrooms for homeless people sounds a long way off the image of power-hungry elites using philanthropy as a devious strategy to cement and extend their influence, that is because it is. The Garfield Weston Foundation does not fit the picture of self-dealing elites endangering democracy, and – despite the foundation's size – is not mentioned in the critiques of philanthropy that have been flying off the shelves in bookstores.

Many big donors provide funding for similarly prosaic items and mundane costs. The Laboratory Refurbishment Grants provided by the UK's Wolfson Foundation between 1998 and 2017 included £5 million to upgrade the UK's leading infectious disease laboratories, which not incidentally provided scientists with better conditions in which to focus on developing Covid-19 vaccines in 2020. A widely noted impact of grant-making during the global pandemic has been a greater willingness by the majority of big institutional donors to provide core and unrestricted funding (Finchum-Mason *et al.* 2020). Paying the rent, salaries and utility bills for nonprofit organizations literally enables them to keep the lights on and the Wi-Fi connected so that they can do their work. As one major donor told me: "I like supporting those pieces of work that are too boring for other funders." Core funding also requires and demonstrates trust in recipients, as evidenced by MacKenzie Scott whose entire $5.8 billion of grants in 2020 were made with no strings attached (Dale 2020). This method of providing financial support highlights the extent to which donors are willing to share power with those they fund in order to achieve their objectives, because they know that their money only represents a latent value which needs the assistance of others to be realized.

Despite the typical conceptualization of philanthropy "as a world of donors" (Ostrander & Schervish 1990: 67) in which the ascendancy of philanthropists appears to be absolute, the reality is that there are many other necessary and influential agents who play essential roles in alerting donors to causes and projects that need funding, developing potential solutions and enabling the funding to be received, spent and reported on. Yet despite the obvious presence and role of these other actors, including all those who mediate and enable philanthropic activity as well as the end beneficiaries, philanthropists continue to be understood as possessing a singular power to shape the world according to their whims. It is obviously true that possessing financial resources gives wealth holders more options, nicely summed up in Schervish's concept of "hyperagency", which describes the enhanced capacity of the wealthy to determine the conditions under which they live (Schervish 2000: 20). But the belief in absolute philanthropic power is so widely held that debates jump straight ahead to whether that power can be, or should be, wielded for good, rather than questioning how much power one can have when one's assets are merely currency that is impotent without those able and willing to spend it.

The leadership of each nonprofit can accept or reject donations according to their judgement of what is in the best interests of their organization, including lack of mission alignment (for example a tobacco company wishing to donate to a lung cancer charity) and reputational risk (for example accepting money from a "tainted" donor that would result in losing other support). Recipients' ability to exercise discernment is longstanding. Many people are aware that Andrew Carnegie funded 2,500 libraries around the world, but it is less well known that 225 communities turned down the offer, usually owing to local preference to prioritize developing other facilities and reluctance to fund ongoing maintenance costs, and occasionally because of concerns about the donor and how he made his money (Krass 2002: 422).

Overstating the power wielded by philanthropists is also evident when we consider how much non-governmental power resides outside of the universe of philanthropists, notably in commercial "special interest" groups. Private donors' funding of advocacy efforts is of particular concern to critics focused on illegitimate philanthropic power, yet expenditure on lobbying in Washington, DC by all nonprofit institutions combined (i.e. on every single cause promoted by philanthropists) was lower than that spent by any one industry across the two years of 2018 and 2019. The pharmaceutical/health products industry spent almost half a billion dollars ($446,168,010), while total nonprofit lobbying amounted to $96 million – only just over half of what the air transport industry spent advocating for itself ($151 million) (all figures from Evers-Hillstrom 2019). These figures remind us that many non-governmental actors enjoy power and influence, including those promoting business interests as well as celebrities, campaigning journalists, public intellectuals and community activists. Possessing influence beyond the ballot box is not a unique feature of philanthropy. Furthermore, ideational or policy-oriented philanthropy is a minor element of wider philanthropic activity, especially outside of the US. If this – or any other – type of philanthropic expenditure is widely viewed as unacceptable then the appropriate response is to tighten the rules on what counts as tax deductible (as argued by Callahan 2017) and take care not to overstate the problem, because "we run the risk of exaggerating the degree to which philanthropy is focused on, or even big philanthropy is focused on, direct policy advocacy" (Buchanan, quoted in Matthews 2019).

Further examples help keep things in proportion: in the US in 2019, the oil and gas industry spent $92 billion on lobbying alone, whereas in the same year all environmental causes (including animal welfare) received $14.6 billion in philanthropic donations, which covers their core costs, front-line work and advocacy efforts (Giving USA 2020). To expend more worry about the far feebler "power" of donors' funding efforts to combat climate change than about the power of the industry causing those problems seems a very curious prioritization. It also raises the question as to what else private individuals can do if they are concerned about long-term and supranational issues over which their domestic vote has minimal influence: "Can you really contribute to change in an area such as global warming without influencing public policy?" asks Phil Buchanan (2019a: 163).

From September 2019 to March 2020, Australia suffered extensive bush fires which destroyed 17 million hectares of land and 3,000 homes, killing 33 people and a huge amount of wildlife. This disaster led to AUS$640 million in philanthropic donations for relief and recovery efforts (ACNC 2020), including high-profile gifts from celebrities around the world. Yet, as the fires were exacerbated by the hotter and drier conditions created by climate change, it would be illogical to cheer the funding of relief while handwringing over the funding of preventative efforts. This is why the Australian High Court has ruled that the latter is permissible, as Krystian Seibert of Philanthropy Australia explains:

> Philanthropy is involved in these efforts [to protect the environment] for good reason. Take the example of a factory polluting a river. You can spend lots of your money downriver funding the installation of water filters and treating affected wildlife. Or you can fund efforts upstream to ensure the factory complies with the law, or if the law doesn't stop the pollution, efforts to change the law … Advocacy is an entirely legitimate and appropriate way to pursue charitable objectives, including protecting the environment. Indeed, in 2010 the High Court held that the undertaking of advocacy by charities was essential to Australia's system of democracy. (Seibert 2017)

It makes no sense to problematize – or even curb – philanthropic funding of lobbying and advocacy efforts, given they have far less resources and far more redeeming features than the "profit calculation" that propels private sector lobbying. Where there is justified concern about the improper use of private power, the solution lies in stronger regulation – for example, under UK charity law a political purpose is incompatible with having charitable status, and activities that might unduly influence the political process are prohibited (Breeze & Ramsbottom 2020; Prochaska 2002: 6).

The particular problem of how richer parents can use philanthropy to channel more funds to already-advantaged schools is a commonly cited example of improper power in the hands of private donors (this example is first set out in Reich 2005). But this example also illustrates how the issue of power in philanthropy is overstated, as well as assuming that the US experience (in relation to both philanthropy and the system for funding public schools) is typical. US public school funding comes from local property taxes – which are much lower in poorer areas, leading to the "savage inequalities" described by Kozol (2012). Spending per head is higher in wealthier communities because they enjoy a larger tax base and lower demands on public spending for welfare needs, while children attending schools in poorer districts are adversely affected by the converse double whammy of a smaller tax base which is stretched thinner owing to greater local needs. School finance reforms have helped tackle inequality in educational provision, but half of US states have not implemented such reforms (Lafortune *et al.* 2018). So the heart of the problem is the underfunding of public schools, especially in poorer areas, and the solution must therefore focus on changing how US public schools are funded. Philanthropy is obviously not the cause of the funding and attainment gap between richer and poorer American school pupils, which can only be solved by wider and deeper school finance reforms. The UK also has a problem of advantage begetting advantage, as richer parents can and do donate more to their children's schools (Body *et al.* 2017), but this is mitigated by two factors: government funding of state schools far outweighs their philanthropic income at around £6,000 per pupil per year (IFS 2019) compared to average fundraised income of £43 per pupil per year (Body *et al.* 2017: 262), and the government provides additional funding (the "pupil premium") for those schools serving the most disadvantaged pupils (DfE 2020).

This example leads into the third plank of this critique: that regardless of its role in undermining democracy or exercising power, philanthropy is problematic because it is insufficiently concerned with tackling poverty and inequality.

Against the claim that philanthropy is insufficiently concerned
with inequality

In the public imagination, to be "charitable" implies helping the poor, so it comes as a surprise to many to learn that there is no historical precedent or legal obligation for philanthropy to be redistributive or focused on poverty and inequality. The words "charity" and "philanthropy" may bring to mind images of the rich helping the poor, but philanthropic activity has always operated on a much broader canvas to ameliorate problems and create benefits across society. Current UK charity law identifies 13 categories of charitable purpose, including "the relief of those in need by reason of youth, age, ill-health, disability, financial hardship or other disadvantage", which is a good fit with the public understanding of charity, but also includes non-needs-based purposes such as "the advancement of the arts, culture, heritage and science", "the advancement of animal welfare" and "the advancement of environmental protection". The list of qualifying causes is similar in other countries, and wherever they appear these category labels cannot elucidate which people benefit from the donation. An example is helpful to illustrate that the way we record and study philanthropy by cause area (arts, welfare, education and so on) causes a "category error" that gives a mistaken impression as to the destination of philanthropic gifts.

Dr Helen Bowcock established the Hazelhurst Trust with her husband Matthew in 2001 with proceeds from the sale of their software company. One of the main beneficiaries of the Bowcocks' donations is Watts Gallery near their home in Surrey, England. While this charitable choice – an art gallery – appears to fit the stereotype of "elite donors giving to elite causes", a closer look at the purpose and outcome of their giving tells a different story, as Helen explains:

> We haven't made grants for the art itself, all of our donations fund learning and outreach activities. This includes working with women in two local prisons to develop their skills, confidence and perseverance so they can exhibit and sell their work, and also helping young people who had withdrawn from school to return to education through art. This isn't about giving money for elite activities as could be assumed, it's about improving lives and helping to create a better society.

When I worked as a fundraiser for a youth homelessness charity in London, a renowned UK philanthropist, Paul Hamlyn, paid for all the seats at certain performances in London's Royal Opera House and the National Theatre to be donated to organizations such as ours, so that the most marginalized young people could experience a live show. I remember the buzz when a group of our residents returned to the hostel after watching their first ballet. Whatever impact or future repercussions that experience had, it is simply inaccurate to assume that all arts philanthropy constitutes "recycling within elites" as many scholars contend (e.g. Odendahl 1990; Ostrower 1995).

The same category error recurs in other cause areas: donations to universities may beef up juicy endowments or pay for new buildings, or they may support students who might otherwise be excluded from accessing the best education because of poverty, racial or other injustices. But it may also be the case that the endowment generates the interest for those scholarships, and that the new buildings on campus are the site for those students to do their most inspired and enjoyable learning. There is no simple way of calculating "who benefits" from philanthropy, or attributing outcomes to particular donations because benefits may occur indirectly and the outcome can be months, years or decades after the philanthropic intervention.

In some cases addressing inequality is the core concern of the biggest donors. The motto of the Bill and Melinda Gates Foundation is "all lives have equal value", and the Gateses' explicit goal to "dramatically reduce inequity" (Gates 2015) can reasonably lay claim to success in tackling some types of inequality in some places, such as reducing unequal health outcomes for people living in poor countries who might otherwise have died or suffered from polio, malaria, HIV, complications in childbirth or preventable childhood diseases. When Mark Zuckerberg and Priscilla Chan established the Chan Zuckerberg Initiative in 2015, their rationale, as set out in a letter to their newborn daughter Max, was "to create a more equal world" (Zuckerberg & Chan 2015). And the Irish American founder of the Duty Free Shoppers group, Chuck Feeney, who gave most of his billions away anonymously, made all of his final grants to organizations seeking to achieve equity.

Using the fruits of inequality to advance equality is, of course, a scenario that prompts much debate about the logical coherence and moral integrity of phil-anthropy. It is also another longstanding debate, with no easy resolution. An in-depth study of how wealthy US women from 1870 to 1967 funded a range of connected causes – suffragism, higher education and reproductive rights – to successfully advance the political, economic and social rights of all women, clearly demonstrates that money played a vital role in securing women's rights. Yet the leveraging of financial inequality to tackle other kinds of inequality caused discomfort and resentment, especially when donors advanced their preferred strategy or leadership. This is why the author of that study refers to both the "possibilities and problems" of philanthropy (Johnson 2017: 97). Yet she also shows how "money power" was wielded for the cause. For example, in 1892 Mary Garrett donated the lion's share of the $500,000 target to estab-lish a new medical school at Johns Hopkins University on the condition that women students be admitted on the same terms as men (Johnson 2017: 147).

And Katharine Dexter McCormick's tenacious and single-handed funding of the development of the oral contraceptive pill in the face of the disinterested male scientific establishment was driven by her goal of reproductive freedom for all women (Johnson 2017: 199–222). Despite their financial advantages, wealthy women also experienced sexism and lack of control over their lives, including educational opportunities, career aspirations and reproduction. Using their wealth to fund "coercive philanthropy" that pushed women's rights in the face of entrenched sexism, enabled "wealthy allies" to transform society for all women.

Critics also take to task those donors whose philanthropic effort is not designed to have any specific impact on inequality, such as the three philanthropists we met at the start of this book whose efforts have helped young women to leave sex work, have created a more uplifting environment for young people with autism and have helped avoid mass shootings in UK schools. These are clearly all worthwhile outcomes, despite none of them being specifically focused on solving, or even mitigating, inequality. "Damned if we do, damned if we don't" is a refrain familiar to many who are castigated whether they give or not, and it also applies to whether their giving is focused on equality or not.

The assumption that philanthropy's sole purpose is to tackle inequality is another "straw man" tactic that misrepresents philanthropic intentions as a single and unvarying aim, and holds donors to account for failing to meet a goal that most never set out to achieve. While inequality is a clear threat to democracy, it is less clear why philanthropy is in the firing line rather than the machinery of government, which has far more levers to pull to address inequality, notably tax and spend policies. There is also little credit for philanthropy's role in diverting money from purely private to public ends, and reducing the impact of what Thomas Piketty has described as the key mechanism behind inequality: intergenerational wealth transfers (Piketty 2014). Inheritance is the principal mechanism for wealth accumulation among the global elite, and this exclusive cascade of wealth is set to increase dramatically in the coming years, which undermines efforts to enable social mobility based on individual effort and meritocracy. In the US, at least $34.5 trillion of household wealth will be transferred between 2007 and 2061 (Havens & Schervish 2014: 22), and the equivalent figure in the UK, for the shorter time period of 2017–37, is £5.5 trillion (Kings Court Trust 2017). I have interviewed philanthropists who have given away almost all of their wealth for the express purpose of avoiding intergenerational injustice. Establishing a philanthropic foundation as an alternative to passing wealth on to already-privileged descendants slows or interrupts the transition of capital from one generation to the next but is also construed as a way of exercising power and influence over future generations, as discussed in the final element of the response to the academic critique.

The "dead hand" of philanthropy or government

The perceived problem of conducting philanthropy through the foundation form is as old as the foundation form itself. The foundation form was viewed from the outset as "a 'Trojan Horse' ready to undo democracy" (Zunz 2011: 21). When the general purpose private philanthropic foundation was first proposed in the early twentieth century, there was "deep resistance and democratic skepticism" (Reich *et al.* 2016: 18). The example most commonly pointed to is the opposition faced by John D. Rockefeller in 1912 when he attempted to secure congressional approval to incorporate a foundation with a historically large endowment and open-ended purposes. This plan encountered much opposition including from Reverend John Haynes Holmes, a Unitarian minister and former chair of the American Civil Liberties Institution, who described the idea as "repugnant to the whole idea of democratic society". Three years later, Senator Frank Walsh argued that all foundations "appear to be a menace to the welfare of society" (cited in Reich 2018: 4–5). A century later, pointed questions are still being asked about the existential rights of philanthropic foundations: "Who do foundations think they are? Why do they even exist? Why do democratic societies accept, even foster, the presence of 'aristocratic institutions' that control large amounts of capital, in perpetuity, with few constraints on how their assets may be used? On what grounds are institutions that control vast wealth able to secure the consent of society and government?" (Heydemann & Toepler 2006: 3).

This longstanding concern is acknowledged by philanthropists who set extremely loose priorities such as "the welfare of mankind" in order to allow maximum flexibility to those charged with distributing the funds in the future. The UK philanthropist Joseph Rowntree, whose fortune came from chocolate and whose giving was guided by his Quaker beliefs, pre-empted this concern in the 1904 Memorandum setting up his trust in which he explained that his words were only intended to be helpful in explaining why he created the trusts and who clarified that: "I wish it to be distinctly understood that it is of no legal or binding force in any way or direction, and is not intended to restrict or extend the full discretion given to the Trustees and Directors" (Rowntree 1904).

Growing interest in "life-limited" foundations, which spend all of their funds within, or soon after, the lifetime of the donor, is another solution to this problem (RPA 2020), for example the Gates Foundation is committed to close within 20 years of the death of the last of the three founding trustees (Warren Buffett, Bill Gates and Melinda French Gates).

Not only can the "dead hand" problem be pre-empted and solved by thoughtful donors, in the context of the charge that it is "undemocratic" it is worth noting the equivalence with mandatory spending decisions which now comprise a majority of the US federal budget. Unlike discretionary spending decisions, which are in the hands of current elected politicians, mandatory spending gives greater power to previous lawmakers who can tie the hands of their democratically elected successors and affect citizens today. Many items of mandatory spending would be supported by progressive people, among whom I count myself, such as social security, Medicare/Medicaid and unemployment compensation. I am glad there is some stability and predictability in the provision of such items, just as I am glad that the historic endowments of foundations enables the continued funding of many essential and life-enhancing activities. But it is unfair to only call attention to the presence of "historic" power in the philanthropy sector when it clearly also dominates other sectors.

Where does this review and defence of the three planks of the academic critique take us? Clearly there is some merit in the concerns, equally clearly some claims are misdirected, overstated and fail to recognize the unique role and limitations of philanthropy. The circle can be squared if we draw on existing scholarship that helps us to rethink the issues and learn to live with the paradoxes inherent in embracing philanthropy within democratic societies.

Embracing the paradox of philanthropy

The paradox of philanthropy is that it simultaneously detracts from and supports democracy. This paradox is set out by another Stanford scholar, Bruce Sievers, who argues that democracies need a thriving civil society, yet some of the funding for that civil society comes from a powerful, unaccountable and wealthy elite (Sievers 2010).

The ways in which private philanthropic action can support and enable democracy have been described and documented many times over the past two centuries, from Alexis de Tocqueville's study of *Democracy in America* (1838) which famously celebrates the crucial role of voluntary associations in enabling representative democracy to succeed in the new republic, to Robert Putnam's influential studies of Italy and the US which show how the social capital and mutual trust generated through voluntary interactions "makes democracy work" (Putnam 1993, 2000). Philanthropy helps creates social capital by fostering relationships with, and trust in, fellow citizens beyond immediate family and friends, and it also funds activities that enable democracies to exist and flourish by providing a forum for individuals and communities to advocate for change (Payton & Moody 2008: 156–7). For both these reasons, Rob Payton and Michael Moody conclude that "democracy needs philanthropy" (Payton & Moody 2008: 157). It is also useful to remember that civil society organizations are a distinguishing feature of free societies, and were not permitted to exist in totalitarian societies such as the Soviet Union or Communist China.

Philosophers and politicians have also articulated the benefits of philanthropic activity. In the nineteenth century, John Stuart Mill noted the political significance of philanthropy as a check maintained over those who rule, which requires intelligence, activity and public spiritedness among the governed (Prochaska 2002: 16), while the architect of the UK welfare state, William Beveridge, confirmed that "philanthropy will still be needed. It will be needed to pioneer ahead of the state" (cited in Cunningham 2020: 183). Contemporary politicians, whose law-making enables and regulates the philanthropy sector, continue to assert that democracy needs philanthropy, such as Vice-President Kamala Harris' reflection on the value of philanthropic action during her time in office as district attorney:

> We also need to keep the pressure on from the outside, where organizations and individuals can create meaningful change. When I was attorney general, I made sure ours was the first state law enforcement agency to require body cameras for its agents. I did it because it was the right thing to do. But I was able to do it because the Black Lives Matters movement had created intense pressure. By forcing these issues onto the national agenda, the movement created an environment on the outside that helped give me the space to get it done on the inside. That's often how change happens. And I credit the movement for those reforms just as much as anyone in my office, including me.
>
> (Harris 2019: 72–3).

Black Lives Matter is a grassroots movement reliant on activists and volunteers. But it also requires funding, just as previous progressive movements that defeated the slave trade, secured votes for women and achieved same-sex marriage needed to pay for their core costs (such as offices and utility bills) and campaigning materials, as well as to hire venues, cover travel costs, conduct research and fund salaried organizers. Much of this funding comes from the mass of small contributions by non-wealthy donors, reflecting the reality that mass philanthropy typically outnumbers big philanthropy. But some campaigning nonprofits get funding from big donors, such as the American Civil Liberties Union's (ACLU) multi-million dollar support from the Ford Foundation and George Soros' Open Society Institute. We also know that some rich and famous individuals contribute large sums to these campaigns because traditional and social media provide details of their donations to organizations such as the ACLU, Black Lives Matter and the George Floyd Memorial Fund. In "normal times" the role of private giving in supporting efforts that put pressure on elected representatives is what prompted former New York mayor and now Giving Pledge signatory Michael Bloomberg to describe philanthropy "as a way to embolden government" (Allen 2015). Herein lies the paradox because these big individual and institutional donors, who already hold a disproportionate amount of power and are not accountable to an electorate or shareholders, are needed – and indeed encouraged – to help facilitate citizen engagement to take on historic and contemporary vested interests in relation to slavery, sexism, racism, homophobia and other forms of government-sanctioned bigotry.

Those who argue that big philanthropy is a threat to, and inimical with, democracy have overlooked the important point that democracy is a dynamic and constantly developing notion, rather than a fixed and constant concept. This is easy to see with a great deal of distance: no one wishes to stick to the original 1776 meaning of the words in the second paragraph of the United States Declaration of Independence, that "all men are created equal" when Thomas Jefferson only meant biological, "free" men who own property. But the journey towards universal suffrage and greater equality required philanthropic support, because enslaved people, women and non-property-owning men did not have any power or voice within the "democratic" system of the time (Davies 2015, 88–9). The journey continues today, with private funding for initiatives promoting further changes to the electoral system such as lowering the voting age to 16 and re-enfranchizing people with historic offences, as well as funding efforts to defend and extend equal rights to all. Philanthropic involvement in politics and policymaking is not – or should not be – about trying to get a particular party into power, rather it is about improving the process. Philanthropy in the service of democracy confounds the simplistic assumption that philanthropic and democratic solutions are inevitably opposed.

Democracy is not the same as raw majoritarianism. Given that democracy can be – and often has been – improved by outside pressure (the gadfly defence), the question of whether democracy can tolerate philanthropy can also be reversed to ask whether democracy can function and thrive without philanthropy. The usefulness of asking both these questions is what constitutes the paradox of philanthropy's role in liberal democracies. Rather than seeing philanthropy as a threat to democracy, it makes more sense to view philanthropy and democracy as mutually – if sometimes fractiously – interdependent, and to understand both as dynamic, contextual and in need of ongoing improvement from external pressures.

Rather than seeking to definitively prove that philanthropy is either an obstacle or an asset for democracies, we can take a more expansive view that it can be both, and that the challenge is to minimize problems through improved regulation and legislation, while enabling the positives to flourish through better donor support and education. In this way philanthropy can be understood and appreciated as a beneficial anomaly in democratic societies (Whitaker 1974a).

The problematic consequences of the academic critique

The result of the triad of accusations that philanthropy is undemocratic, an exercise in power and insufficiently concerned about inequality, is to deny the virtue that might otherwise be seen and valued in philanthropic acts.

Academic scholarship does not exist solely in the realm of ideas; our work can be – and often is – used in the public and private spheres by people whose job it is to shape public opinion and produce policy. Academic critiques reach the general public when scholars contribute quotes and opinion pieces for media outlets, speak at public and nonprofit sector events, participate in panel debates, write books that succeed in the trade (non-academic) press and attract a following on social media. What academics say and how they say it matters in terms of shaping the general understanding of, and attitudes towards, charitable giving, which in turn influences the context in which people decide whether or not to be philanthropic, as well as their enthusiasm for supporting policies that encourage or discourage philanthropy.

Academic critics may be clear that their focus is on "big" philanthropy, notably that which is conducted through the foundation form or in pursuit of influencing policy, but that three-letter adjective "big" easily gets lost when ideas enter the noisy square of public and political debate, and the slippage that tars all philanthropy with the same brush is unfair and damaging: "They slip too easily from judgments of big philanthropy to judgments of all philanthropy. This simplistic stance threatens to undermine the significant historical and social role philanthropy can, has, and should play in our democracy" (Moody & Martin 2020).

Problematizing philanthropy per se and associating it with undesirable concepts such as "undemocratic", "elite power" and "unconcerned about inequality" results in damaging the overall reputation of philanthropy and making it a less attractive option for those who might otherwise have chosen to give some of it away, which ultimately causes most harm to those people, communities and environments most in need of private support.

It is a conscious choice to highlight the limitations of philanthropy without also noting its value, or acknowledging the limitations of government and the market. The foregrounding of negatives – that philanthropy is *not* democratic, *not* concerned about power dynamics and *not* focused on equality – is not evident in the way we label or think about the value of the other sectors and their necessary role in wider society. All three sectors of society (government, business and philanthropy) make a valuable contribution, and each also has limitations. Imperfections, inadequacies and the potential for advantage-seeking behaviour are clearly not unique to the world of philanthropy; they are a feature of all three sectors. The problematic aspects and impacts of philanthropy are real, but ought to be compared with the reality – rather than idealized versions – of the government and the market, and are best dealt with through better legislation and regulation, as they would be in the other two sectors (for example there are curbs on monopolistic practice in the market and there are term limits for those holding high offices of state), rather than through destabilizing philanthropy by casting generalized aspersions and delegitimizing a potentially useful social activity.

Critical scholarship is, of course, valuable. It helps advance understanding by probing beyond what is superficial and immediately obvious to draw out the structures, relationships and consequential hidden interests that have hitherto been overlooked (Gharabaghi & Anderson-Nathe 2017). However, that purpose is moot when the "big reveal" that philanthropy is not run strictly in line with democratic principles, that donors get something out of giving and that it does not always tackle inequality is already well known and understood. These points have long been readily acknowledged by all concerned, including donors, and best practice in the sector already involves proactively seeking ways to identify where harmful dynamics occur and making progressive change to improve philanthropic impact. The "awesome responsibility" felt by big donors, and their concern to "maximize the good of giving" (Buchanan 2019a: 1), means it is time to move on from pointing out obvious flaws and focus instead on designing new and better ways of doing philanthropy by engaging with the practical reality of improving an imperfect but worthwhile practice.

Conclusion

The defence against the academic critique acknowledges some truth in the three key concerns about philanthropy – it is undeniably undemocratic in some regards, it does involve some exercise of power and it is not always concerned with poverty and inequality. But there is a robust response to each of these concerns which enables us to view the role of philanthropy in a democracy as a beneficial anomaly, as first posited five decades ago (Whitaker 1974a), because:

- *Philanthropy is compatible enough with democracy to be defensible.* Donors are not above the law because their philanthropic actions and the availability of charity tax breaks are decided by elected representatives. Further, philanthropy can – and often has – played a positive role in democratic societies by improving the processes of democracy, drawing attention to new and overlooked problems, and funding the development of solutions that governments or the market can then take to scale.
- *Concerns about the exercise of power are overstated.* While it is clearly the case that all wealthy people (philanthropic or not) enjoy more power than

the non-wealthy, money only has a latent value because donors and doers are mutually dependent. Further, it is also the case that many other non-governmental actors have power in society yet lack a democratic mandate, and it is unclear why philanthropy has become the chosen target for concerns about power.

- *Despite widespread assumptions, there is no legal or moral obligation for philanthropy to be focused on poverty and inequality.* Philanthropic activity operates on a much broader canvas to ameliorate problems and create benefits across society. And the existence of philanthropy helps to divert resources from private to public hands, which mitigates the key mechanism behind inequality: the intergenerational transfer of wealth.

As well as dealing with these three objections, it is also important to note the conscious choice in overlooking alternative – and more positive – drivers and impacts of philanthropy than reinforcing power and advancing elite interests. In addition to making sense of grief, as illustrated by the story of the Stanfords at the start of this chapter, philanthropists describe being motivated by a range of factors including gratitude, empathy, compassion, religious conviction, a sense of duty, awareness of need and anger at the existence of unmet needs. It is also a choice to decide whether or not to highlight positive outcomes of philanthropy such as advances in medical research and healthcare that have saved and lengthened millions of lives, as well as the provision of civic infrastructure and the funding of civil society organizations that have improved the quality of life for generations of people over time and across the globe.

The impact of associating philanthropy with words such as "undemocratic", "power" and "unconcerned about inequality" is to plant seeds about the rightness of philanthropic action which, as I discuss further in Chapter 6, is a textbook example of the strategy of "denying virtue" by favouring alternative self-interested explanations such as the pursuit of power, influence and other personal benefits. This constitutes the first trick up the sleeve of those intent on derogating do-gooders. Before that, Chapter 4 looks at the insider critique, which focuses on another set of concerns about philanthropy, in particular the "misdirected" distribution of philanthropic donations.

4

THE INSIDER CRITIQUE

The question I have been asked most often during both halves of my career, first as a fundraiser and now as a philanthropy scholar, is: "Why do people give?" Often it is a genuine enquiry into the most common reasons that prompt people to donate their own money voluntarily. Sometimes it is phrased as a challenge, goading me to expose the "real", self-interested motivations that the questioner believes prompt donations, such as dodging tax or as a cover for bad behaviour.

Luckily for me the question "why do people give" has a simple answer that is supported by reams of research, as well as by a moment's reflection on your own charitable donations: people primarily give for personal reasons. Most of the time, most people donate to issues and causes that have touched their lives, for better or worse. This is why Cancer Research UK is the top fundraising charity in the UK, because half of us will receive a cancer diagnosis at some point in our lives, and everyone has loved ones with this disease. Children's charities and animal welfare charities are also among the most popular fundraising causes because of our universal experience of being a child, the commonplace experience of being a parent and the widespread ownership and enjoyment of pets. Nonprofit organizations focused on cancer, kids and kittens achieve widespread support because they are aligned with common personal experiences and preferences, and because it is easy to feel affinity with their beneficiaries (Breeze 2013). Some of the most significant and well-known major philanthropic efforts are driven by the same sort of personal factors.

When John D. Rockefeller's baby grandson Jack died of scarlet fever in 1901, he "grieved profoundly" and decided to establish the first institute in the US to focus on biomedical research (Hirsch 2011: 278). Since 1910, the Rockefeller Institute for Medical Research has produced 26 Nobel Prize winners, played a key role in discovering DNA and advancing the science of cell biology, and contributed to understanding and curing a range of diseases including meningitis, pneumonia, African sleeping sickness and cancer (Rockefeller University, n.d.).

Scottish-born Andrew Carnegie grew up in deep poverty, and began work in a cotton factory aged 13 soon after his family moved to the US seeking a better life in Allegheny, Pennsylvania. Through his job the teenage Carnegie met Colonel James Anderson, a wealthy iron manufacturer who had a large personal library in his home. On Saturdays, Anderson allowed local "working boys" to visit and borrow his books. Carnegie seized the opportunity to gain knowledge and improve his life chances and, after creating his enormous wealth, he funded the building of 2,500 public libraries around the world, starting with his birthplace in Scotland, where the Carnegie library in Dunfermline opened in 1883. Carnegie also drew on his past for another early philanthropic act. Opposite the humble two-room cottage in which he was born stand huge iron gates that kept local people out of the Pittencrieff Estate – 76 acres of beautiful outdoor space that was solely for the enjoyment of its wealthy owners, until 1902 when Carnegie bought the land as a gift for all the children of Dunfermline to enjoy.

Fast-forward a century and the same personal motivations predominate in contemporary philanthropy, as exemplified by Heather Beckwith, who told me:

> My grandson Oscar was born with a rare and complicated genetic syndrome called Crouzon. All of his life he has been a patient at the famous London children's hospital, Great Ormond Street Hospital (GOSH), so I decided to donate £1 million to GOSH as part of my way of coping with very sad circumstances. I wanted experts at a centre of excellence to be able to work through the understanding of this condition and research the genetics, with the eventual aim of preventing it in the future. I don't anticipate them finding a cure in my lifetime, but at least by starting to fund this now, rather than waiting any longer, there's a slim chance of seeing some results. Personal reasons are the most powerful factor behind my giving. Perhaps if I had a family member with a different health problem, like autism, then I would be supporting a charity that helps autistic children rather than GOSH. But this is the situation that I find myself in and I believe that many philanthropic acts are driven by the kind of personal experiences that our family has, unfortunately, experienced.

Heather Beckwith's point is that philanthropy is personal. People give to what they know and care about, as a result of their own experiences. Removing or reducing that subjectivity which, according to critical voices predominantly from within the nonprofit sector, leads to giving being "done wrong", is the central aim of the insider critique.

The insider critique of philanthropy

The core premise of the insider critique is that philanthropic spending is not distributed optimally and that more "rigour" should be exercised by private donors to align their philanthropic responses with the needs that exist in the world. The nature of the proposed "rigour" has changed over time in different versions of the insider critique, from the "scientific philanthropy" of the late nineteenth century, which drew on data and ideas from the then-new social sciences, to the call to make philanthropy more "strategic" or "business-like" in the late twentieth century, to the current dominant iteration known as "effective altruism", which advocates the use of applied moral philosophy and quantitative metrics to reach "better" giving decisions. However solutions are framed, the goal is to correct the situation in which "charitable donations find their way to grantees through a haphazard combination of luck, charisma and razzmatazz that is poorly suited to the importance of their work" (Goldberg 2009: 29).

This critique has primarily been articulated from within the philanthropy sector by those whose work involves running nonprofit organizations and infrastructure bodies, making institutional grants and advising individual donors, hence it emerges from "insiders" within the realm of nonprofit and philanthropic action.

The charge that philanthropy is overly driven by emotional rather than rational thinking is supported by research showing that the way "high-capacity donors" choose what and who to support is overly reliant on personal connections and recommendations, and often results in worthy organizations, whose work falls outside of donors' personal networks or experiences, being overlooked (Andrews *et al.* 2020). Although some insider critiques simply call for a better balance between "heart" and "head" in giving (Connolly 2011), others take the more strident position that any personal investment in a cause is indefensible and self-indulgent, urging donors to only use evidence-based metrics to allocate and monitor their philanthropic spending (MacAskill 2015).

There is not just one, single insider critique; rather, there have been many different voices offering ideas on how to "do philanthropy better", including the historic promotion of "scientific philanthropy" and three concepts that have successfully landed in the public consciousness since the start of the twenty-first century: strategic philanthropy, philanthrocapitalism and effective altruism.

Scientific philanthropy

As capitalism began to dominate the economic systems of many countries during the seventeenth and eighteenth centuries, the ideas and principles of political economy also gained growing adherence across society, including among philanthropists. The belief that the invisible hand of market forces secures maximum benefits led many to question the value of indiscriminate charity. Random almsgiving, such as giving coins to beggars, was increasingly criticized as fundamentally unhelpful because it made recipients dependent on donors, and further demoralized the poor rather than enabling them to improve their situation. The nineteenth-century attacks on philanthropy discussed in Chapter 2 often come from the perspective of proponents of political economy, most notably the philosopher John Stuart Mill who was concerned that "superficial" and "pseudo-philanthropy" interfered with the iron laws of political economy (Cunningham 2020: 114). Mill also highlighted the problem of the mismatch between social needs and the distribution of charitable resources, noting that charity "almost always does too much or too little: it lavishes its bounty in one place, and leaves people to starve in another" (Mill 1848).

The integration of political economy thinking into philanthropic practice gave rise to warnings about the dangers of "misguided" and "ignorant" charity work that can do more harm than good. It promoted the benefits of "knowledgeable" and "scientific" philanthropy which provides help – such as education and apprenticeships for children, housing with affordable rents and teaching household-management skills to help the poor avoid debt – without undermining the workings of capitalism.

These debates led to the late nineteenth-century creation of Charity Organization Societies (COS), which sought to correct the "misplaced priorities" of contemporary philanthropists by coordinating donations to support the "deserving" poor, and focus on efforts that advocate the values of hard work and thrift to cultivate self-sufficiency and personal responsibility. As with all permutations of the insider critique, COS wanted to reform how people give by showing them how to "do good better" using "scientific principles" to target assistance where it was most needed and would be most effective. But COS failed to convince most donors that this was a better way to channel their altruistic impulses, and it was famously resented by beneficiaries who felt unreasonably scrutinized and judged, and decided that the acronym COS actually stood for "Cringe or Starve". In a similar vein, the Irish American poet John Boyle O'Reilly derided proponents of this movement on the other side of the Atlantic, with this couplet in his 1896 poem "In Bohemia": "The organized charity, scrimped and iced | In the name of a cautious, statistical Christ."

In the twentieth century the baton of scientific philanthropy was taken up more enthusiastically by institutional, rather than individual, philanthropy. Progressive-era foundations deployed highly bureaucratized processes and relied on "experts armed with data" to understand and address the social problems facing rapidly urbanizing and industrializing societies (Ealy 2014: 87–8). Thus technocracy has long been promoted as the best way to apply finite philanthropic resources to infinite needs, and this approach has come to the fore again in more recent manifestations of the insider critique.

Strategic philanthropy

As the name suggests, "strategic philanthropy" involves creating and implementing a strategy to guide philanthropic activity. Donors throughout history might lay claim to have, or be described as having, a strategic approach. Andrew Carnegie's roll-out of the design for building and running libraries across the word clearly did not happen by accident. But the label came into general use at the turn of the millennium by those who viewed themselves as "new philanthropists" and wished to indicate a break with the perceived random almsgiving or "spray and pray" efforts of their philanthropic predecessors. Strategic givers are encouraged to give careful consideration to questions such as choosing beneficiaries and the best vehicle, style and time frame for their giving, as well as using a theory of change to plan the steps to achieve intended outcomes, with the caveat that there are no universally appropriate answers to such questions (Frumkin 2006). The language used by strategic donors – which includes logic models, leverage and theories of scale – echoes the kind of jargon used by managers and consultants in the for-profit sector. Perhaps for this reason, strategic philanthropy has been particularly dominant within the corporate realm as a means of demonstrating that company funds are being "well spent" to achieve both social and business goals (Porter & Kramer 2002).

Self-defined strategic philanthropists tend to make their wealth young, pursue a cosmopolitan lifestyle and seek greater control over, and tangible results from, their donations. They also typically wish to give their time and expertise alongside their money. Charles Handy describes these new philanthropists as:

> individuals, still in the prime of life, … they now want to use their money, their skills and their abilities to get things done to create something transparently useful in society. They talk of making a difference, of giving something back, but they aren't satisfied by writing cheques to worthy causes, valuable though such charity can be. These people want to be in the driving seat because that's where they belong.
>
> (Handy 2006: 8–9)

The academic centre at the University of Cambridge, launched in 2020, is named the Centre for Strategic Philanthropy and aims to promote "impact-driven giving that is evidence-based", citing the university's vice chancellor's view that "Global philanthropic capital must be used effectively and for maximum impact" (CSP n.d.).

These sentiments and goals are shared by donors using labels such as "high-engagement philanthropy" and "impact philanthropy", and are also evident in the style of philanthropy termed "philanthrocapitalism" by commentators.

Philanthrocapitalism

The defining feature of the philanthrocapitalist approach is the application of business methods to philanthropy. The term was coined by the journalist Matthew Bishop and the economist turned nonprofit leader Michael Green, who described a trend of donors seeking to "improve philanthropy" by applying their money-making skills to giving (hence the neologism philanthro-capitalism). Philanthrocapitalists are said to "think long-term, to go against conventional wisdom, to take up ideas too risky for government, to deploy substantial resources quickly when the situation demands it – above all, to try something new" (Bishop & Green 2008: 12).

The search for novel money-making methods is the goal of venture capitalism, the principles of which are harnessed in the idea of "venture philanthropy". This involves investing philanthropic capital and expertise in promising ideas, nonprofit organizations and leaders to quickly take their work to scale. The difficulty in raising capital to fund the long-term development of successful nonprofit organizations has led to various proposals for a sector-targeted investment bank, individual "angel investors" and even a nonprofit stock exchange. The use of market mechanisms to improve the allocation of philanthropic capital is intended to drive funding to the most effective nonprofits rather than those lucky enough to have secured support through arbitrary reasons, such as personal connections.

Eliminating entirely the role of personal connections in distributing philanthropic funding is the central goal of "effective altruism", a third approach to "doing good better".

Effective altruism

Effective altruism is a philosophy and a social movement that urges people to do the most good that they can, on the basis of careful reasoning and reliable evidence (Singer 2015: 4–5). The founder of this movement, Australian philosopher Peter Singer, often asks his students and audiences this question: if you walk past a pond and see a child drowning, would you jump in to save it, even if doing so would get your clothes muddy and make you late for your next appointment?

As everyone agrees that there is a moral obligation to save the drowning child in front of us, even if it incurs the trivial cost and bother of getting clothes cleaned, Singer argues there is an equal obligation to save the lives of unknown dying children in a distant country, whose lives can equally easily be saved by donating to pay for cheap, proven interventions, such as malaria nets or deworming treatments.

In addition to highlighting the irrelevance of proximity and visibility of suffering, effective altruists also argue that some philanthropic goals and causes are more worthwhile than others, so donors have a dual moral imperative to fund the most effective ways of helping the most important issues. To illustrate how this works in practice, Singer compares different giving choices, such as contributing $100,000 to help build a new wing in a local art museum or covering the cost of treating trachoma (a cause of preventable blindness that typically affects children in developing countries) which costs $100 per person. Preventing sight loss for 1,000 people has a greater moral claim on the donor, or, in Singer's words, "a donation to prevent trachoma offers at least 10 times the value of giving to the museum" (Singer 2013). A related example offered by Singer notes that the $40,000 cost of providing one guide dog for a blind person in the US or UK is the same as preventing 400 people from going blind in a distant, developing country. I once interviewed a donor to Guide Dogs for the Blind, who told me: "My wife is blind, she has a guide dog and she gets a range of support from the Royal Institute for the Blind. I wouldn't say we wouldn't have supported blind charities if she wasn't, but obviously that gives us a particular interest in that charity." This kind of personal connection is exactly the issue that effective altruism is trying to tackle.

Another example is offered by the leading UK advocate of this approach. Will MacAskill recounts the time he visited the Hamlin Fistula Hospital in Ethiopia. Fistulas are caused by tearing during childbirth and also by sexual abuse and rape. They cause immense physical pain and the women affected are often unable to work and may even be ostracized from their communities. MacAskill writes: "I'd visited this hospital, I'd hugged the women who suffered from this condition, and they'd thanked me for visiting them. It had been an important experience for me: a vivid first-hand demonstration of the severity of the problems in the world. This was a cause I had a personal connection with" (MacAskill 2015: 48).

But MacAskill did the maths and worked out that he could help more people if he donated elsewhere so he chose not to support the Fistula Foundation, because "I would be privileging the needs of some people over others for emotional rather than moral reasons … It was arbitrary that I'd seen this particular problem at close quarters" (MacAskill 2015: 48-9).

The maths that enabled MacAskill to reach this decision is borrowed from the discipline of health economics in which the quality-adjusted life year, or QALY for short, is a year of life lived in perfect health. Philanthropic interventions can either extend the amount of time someone lives, or they can improve the quality of life during the time someone is alive, so 20 QALYs could either be 20 extra years of life, or living an extra 40 years with a quality of life improvement from 50 per cent to 100 per cent. To show how QALYs can help with philanthropic decisions, MacAskill offers the example of paying $10,000 for antiretroviral therapy for a 40 year old who has AIDS, or paying the same amount for surgery to prevent blindness in a 20 year old. The antiretroviral therapy will add five years to the lifespan of the 40 year old who would otherwise die at 45, and their quality of life will increase from 50 per cent to 90 per cent. The 40 per cent improvement in quality of life for the first five years plus an extra five years of life at 90 per cent health equals 6.5 QALYs ((40% × 5) + (90% × 5) = 6.5). The 20 year old will, on average, live to the age of 70. Surveys show that people rate the quality of life while blind at 40 per cent, so preventing blindness in a 20 year old increases quality of life by 60 per cent for 50 years, which equals 30 QALYs (60% × 50 = 30). Therefore, the donor should fund the eye surgery because it yields over four times the benefit of paying for the antiretroviral drugs (MacAskill 2015: 42–3).

The methodology of calculating the "best" use of donations is under constant review within the effective altruism movement, and includes attempts to capture the amounts of money that recommended nonprofits are capable of absorbing at any given time, the marginal utility of donating additional dollars to recommended nonprofits, and attempts to capture the returns on funding advocacy activities.

Although the effective altruist's approach to making philanthropic decisions using a calculator feels novel, its thrust is in line with repeated attempts across time to improve philanthropy by making it more organized, strategic, effective and impactful in order to do the most good with limited resources.

Defending philanthropy against the insider critique

The proposition that giving should do as much good as possible is entirely uncontroversial. Every donor, whether giving large or small amounts, hopes that their money will be used well. But translating that uncontentious sentiment into specific guidelines for how to conduct philanthropy is stymied by three challenges: normative, reductionist and attribution challenges. After discussing these three challenges I set out an additional concern that, rather than improve giving, insider critiques may deter people from starting or scaling up their giving for fear of "getting it wrong".

The normative challenge

There is an old joke about a traveller who is lost and asks a local how to get to his intended destination. "Well now," says the local, "If I wanted to get there, I wouldn't start from here." The joke, of course, is that the traveller has no choice but to start from where they currently are. So too, advice to improve philanthropy needs to be based on how donations actually happen in practice.

As the examples at the start of this chapter illustrate, and as a large body of research shows (see also, e.g., Berman *et al.* 2018), philanthropy involves intensely personal and subjective choices. John D. Rockefeller, Andrew Carnegie and Heather Beckwith were responding to the hand that life had dealt them. Each of us has life experiences that result in stronger connections to certain issues, places and values, which in turn shapes our "philanthropic autobiography" (Payton & Moody 2008: 21–3). Another way of putting this, based on extensive studies of wealthy donors in the US, is that generosity thrives when donors identify with the needs of beneficiaries (Schervish 2007). Very few people who had visited the Ethiopian Fistula hospital, seen the good work done there and hugged the patients would then refuse to give any support because a better "donating deal" lay elsewhere. Indeed, such an approach would be incompatible with many religious and humanitarian teachings that advocate the merits of all efforts to help: from verse 5(32) in the Quran that "whoever saves one – it is as if he had saved mankind entirely"; to the words of Anne Frank, "How lovely to think that no one need wait a moment, we can start now, start slowly changing the world!"; to Mother Theresa's admonition to "Never worry about numbers. Help one person at a time and always start with the person nearest you." As Berger and Penna (2013) point out, there is no "Sophie's choice" moment in philanthropic giving – we can support as many causes as we choose, so it is specious to suggest that we must choose between supporting an art gallery or funding malaria nets, we can – and many do – fund both.

The perils of taking a utilitarian approach that reduces morality to a data-driven calculation are nicely highlighted in Giles Fraser's take on the drowning child analogy. Pointing to the way that proximity and specific relationships tend to generate empathy and moral concern, he asks whether anyone would choose to save a large bag of money from a burning building rather than saving their neighbour's terrified child, even if the contents of the bag could be donated to save the lives of a thousand strangers (Fraser 2017). Seeking the most beneficial bangs per donated buck is clearly not the only, or even a very common, way for people to make giving decisions. And this is not primarily (as is often assumed) because donors do not have access to robust information with which to make charitable choices. That hypothesis has been tested by a number of multi-million dollar efforts around the world, including a $12 million investment by the William and Flora Hewlett Foundation to fund publicly accessible information about the financial performance and social impact of nonprofit organizations. This initiative ended because there was no discernible impact on changing donor behaviour (Donovan 2014).

There are many other consequential aspects of our lives that are similarly path dependent and rooted in personal choices and connections: our careers, life partners and where we live are not selected after a full survey of all possible options; rather, we start from where we are, and make decisions based on what and who we know. This is not just a pragmatic attempt to avoid "analysis paralysis", it is also an acknowledgement that there is no one "right" answer to all of these major life decisions. We can applaud the work of a surgeon operating in a war zone without criticizing them for not choosing a career in diplomacy to prevent conflicts from happening in the first place.

But of course what is normative is not necessarily right, so let us explore the other challenges of the insider critique.

The reductionist challenge

John K. Castle is descended from one of the original founders of Yale University. He endowed a lecture series to honour his ancestor, the Reverend James Pierpoint. Peter Singer was appointed the Castle Lecturer in 2013 and he gave three lectures on "altruism" and "effectiveness" that formed the intellectual basis for the "effective altruism" movement. There is an irony that Castle's philanthropic act helped develop a critique that argues strongly against the sort of funding that enabled the lecture series, because donations to universities are not cheap life-saving or life-enhancing interventions. The larger lesson is the multiple, unpredictable implications of any particular philanthropic gift. Just as the flap of a butterfly's wings may or may not set off a tornado in Texas, so too we cannot know exactly what will be set in train by a donation, nor the precise steps that will definitely lead to a desired outcome.

The focus of the insider critiques on rigorous, data-driven and business-like approaches often comes unstuck when confronting the reality of complex philanthropic goals and how social change happens in practice. The reductionist challenge is that making the world a better place is clearly not a simple proposition. Philanthropy often tackles complex, entrenched, "wicked problems" such as ending child poverty or providing affordable housing for all, that have so far defied government or market solutions. Philanthropy also responds to newly emerging issues, such as closing the digital divide, that are therefore less well understood, and to supranational issues such as climate change and the refugee crisis, which require solutions that transcend the remit of any one elected government.

This point is well made in a cartoon pinned to the noticeboard above my desk, which depicts a bunch of clipboard-carrying bureaucrats telling the Indian civil rights leader Mahatma Gandhi: "We won't fund you because we can't see the link between spinning and bringing down the Empire." The "greatest achievements" of philanthropy discussed in Chapter 1 – including helping to end slavery, building civic infrastructure, mapping the human genome, promoting fair trade and changing public attitudes and policy to secure greater equality – were all value-laden missions that involved long timescales, non-linear interventions and interactions with huge numbers of human beings, and therefore unquantifiable and unpredictable dimensions. Such goals could never be captured by easily definable inputs and predictable outputs within a closed system, yet philanthropic funding played a role in making each of them happen.

This is not to dispute the value of well-run and efficient nonprofit organizations that achieve maximum impact, because clearly both donors and doers want money to be spent well, but only in so far as it helps achieve ultimate goals that are unlikely to be captured in the "bottom line" model of business. For example, I have met many philanthropists whose chosen focus involves helping people with deprived and chaotic backgrounds who have ended up in the care system, in prison, experiencing homelessness and dealing with debilitating addictions. It is reasonable to track metrics such as the numbers of people that their projects reach, how long they engage with the programme and immediate outcomes in relation to, for example, avoiding reoffending, securing a tenancy or staying clean. But both funders and front-line practitioners involved in this work seek far more ambitious and wide-ranging transformations: that their clients go on to lead fulfilling and flourishing lives, that intergenerational cycles of deprivation are ended and that wider social attitudes change to see the value of avoiding such harms in the first place, offering swift and generous support when needed. Such large-scale transformations in how people think, act and are treated, and in how we treat each other, cannot be captured by a narrow business model reliant on target-driven metrics. Nor can organizations that boast the "best" financial ratios and lowest overhead costs be assumed to be best placed to achieve donors' ultimate philanthropic goals. As Susan Berresford, former head of the Ford Foundation, notes: technocratic approaches sound promising and can at times be valuable, but overall it "miniaturizes ambition" and has a "deadening effect" on nonprofit innovation (Berresford 2010). Bruce Sievers advises philanthropy to avoid emulating business models and to resist the lure of "conceptual fads" such as cost–benefit analyses because that encourages nonprofit leaders to manipulate meaningless metrics to placate funders, and leads to the neglect of high-potential social change activity, such as supporting the infrastructure of civil society, improving public broadcasting and promoting intercultural understanding (Sievers 2004). The goals of philanthropy include general human advancement, concern for future generations and environmental sustainability, and should not be reduced to activities that are amenable to instrumental, measurable objectives.

Philanthropists themselves are often acutely aware of the inadequacies of the business model when pursuing social change and should not be held responsible for jargon and approaches that are encouraged by consultants and commentators. The word "philanthrocapitalism" was coined by the journalist Mathew Bishop and the then economist, now nonprofit leader, Michael Green, not by donors. The suggestion that philanthropy justifies capitalism, and that the "rich can save the world" (as the short-lived subtitle of the first edition of Bishop and Green's 2008 book declaimed), are not commonly articulated by philanthropists (in fact I have never heard a big donor express that view), and yet they are nonetheless held accountable to that sentiment.

What donors do more commonly express is connection to, and identification with, others with whom they feel an affinity through shared life experiences. This is how giving differs from consumption: a donation is not an attempt to buy a specific outcome, rather it can be an act of solidarity or allyship, an expression of sympathy or a desire to demonstrate gratitude. Behavioural economists find that giving decisions in the US are driven less by a rational analysis of how to achieve maximum impact and more by a desire to join with others who share a similar outlook on how the world should be (Karlan & List 2007). As one of the authors of that study reflects: "Giving is not about a calculation of what you are buying. It is about participating in a fight" (Karlan, cited in Leonhard 2008). While the insider critique urges donors to always think strategically in order to align their response with the most urgent needs, this approach overlooks the values of connection, compassion and consolation that are integral to the philanthropic response.

As well as failing to take account of the expressive and emotional functions of philanthropy, the modern insider critique also largely overlooks the potential for private giving to tackle problems at their source rather than administering "band aid" solutions. The case that prevention is better than cure has been set out many times, perhaps most concisely and evocatively in Joseph Malins' 1895 poem, whose final couplet argues: "Better put a strong fence around the top of the cliff | Than an ambulance down in the valley."

The difficulty in measuring the outcomes of problems that are averted rather than administered (who knows how many people the fence saved, whereas the bodies in the ambulance can be easily counted), and the lack of certain and identifiable outcomes when funding advocacy rather than direct assistance, means that effective altruism stands particularly criticized for failing to tackle deeper structural problems. Reducing philanthropy to a lives-saved-per-dollar calculation denies donors the chance to play a wider role in systemic change and help build a better society – always bearing in mind the very different ways that people define "better". As a study of compassion and how best to care for strangers concludes, in relation to effective altruism: "The Singer principle of preventing badness would seem to override the question of how to promote the good and how to foster human flourishing" (Murphy 2018: 84).

The lack of nuance in critiques of philanthropy is especially apparent here because the role and purpose of philanthropy is about so much more than extending lifespans. Judging all philanthropic decisions on a lives-saved-per-dollar basis fails to appreciate that, among many other things, the philanthropy space is where we practice empathy, demonstrate solidarity and shape the kind of society we want to live in. A narrow, unreflective focus on direct aid can also prompt concerns that donors do not understand – or support – the need for broader efforts to make the world more just: "Calling on the wealthy to address the world's [existing] problems as effectively as possible is hardly challenging them. It means accepting the world as it is and calling on the winners to offer palliative care to the losers" (Pickering 2016).

In reaction to the emaciated interpretation of philanthropy offered in reductionist insider critiques, others are engaged in self-defined "radical philanthropy" that is focused on tackling structural problems and seeks to transform the institutions of the current economic system: "what sets radical philanthropy apart is that it recognizes the centrality of the cumulative and interconnecting forces of free market capitalism, colonialism, neocolonialism, and imperialism in making and maintaining global poverty. It also recognizes that poverty has other cross-cutting dimensions, including the intersectionality of race, class and gender" (Herro & Obeng-Odoom 2019: 882).

Such approaches highlight the third challenge inherent in the insider critique: how to attribute credit to philanthropic interventions that are engaged with enduring and expansive issues, and are also the concern of government and market action.

The attribution challenge

The attribution challenge is that we cannot always know for certain precisely what input causes what outcome. It is not easy to identify clear causal relationships, especially when a large number of different donors and philanthropists – as well as governments and market actors – are simultaneously pursuing complex goals such as reducing child mortality or raising education levels.

Using the metrics-based method promoted by effective altruism to evaluate and compare charities, donors are encouraged to support a very small number of organizations focused on preventing disease and early deaths among children in developing countries, as this almost always results in a higher QALY than any other type of intervention. The Anti-Malaria Foundation provides insecticide-treated nets in sub-Saharan Africa for just $5 a piece. This organization is one of the small number of organizations that is highly rated by effective altruists because they offer such a cheap way to save lives – the comparison with how many of us spend a similar sum on a daily coffee is a useful reminder of our privilege and obligation to make better decisions about how money is used. But behind easily fundable interventions such as malaria nets are a host of other far more expensive contributions, including the scientific research that conclusively proved it is mosquitoes that transmit malaria, conducted by a researcher at the Liverpool School of Tropical Medicine, Sir Ronald Ross, winner of the Nobel Prize in Physiology or Medicine in 1902 for this discovery. As noted above, donating to universities is not a favoured option for effective altruists but the $5 intervention is dependent on that earlier, and far more expensive, scientific effort. The donor who funds the cost of the malaria net is standing on the shoulders of the scientists whose research led to the treatment breakthrough, and is also reliant on the contribution of those who designed the net, those who manufacture it, the distribution network and the educators who show the beneficiary how to use it. And it is also reliant on the funders who enabled the work of those other people, from donations to universities, to scholarships for talented designers, to funding for distribution networks for medical supplies in countries lacking a health infrastructure.

It is obviously easier to quantify the direct impact of a malaria net than the exploratory funding for research that ultimately enabled the $5 nets, but in these beautifully phrased words, attributed to Albert Einstein: "Not everything that can be counted counts, and not everything that counts can be counted." There is therefore a measurement problem at the heart of the insider critique that overlooks the full cost and complexity involved in achieving public goods. This results in channelling funds to those causes and organizations that can demonstrate the greatest impact per dollar spent *today*. This approach risks underfunding the groundwork, including research and development as well as advocacy, campaigns, coalition building and other long-term efforts that are needed to work towards solving the biggest and most intractable problems, whose impact may not be realized for many years. The need for systemic solutions and institutional reform (sometimes described as the advantages of "wholesale" over "retail" philanthropy) have long been understood as capable of delivering greater "returns" than direct aid to the global poor. Yet the inability to quantify and feel ownership over the outcomes of diffuse aid creates a paradox for effective altruists, who seek maximum effectiveness from their giving – but only if they can count and possess it. This proprietary instinct is problematic in modern society, which only functions because of the division of labour. None of us are self-sufficient: we cannot produce all that we need for ourselves, nor can we single-handedly assist others. Collaboration is the natural state for donors, as American philanthropy commentators Thomas Tierney and Joel Fleishman note: "One of philanthropy's great ironies is that very little can be accomplished by individuals acting on their own, even when those individuals are extraordinarily wealthy. The grander your ambitions, the more certain it is that success will require working with and through a broad range of other players, including … other donors who are passionate about the same issue" (Tierney & Fleishman 2011: 13).

The suggestion that we can operate as "heroic individuals", able to save a life entirely on our own, is to disregard all that is known about how modern society works and how change occurs. We need others to make our contribution possible, and we need to trust that others will do their part. As US donor Carrie Morgridge writes: "There's no such thing as a stand-alone philanthropist. But your gift and mine, together with many others, can work miracles" (Morgridge 2015: 150). The insider critique promotes an individualistic and isolationist approach that fails to understand our interconnectedness and the need for trust in others. MacAskill could have supported the Fistula Hospital in Ethiopia if he had had confidence in the presence and generosity of other donors to support the "better value" causes directed by his calculations.

The measurement problem also extends to the ethical and practical issues raised by this approach. The "gold standard" for designing effective interventions involves a randomized controlled trial (RCT) which identifies the best solution by exposing random samples to different interventions and comparing the results. RCTs are successfully used in clinical trials to test new medicines but their suitability for non-pharmaceutical scenarios is contested on a number of grounds: they are extremely expensive to run; it is hard, if not impossible, to isolate the variable being tested; and it is unethical to deny help to some people by allocating them to a non-treatment group (Hobbes 2014). A letter signed by leading economists, including three Nobel Prize winners, highlights the problem of "tortuous impact assessments", because "truly random sampling with blinded subjects is almost impossible in human communities without creating scenarios so abstract as to tell us little about the real world. And trials are expensive to carry out, and fraught with ethical challenges" (*Guardian* 2018).

The other key tool of effective altruists – the QALY – was developed for evaluating health interventions but, as this book explains, the philanthropic impulse prompts action across a far wider set of issues. People do not only give to keep people alive, they give to make life worth living. When we consider the scope of work funded by donors in practice, it is clear that there is no meaningful way to compare the different outcomes achieved by all kinds of philanthropy. Is success in decreasing loneliness better than success in improving air quality? Is widening access to the arts more valuable than social inclusion in sport? A calculator cannot help us to answer these questions because they are reliant on personal values, passions and different visions of the good society, as well as on realistic assessments of what we can each best contribute to realizing that vision.

Not all donors seek to make causal claims and attribute all good outcomes to their donations. The strapline of the Rank Foundation in the UK is "a pebble in the pond", representing the idea that their funding is a moderate contribution that will eventually create larger ripples. Caroline Broadhurst, the foundation's deputy chief executive, told me: "We use the pebble analogy because we know that the valuable social impact is created by the skills, drive and expertise of the charity and social leaders themselves. We play a role, bringing financial and non-financial support, and we let our work speak for itself."

Seeking to make a contribution rather than to claim attribution is a realistic way to describe giving, recognizes the complexity of making change happen and avoids the problem of hubris and "heroic individualism".

Another approach taken by many philanthropists and donors is to pursue "double impact" by helping meet immediate needs while also tackling the root causes, pursuing both amelioration and systemic change simultaneously. As Vicky, who works at a nonprofit supporting women affected by domestic abuse, explained to me: "we work to meet the immediate needs of women and families by providing shelter, food, emotional support, and a variety of community resources. However, we also offer a variety of outreach services, work to dismantle the stigma surrounding abuse, raise awareness about the issue of violence against women, and work directly with the abusers themselves."

This has also been described as taking a "zoom in/zoom out" approach: zooming in to pay attention to meeting immediate needs while also zooming out to understand what policies, structures and systems need to change to end the perpetuation of those needs. For example, community food programmes can meet the immediate nutritional needs of people who are unable to afford food, while also participating in poverty advocacy work, for example by publishing details of demand for their help and the drivers behind food poverty.

These examples show the benefits of taking a broader and more flexible approach to working out what constitutes "doing good better".

The problematic consequences of the insider critique

The normative, reductionist and attribution challenges inherent in the insider critique of philanthropy leads to a number of problematic consequences for donors, doers, nonprofit leaders and wider society.

While the intention of the insider critique is to improve the practice of philanthropy through a more efficient allocation of donations, it has the unintended consequence of adding fuel to popular notions that most giving is misguided, and therefore risks delaying or even deterring people from putting their generous intentions into practice. It also adds to the costs of fundraising and running a charity because providing robust evidence of impact is not cheap, made more galling by the lack of take-up by donors using such data to inform their giving decisions.

Delaying and deterring giving

I often ask philanthropists what advice they would give to other people who are considering giving away significant sums of money. Their response can be summed up in two words: "just start". The value of undertaking donor education, seeking advice, doing research on the issues and potential solutions, evaluating outcomes and acting on the results are all also noted but – crucially – not at the expense of getting started. As UK philanthropist Trevor Pears told me:

> A good place to start is with *I don't know* but decide to commit to start anyway. You can navel-gaze and ask a million-and-one questions but not start because you don't commit. So I would say: *get on the journey, make the commitment, go.* I don't think you can learn how to be effective in philanthropy by sitting behind a desk. You've got to get out and physically see and engage and feel and touch and you'll learn through what you see and do.

Kris Putnam-Walkerly has advised individual and organizational donors for two decades. In her book, addressed to those seeking to become more effective givers, she warns against the dangers of acting too slowly, with excessive bureaucracy and a fear of getting it wrong, noting: "The fear of failure is real and prevalent. Philanthropists respond to this fear with a scarcity mentality – they hold back themselves and their resources … They engage in labor-intensive efforts dancing around the question: conducting excessive research and data analysis to unearth every facet of an issue before deciding to launch the initiative … or simply never trying" (Putnam-Walkerly 2020: 25).

The desire to improve giving and achieve effective outcomes is widely shared by donors, so the insider critics are pushing at an open door. But emotive and overly critical language, including accusing donors of being responsible for harm and even deaths if they choose to fund the "wrong" nonprofits, risks turning philanthropy into a test that is easy to fail. Judging other donors on the merits of their giving is a long way from the original meaning of philanthropy as "love of humankind". Instead of encouraging more people to give more, it puts up barriers and might reasonably leave potential donors deciding it is better not to give at all than to risk "getting it wrong".

Increases the costs of fundraising and running a charity

Raising funds for good causes is challenging enough without having to confront new objections from donors who have heard the data-driven siren call, and feel compelled to see "proof of impact" in order to be, and be seen to be, a savvy "new" philanthropist. The desire for certainty in an uncertain world is understandable, yet there is a growing concern among fundraisers that the main beneficiary of the insider critique is the "impact industry", whose work is paid for by money that would otherwise have been available to fund the work that the charity exists to do.

Is that an overstatement? Sara runs a very small charity that works with children aged 4–11 in one of the most deprived areas of England, whose families are often from immigrant and refugee backgrounds and who face multiple challenges in relation to income, health and local high crime rates. After a career singing in opera houses around the world, she has settled back in her home town to develop an in-school singing programme aimed at improving the life chances of these children. The children grow in confidence and self-esteem, and have been given opportunities to perform locally and nationally, including singing for the Pope during his UK visit in 2010, and singing live on the BBC Christmas midnight mass programme. The annual running costs of the project are around £24,000, half of which comes from the government. Fundraising to cover the other half takes up a lot of Sara's time, and she told me about a potential donor who said: "I can see you're doing a brilliant job, I've watched the children perform and I want to help. But instead of giving you the other £12,000 that you need for running costs, I'd prefer to give the same amount – £12,000 – to spend on doing research. I've heard that if you can prove your model makes a lifelong difference, then you can use that data to persuade other people to fund your running costs."

Unsurprisingly, Sara said no. Impact measurement is important but has to be kept in proportion, especially for small nonprofits where the staff members would have to commission and oversee the study while also still needing to fundraise for core costs and run the project. Not only would it be disproportionate to spend time and money in this way, it would take decades to prove "lifelong differences" and the flexibility required to be responsive to changing needs means the goalposts would be constantly moving, as Sara explains:

> The success of this project is down to our ability to tweak the model constantly in response to local, changing need, which would be much harder if we had funders breathing down our necks asking if we'd met our targets. The fluidity we have allows us constantly to ask "what's best for the children right now?" For example, in 2020 we needed to quickly develop and implement new ideas to maintain our project during lock-down and will change what we do again to help the children recover from the pandemic. Expensive data collection on what we were doing pre-Covid would be mostly irrelevant now.

It is also unfair to the donor, whose expectation that their research would magic-ally unlock donations from others may well be disappointed. Providing robust data takes a lot of time and money, and ironically there is a lack of evidence that such evidence makes the difference that its adherents assume. The working hypothesis is that the inability to identify effective charities holds otherwise gen-erous people back from giving, and that proof of impact will unlock donations. Yet studies show that donors' expressed preference for proven impact may be "cheap talk" rather than a genuine barrier. Adding scientific information to direct mail solicitations was found to have no effect on the average likelihood of giving or average gift amount (Karlan & Wood 2017), and another study concluded that "even when effectiveness information is made easily comparable across options, it has a limited impact on choice" (Berman *et al.* 2018: 834). Research highlighting the persistence of subjectivity in charity choices even when information is freely and easily available, shows that the nonprofit sector is not helpfully viewed as a market in need of correction by the provision of more information.

"Personal" philanthropy results in greater good

Indeed, there is an alternative hypothesis worth investigating: that giving driven by personal experiences and connections results in larger overall amounts of good being done. People give more, and more enthusiastically, when they feel truly connected to a cause, trust the organization and enjoy interacting with their staff, volunteers and fellow donors. This is the basis of the dominant paradigm in fundraising that is known as "relationship fundraising" which encourages fundraisers to build long-term authentic relationships with their supporters, engaging them in the work of the organization, so that they feel part of the team that is achieving meaningful results. This approach stands in contrast to "transactional fundraising", which treats donors like ATMs that are tapped for cash as the need arises.

UK philanthropist Richard Ross explained to me how being involved with the scientists and medical research that he funds helps to sustain and grow his interest and commitment:

> Contributing to this life-changing work is extremely interesting, constructive and totally worthwhile … I know how fulfilling and exciting it is for the donor to have been part of this process of discovery … For me it is not just a case of giving away money, it's about meeting the researchers we fund, being involved in what they're doing and being part of it. Meeting people like neuroscientists is more interesting than anything I will ever do in any other part of my life … it's a wonderful extra dimension to life. If you can find a focus for your philanthropy, and spend time and energy working at it so that it becomes an integral part of your life, you'll be helping others and you'll get more pleasure from your giving than from anything else you've ever done.

Ross's evident passion for his chosen cause, and the virtuous cycle of giving more as he gets closer to those he funds, is shared by many other big donors. Arts organizations are particularly well suited to engaging passionate supporters. Joan Weill gave $20 million to a dance company in New York, explaining that, "If I came back in my next life, I'd come back as a dancer" (Lewis 2006). Edyth Broad commented (presumably tongue-in-cheek) that she and her husband gave $6 million to the Los Angeles Opera because they wanted to watch Wagner's *Ring Cycle* without travelling to Europe (Wyatt 2006). And UK banker Martin Smith's significant support for the Orchestra of the Age of Enlightenment led to an invitation to fulfil his lifelong dream by conducting them playing the Overture to *The Marriage of Figaro* for his fiftieth birthday (Church 2005). Smith invited his friends and professional contacts to attend this and subsequent events on later significant birthdays, which not only gave him huge pleasure but also resulted in considerable sums being raised for the orchestra. In all these examples, the donors' passion for the art form and their sustained financial support goes hand in hand.

Passion-driven philanthropy, rather than donations prompted by a utilitarian calculus, are also more likely to extend beyond money to the giving of time, expertise and connections which can be even more valuable to recipient organizations and causes. As Paul Ruddock, who lives between London and New York, told me: "I think that philanthropy has four elements to it: giving money, getting money, giving skills and giving time. For both my wife and I, it's never just about giving money. We are also prepared to help raise lots of money, as well as using our skills to help the organizations that we support."

Although Ruddock and his wife have donated over £40 million, they also have significant value as board members, ambassadors and volunteer fundraisers. This is another nuanced aspect that is overlooked by the insider critique: philanthropy is not just a financial transaction, it is much richer (pun intended) than that. Donors give their non-monetary resources of time, talent, knowledge and contacts to causes that they also have genuine connections to, and a passion for. It is hard to sustain and grow our own commitment, or to enthuse friends to support a cause that has been chosen by a formula rather than a cause that is supported because of a deep and abiding personal connection.

Encouraging people to give to the things they know and care about – or at least not criticizing them for doing so – leads to greater donor engagement, more generous giving and a stronger philanthropy sector overall. As Berger and Penna conclude: "The superficially enticing 'logic' of effective altruism ultimately leads to a moralistic, hyper-rationalistic, top-down approach to philanthropy that can kill the very altruistic spirit it claims to foster" (Berger & Penna 2013).

Conclusion

The reflection that "It is more difficult to give money away intelligently than to earn it in the first place" (attributed to both Andrew Carnegie and John D. Rockefeller) continues to be echoed by donors today Giving is hard enough already, both to do it well and to make it a priority in the face of competing demands on our time and wallets, without making it unnecessarily complicated and off-putting. The insider critique adds to the sense that philanthropy is inherently problematic and getting involved is more trouble than it is worth.

Despite this conclusion, the insider critique can also be a force for good. Although it problematizes philanthropy by promoting ideas of "better" and "worse" giving, which could result in delaying or deterring giving altogether, it also seeks to encourage more, and more effective, giving. The ideas it promotes are getting more people thinking and talking about philanthropy.

It is uncontroversial to suggest that donors should be thoughtful and considered in their giving decisions, should take steps to ensure the positive potential of their giving is maximized, and should endeavour to avoid harm. But the insider critique fuels the misconception that the primary goal of philanthropy is to help the poor and tackle inequality. It overlooks the reality of philanthropy as an extremely broad church: there are infinite ways to contribute to a (subjectively defined) "better" society. There is no perfect formula for working out how to be generous, and philanthropic one-upmanship ("my cause is worthier than yours") is demoralizing for existing donors and discouraging for those yet to start giving. This is why I agree with Katherine Fulton that "Strategic philanthropy, in the wrong hands, can suck the soul out of giving, choosing instead to make investments in technical fixes that can never catalyze true, lasting transformation. Great philanthropy transcends business-like transactions and instead requires wisdom, imagination, and courage" (Fulton 2018).

The result of the insider critique is to frame most giving as misdirected, with inadequate outcomes of philanthropic acts. The insider critique is a textbook example of the strategy of trivializing donors' actions as well intentioned but naïve, unaware of the realities of the real world, such that their contribution is negligible or has unintended consequences. This strategy constitutes the second trick up the sleeve of those intent on derogating do-gooders.

There is also an easy and unhelpful slippage from promoting a preferred method of giving to criticizing and assuming ill intent on the part of all other types of donors. On the back jacket of William MacAskill's guide to *Effective Altruism*, the popular science author Stephen Pinker describes the book's approach to giving as "efforts that actually help people rather than making you feel good or helping you show off". The assertion that public and private benefits are mutually exclusive, and the assumption that philanthropy is a facade for self-promotion, are both explored in Chapter 5, which explains and offers a defence against the populist critique.

5

THE POPULIST CRITIQUE

If you were released from prison because a rich donor funded a project that proved you had been wrongfully convicted, would the shape of that donor's ears be of interest to you? If your elderly parent was able to receive music therapy to ease the distress of dementia, how relevant would the funder's poor fashion sense be? If your disabled child got access to extra interventions that improved her health and happiness, would you care that the services were funded by someone who'd gone through a very messy divorce?

These questions may sound ridiculous but John Arnold, Tom Hunter and MacKenzie Scott have all had aspects of their appearance and private lives raked over in the media in connection to their significant philanthropic efforts. John Arnold, who along with his wife Laura funds the Innocence Project and other successful criminal justice reform projects, was described as having the "jug-eared face of a Division III women's basketball coach" (Arnold 2014). Scotland's first home-grown billionaire, Sir Tom Hunter, who gave £1 million to Music for Dementia and the Alzheimer's Society after losing both his parents to Alzheimer's, was mocked for wearing "lurid" colours and looking "as if he has been basted in glue and rolled around a branch of Topman" (Caesar 2006). MacKenzie Scott's announcement of her $5.8 billion of giving in 2020 was accompanied in many media articles with reference to her "spectacularly public" divorce from Amazon founder Jeff Bezos, and her philanthropy was interpreted as "fuck-you money" designed to show up her less philanthropic (so far) ex-spouse (Bryant 2020).

Ad hominem attacks on philanthropists, and assumptions they have disingenuous motives, are longstanding, as shown in Chapter 2. There is nothing new about these kinds of comments, but the rise of populism at the start of the twenty-first century has included a hardening of attitudes towards philanthropy and philanthropists, as charitable giving has become framed as yet another battleground between the will of ordinary people and corrupt or self-serving elites (Lewis 2019).

At root, populism is the denial of complexity, providing satisfying but erroneously simple answers to exceedingly complicated problems. This book argues that philanthropy is far more complex than most people realize, and requires far more nuance than many critics appreciate. Populism also involves an unhelpful division of the world into "us" and "them", and the scapegoating of people and institutions that are held accountable for whatever the critic believes is wrong with the world. This results in the "othering" of rich elites, whose giving is assumed to be qualitatively different to giving by non-elites, and also results in holding philanthropists more culpable for problematic social and economic structures than the non-philanthropic rich, which results in undermining the value of the philanthropic impulse in contemporary society.

The populist critique of philanthropy

Populist critiques range widely in scope and gravity, from trivial jibes at donors' mannerisms to profound accusations that their philanthropic acts create and sustain the apparatus of justification for exploitative capitalism. Populists problematize both the accumulation and the distribution of wealth, advancing the view that rich donors have secured their fortunes immorally and suggesting that their philanthropic distribution is an attempt to cover up their ill-gotten wealth, as well as to mask self-interested hidden agendas and ulterior motives. Populist critiques call out both intentional and unconscious harms that either way result in the donor being the prime beneficiary. The cumulative result is to nurture dislike of donors and hostility to the outcomes of their philanthropic acts.

There are obvious overlaps with the academic and insider critiques because populists also draw attention to concerns that giving is undemocratic and misguided. For example, a piece written by media polemicist Simon Jenkins leads with: "It's up to government to tax and spend for the good of all, and not the mega-rich seeking a warm glow" (Jenkins 2020). But populist critiques are centred on a different concern: that philanthropy is a sham, a pretence of selflessness that is fundamentally selfish, a good deed hiding a good deal. The tone of populist critiques is also markedly different. Where academics and insiders typically write from a place of constructive critique, drawing on evidence to make their points, populism is an evidence-free, hyperbolic zone that depicts big donors as ridiculous, immoral and potentially illegal. For example, where the academic Linsey McGoey is concerned that Bill Gates "*might* be inadvertently compounding" inequality (2015: 147, emphasis added), populist writer Anand Giridharadas declaims with certainty that "their do-gooding *is* an accomplice to greater, if more invisible, harm" (Giridharadas 2018b, emphasis added). The crucial three-letter difference between "might" and "is" indicates the slippage from critical scholarship to pernicious populism. In addition to confidently claiming causal effects, populists also assume that donated wealth is tainted, that motivations are self-regarding and that giving is conducted thoughtlessly, as further illustrated in the article by Jenkins, which goes on to describe philanthropists as: "people seeking absolution for their sins. As they take to the hills they throw gold from their wagons … [with] surplus cash secured by dodging taxation, regulation and monopoly control … vaguely thinking about what feels good from the comfort of a California beach or a yacht moored in Monaco" (Jenkins 2020).

Behind the hyperbole and accusations of faux virtue are three specific concerns that recur in populist critiques: hidden interests, hypocrisy and material benefits, which together depict philanthropy as taking disguised as giving – the pursuit of solely egoistic rather than altruistic ends.

Philanthropy involves hidden interests

Seeking a shortcut to the pearly gates, avoiding the taxman, laundering a soiled reputation and buying famous friends are all frequently counted among the assumed hidden interests of big givers.

A mid-twentieth-century book on philanthropy describes a man lying on his deathbed and turning to his priest to ask if giving all of his money to the church might buy him a place in heaven. The clergyman concurs: "It is", he says, "an experiment well worth trying" (Andrews 1950: 36).

In an increasingly secularized world the hidden interest that comes up most often in my conversations with colleagues and neighbours is the belief that philanthropy is primarily a tax avoidance measure. While those advancing this view often struggle to explain how this works in practice (as discussed in Chapter 3, the maths behind this perception does not add up) nonetheless public discussions of big giving – including "below the line" comments on media articles and social media reactions – rarely occur without tax evasion being mentioned as the "real" reason that large charitable donations take place.

Another hidden interest that is frequently identified in popular commentary is the use of philanthropy as a strategy to enhance donors' reputations and polish their image. Accusations that philanthropists are engaged in highly visible reputation laundering to secure public approval are sometimes paired with incompatible claims that donors are undertaking secretive efforts to promote advantageous policies or practices. For example, the "smug-looking" wealthy people whose photographs appear on the Giving Pledge website are accused of using "the name of generosity" to covertly extend their control of public goods and justify a system rigged in their favour (Rhodes & Bloom 2018).

Other hidden interests advanced by critics of philanthropy include social climbing and gaining access to elite networks. Media reports often namecheck donors' famous contacts and symbiotic relationships with other elites, for example reporting that Tom Hunter is "more likely to hobnob with Bill Clinton or Bob Geldof thanks to his high-profile donations to charity" (Mathiason 2006).

Philanthropists are hypocritical

The second frequent motif in populist critiques of philanthropy is that it is fundamentally hypocritical. Big donors are depicted as giving with one hand while taking with the other, using donations as a device to distract and deflect from their unethical behaviour and complicity in creating the social ills they pretend to address. As John Low, then head of the UK's Charities Aid Foundation, explains: "The criticism here rests on a fairly caricatured notion that all philanthropists spend their days making billions by investing in companies that sell weapons to children and then go home and wonder about how best to give their money to address the issue of child soldiers in the developing world" (Low 2012).

When it is not possible to draw a direct line between donors' daily activities and their donations, the accusation of hypocrisy is framed more broadly: that philanthropists benefit from an economic and social system that is rigged in their favour and that creates the problems they then pretend to solve. This is why those who are successful are deemed incapable of credible philanthropy: they cannot want meaningful change to occur because "winners" have such a vested interest in the status quo (Giridharadas 2018a: 259).

Charges of hypocrisy also relate to the amounts that donors give away, which are viewed as "costless" and entailing no sacrifice in the context of their net worth. For example, Jeff Bezos' AUS$1 million in response to the Australian bush fires in early 2020 attracted criticism for representing a tiny fraction of his wealth and was described as "cheap", "stingy" and "rank hypocrisy", equivalent to "5 minutes of income" from the owner of Amazon. A month later, when Bezos pledged an amount over ten thousand times larger, $10 billion, to help counter the effects of climate change, the same charge of inadequacy was made including an article whose headline noted the gift "barely dented" his fortune (Metcalf 2020).

Mark Zuckerberg encountered public scorn online after his donation of $25 million in March 2020 to accelerate treatments for Covid-19 attracted "contemptuous responses on social media" (MacQuillin 2020), including a TikTok video, viewed over 6.6 million times by January 2021, using glasses of water to visualize the gift as a mere drop of water in relation to his overall wealth

(Harris 2020). The 39 further grants for Covid research and relief made by the Chan Zuckerberg Initiative led to no discernible backtracking or recalculating of the censure, nor was this "drop" of a gift contextualized as part of the Chan Zuckerberg's public pledge to give away 99 per cent of their wealth (Zuckerberg & Chan 2015).

Philanthropy creates material benefits for the donor

The third concern that recurs in populist critiques is that philanthropists receive material benefits from acts depicted as gifts. These include tangible outcomes such as tax deductions and having donors' names displayed on prominent buildings, as well as intangible outcomes such as securing goodwill that reduces regulatory and transaction costs. Critics are also concerned that donations are used to stimulate markets in which donors have financial interests, such as supporting global public health efforts in order to gain a "leg up for pharmaceutical companies seeking to expand into faster-growing, lower-income countries" (Bowman 2012). By this account, philanthropy is more akin to a successful marketing strategy than "love of mankind" as it enables donors to continue rigging the system and reaping the benefits.

Media coverage and the populist critique

Media organizations do much to shape the content and set the tenor of the populist critique, and have done so for a long time. Hugh Cunningham's historical analysis of the reputation of philanthropy in nineteenth-century newspapers finds numerous examples of disparaging phrases such as "humbug philanthropy" and adjectives such as "fashionable" and "costless" to highlight that donations help rich people to move in the right circles at little real cost to themselves. He cites an article from the *Liverpool Porcupine* magazine in 1861 which claims that: "The most fashionable amusement of the present age is philanthropy ... No small number of these benevolent persons are philanthropic because it is the fashion to be so; because it brings them into passing contact with this Bishop or that Earl" (cited in Cunningham 2020: 145).

This interpretation of the philanthropic motive permeates beyond newspapers in the same period. Thorstein Veblen's satirical account of the lives of the upper class at the end of the nineteenth century describes philanthropy as "putting in evidence their wealth" in order to win public esteem (Veblen 1994 [1899]: 24). Veblen's portrayal of philanthropy as "honorific waste" and part of the "conspicuous consumption" undertaken by those seeking to flaunt their wealth continues to resonate with contemporary populist critics. Present-day media coverage persists in depicting philanthropy through the prism of wealth, celebrity and fashion. For example, coverage of a major charity event in London carried no details of the cause being supported, and described it as, "the biggest charity bash [where] ... champagne will be guzzled by the bucketload" (Adams 2006) and "where the wealthy gain access to A-list celebrities by pledging money to good causes" (Goodman 2006).

The net result of the populist critique is to question the possibility of any extent of altruism among rich donors, and to promote the interpretation of giving as a cunning ruse. One of the highest-profile populist critics of philanthropy is journalist Anand Giridharadas, whose central claim, conveyed in the subtitle of his book, is that philanthropy is an "elite charade" in which rich donors are funding "fake change" that primarily benefits themselves (Giridharadas 2018a). By this account, philanthropy becomes "phonylanthropy", a faux virtue, a sham act, an illusion and a con that needs calling out.

Defending philanthropy against the populist critique

Offering a defence against the populist critique should be the most straightforward of the three critiques defended in this book because it is an inherently simplistic argument that ought to be easily dismissed. This is especially so for ad hominem attacks that are directed at someone personally rather than their position or actions, which have no place in grown-up debates and need to end. The appearance, likeability or personal travails of an individual donor are irrelevant and should not be factored into an assessment of the rights and wrongs of their philanthropic acts or of philanthropy per se.

Take MacKenzie Scott as an example. Within months of having pledged to give away at least $30 billion (half of her share of the Amazon fortune following her divorce from Jeff Bezos), Scott's first grants totalling $5.8 billion meant she was immediately numbered among the world's biggest private givers. Her giving was not just large scale but also distinctive because she provided unprompted and unrestricted grants to organizations largely working for racial, gender and climate justice, with leaders having lived experience of those issues. This historically large and progressive giving was commended within some nonprofit and academic circles for showing how philanthropy can be done well (Dale 2020) and earned Scott the accolade of "philanthropist of the year" from a leading philanthropy news website (Inside Philanthropy 2020), but her efforts were also called out in high-circulation mass media for lacking transparency (Kulish 2020), and dismissed as a "giving spree" that was either intended to "shame her peers" (Moore 2020) or was a very expensive way of making her ex-husband look bad

(Bryant 2020). Clearly there is a gendered element to this interpretation, as well as typical titillation that sells newspapers and magazines. Both these explanations are sadly predictable, but what is less easy to explain is the crashing silence from those who might have pushed back against the tabloid narrative and seen this as an opportunity to move the conversation on to a more constructive discussion about the role and nature of philanthropy in contemporary society. The next time a new big giver emerges, there is every reason to believe the spotlight will remain focused on the prurient details of their private life and not on their philanthropic purpose.

A more extensive response to other aspects of the populist critique begins with the problem of caricaturing rich donors on the basis of undue generalizations that are not easily reconcilable with what is known about the practice or outcomes of philanthropic acts, nor with how philanthropists describe their own motivation and goals. Next, I contrast the fixed nature and content of populist critiques with the ongoing efforts to improve philanthropic practice. The defence ends with a discussion on the general cultural approval of what "ordinary" donors do, compared with the disapprobation meted out to those writing bigger cheques, which leads into the problematic consequences of this critique.

The populist critique promotes unhelpful and unfair caricatures of rich donors

King Cnut, the Danish-born eleventh-century King of England, attempted to prove to his fawning courtiers that he was not as powerful as they believed, by getting his feet wet while demonstrating he had no ability to prevent the tide coming in. His display of humility has, of course, been misinterpreted as its opposite: a vain king who was surprised to find he could *not* command the tide to stop. The misreading of King Cnut's metaphor is resonant when considering the caricaturing of contemporary philanthropists. Kings and philanthropists can try to be self-effacing but a humble mien cannot be allowed to get in the way of a good anecdote about the foolishness of kings or the hubris of big donors.

The populist critique is riven with caricatures of rich donors that are based on generalizations, selectively chosen examples and evidence-free assumptions about how wealth is accumulated and distributed. One common theme missing from populist critiques but very evident to those of us who work, or conduct primary research, with wealthy donors is their concern about getting it right. They are giving because they want to make a positive difference to causes that they care about, which means philanthropists worry a lot about the decisions they have made to date, and how best to achieve faster and greater impact in the future. The "awesome responsibility [of] … maximizing the good of giving", which requires working hard, thinking deeply and being humble in order to develop the skills and techniques required to be an effective giver (Buchanan 2019a: 1), is a significant departure from the caricature of the self-seeking egotist found in the populist critique.

Populist critics conveniently ignore counterexamples. For example, who has heard of George Eastman, the entrepreneur who made photography widely accessible and gave away around $100 million (c.$1.5 billion in 2020) at the same time as Andrew Carnegie and John D. Rockefeller? His name has disappeared even faster than one of his inventions, the Kodak camera, because he was no fan of the in perpetuity foundation model and donated all of his fortune during his life and in his will. "Men who leave their money to be distributed by others are pie-faced mutts", he declared in 1924 (quoted in Brayer 1996: 346), giving the lie to the suggestion that philanthropists exist in a uniform back-slapping club. Like any slice of humanity, philanthropists include people with varying views, dispositions, abilities and ideological outlooks. They can, and do, disagree with each other about the best way to distribute money, which organizations to fund and which causes matter most. There are philanthropists funding all sides of any contentious issue including access to contraception and abortion, gun control and equalities campaigns. Many big donors are enthusiastic capitalists, others believe in – and are funding – radical social and economic reform. Returning to George Eastman, the assumption that entrepreneurial fortunes are always built on low pay and poor working conditions is undermined by his ethical business practices. In 1898, when he successfully floated his business and became an "overnight millionaire" he gave all his 3,000 employees worldwide a share of the wealth made, with a note reading: "This is a personal matter with Mr Eastman and he requests that you will not consider it as a gift but as extra pay for good work" (Brayer 1996: 178). In 1909 Eastman set up a permanent Welfare Fund to provide sick pay, pensions, disability payments and health care support, years before New York state passed the Workmen Compensation's Law in 1914 (Brayer 1996: 352). The example of George Eastman is not cited as proof that all philanthropists are enlightened and admirable; rather, it illustrates the diversity within the field of philanthropy to which populist critics are oblivious.

Taking a closer look at one of the men he is compared with, John D. Rockefeller is viewed as an archetypal "robber baron" who became a philanthropist in order "to cool public anger" (Giridharadas 2018a: 157). As recounted elsewhere in this book, his foundation was stymied from the start and has faced a counter-reaction of scepticism and populist suspicion that continued throughout the twentieth century (Smith 2001: 39). Yet it is not hard to find evidence that sustains an alternative interpretation: As recounted in Chapter 4, Rockefeller's original motive for funding biomedical research was the death of his baby grandson from scarlet fever; he created his foundation before any tax breaks were available for charitable giving (as did Andrew Carnegie); and he gave $35 million to found the University of Chicago, which as the name indicates came with no demand for naming rights. The Rockefeller Foundation supported African American education during segregation, helped eradicate hookworm in the southern US states and developed the new agricultural science that led to extensive increases in crop production. One of the longest-serving staff members of the Rockefeller Foundation, Dr Norman Borlaug, won the Noble Peace Prize in 1970 for his central role in that "Green Revolution", and has been credited with saving over 300 million lives (Pearce, n.d.). Not a bad outcome for a pie-faced mutt. It is therefore simplistic to suggest that Eastman puts Rockefeller in the shade; they were simply different individuals who chose to organize and conduct their philanthropy in different ways.

Bill Gates and Melinda French Gates' philanthropic interventions in global health are also estimated to have saved lives numbering in the millions, yet elite giving is nonetheless routinely described as "rhetorical" rather than "real" change (a view unlikely to be held by those on the receiving end of life-saving philanthropy), and awareness of positive outcomes is lower than the noise made by those who believe the opposite. The argument that Gates has a vested interest in the Covid-19 pandemic, is culpable for millions of deaths from Covid-19 and will profit from the sale of vaccines and treatments is made by a philanthropically funded nonprofit organization called the Children's Health Defense network, founded by a son of former Senator Robert F. Kennedy, which supports antivaccine campaigners (Wakabayashi *et al.* 2020), illustrating again the inherently heterogeneous nature of "philanthropy" and the futility of simplistic criticisms of such a diverse range of people and actions.

The fact that Bill Gates serves "as kind of an abstract bogeyman" (Whitney Phillips cited in Wakabayashi *et al.* 2020) highlights the irony of viewing image polishing as a central goal of philanthropists. If reputational enhancement was a prime concern, philanthropy would be a redundant strategy by now as it is clearly not working. The polling of public attitudes dispels the notion that rich people can improve their public image by donating from their wealth. Even in the North American context, where it is assumed that philanthropy is more widely celebrated and appreciated than elsewhere, twice as many people think the rich give to benefit themselves rather than to benefit others (Zitelman 2020: 199).

How philanthropists describe their motivation and philanthropic goals

So how do donors themselves explain why they give? In an article written in 1908 John Rockefeller wrote: "The very rich are just like the rest of us; and if they get pleasure from the possession of money, it comes from their ability to do things which give satisfaction to someone besides themselves … The novelty of being able to purchase anything one wants soon passes, because what people most seek cannot be bought with money" (Rockefeller [1908] 2016: 411).

A hundred years later the same sentiment was expressed by British businessman Bob Gavron: "When I made my first million I did two things: I bought a Rolls Royce and I sold it. I realized that whatever I wanted it was not a Rolls Royce. The thing about having a lot of money is that you can do what you want, but you may discover that what you want is relatively modest, and then you have to decide what to do with the rest of it" (quoted in Bradbury 2015).

Donor motivations beyond the caricature

Of course, Rockefeller's and Gavron's explanations of their own giving is not conclusive proof of motivation. They may be lying, exaggerating or unaware of subconscious drivers. But there is no shortage of other accounts by historical and contemporary philanthropists reflecting on why they started and continued giving, including many I have collected in my research, none of which support the hypotheses contained in the populist critique. In this body of data, self-described motivations are extremely diverse, running the gamut from gratitude to compassion to empathy to enjoyment to solidarity. If big donors all have false consciousness in relation to their motives, their "cover stories" are surprisingly varied and uncoordinated. There is a large academic literature on donor motivations which highlights their complexity and variety (for an overview see Bekkers & Wiepking 2011). Here are some examples of these varied motivations in practice.

Gratitude. Many contemporary philanthropists donate to express gratitude to their alma mater, to hospitals that have treated them or their loved ones, and to theatres and opera houses that have provided years of pleasure. Gratitude can also extend beyond interactions with specific institutions. Dame Stephanie Shirley arrived in the UK aged just five years old on the *Kindertransport* train from Vienna to escape the Nazi threat, and attributes her motivation for gifts such as those mentioned in the Introduction to gratitude at being saved, and to prove that her life was worth saving (Shirley 2010).

Compassion. Being moved by the predicament of potential beneficiaries, and feeling a duty or urge to respond, is commonly expressed by big donors. For example, Mike Oglesby, a property developer who focused his philanthropy on people and places in the north of England where his successful company was based, told me:

> There is no doubt that on a personal level it is extremely satisfying to feel that you are making a difference and to see very real results. It is

surprising how often I and my fellow trustees find ourselves in meetings becoming very emotionally involved, and on occasions being reduced to tears. When you are able to help and make a real difference to someone in real need then the experience is one of the most rewarding and satisfying that you can have.

Empathy. Identification with the needs of others is a central explanation for major giving (Schervish 2007). For example, South African businessman Tim Tebeila was born in poverty in rural Sekhukhune and made his fortune in construction, insurance, mining, technology and financial services. Speaking on the pan-African current affairs television programme Africa 360 in 2013, Tebeila explained why his philanthropy is focused on helping the needy in South Africa:

> You don't give because you have enough, and you don't give because you want to please anybody else. You give because you have to do it, in terms of the culture: everybody, in fact every person in the world, was born to become a solution to someone else. So we are giving because we want to provide a solution to a lot of people. In my case, from where I've come from, I've walked in that kind of environment whereby I spent time at some point not having any food. Because of that background, that's why we have learnt to say, you know what: right now I can afford to help them, previously I was just like them, and that also has a great motivation for me, to say "let me touch those lives", because I'm from that particular environment as well.

Enjoyment. Almost every rich donor I have ever interviewed has volunteered the fact that they get a huge amount of enjoyment and satisfaction from their giving. Businessman Barrie Wells, whose philanthropy is focused on arranging days out for very sick children, says:

> It makes me feel incredibly privileged to be in a position to be able to do something so constructive with the money. When I get thanked and hugged I always say: "I'm actually getting as much benefit and happiness out of it as you are" ... The main thing I would tell other people is the sheer amount of enjoyment you get from philanthropy. I'd say: don't think about the money going out of your bank account but instead think about the happiness that will be added to your life.

Jack Petchey, from a poor family in the East End of London, who built successful businesses in car hire, property and tourism, has donated over £100 million through his foundation. When I met him, he was nearing a hundred years of age and still regularly going into his foundation offices for meetings because he enjoys the work so much and is impatient to do more, as he explained: "It feels good to know we are making a difference – it's what gets me out of bed in the morning. In giving, you also receive and the world is a better place for it! I don't want to be the richest man in the graveyard. Actually, I don't want to be in the graveyard at all, I've got a lot to do yet!"

This factor, of philanthropy making life more fulfilling, is also described as the common denominator of those who sign the Giving Pledge, committing to give away at least half their wealth during their lifetimes or at the point of death. As two of the co-founders of the Giving Pledge explain: "The idea of the pledge came out of discussions we had with other givers about what they were doing, about what had worked in philanthropy and what had not worked. Everyone shared how giving had made their lives richer" (Gates & Gates, n.d.)

Solidarity. Akin to empathy, but driven by identification rather than shared experience, donors often speak of turning to philanthropy as the best or only option available when they wish to show their support for a particular region, cause or issue. The outpouring of monetary donations when disasters occur is testament to this urge to do something useful and to express care and concern for those affected. Jonathan Ruffer, who made his fortune in investment management, has focused his philanthropy on the small market town of Bishop Auckland, with which he has no personal connection. He decided to act when he learnt that the town, whose fortunes had been in decline since the demise of the coal-mining industry, was losing one of its remaining assets as its most famous paintings, hung in Auckland Castle, were being sold. "My original intention was to buy the paintings as a way of saying 'I am on your side' to the community" but he went much further – buying the castle and turning it into a major tourist attraction to create jobs and attract crowds to reinvigorate the town (Agerholm *et al.* 2020).

Donor explanations for giving

Rich donors' willingness to participate in studies about philanthropy (Gilding 2010) and to answer direct questions reduces the need for speculation about their motivation. Bill Gates and Melinda French Gates report that they are often asked, "Why are you really giving your money away? What's in it for you?", to which Bill Gates provides the simple reply that it is meaningful work that he enjoys doing. Melinda French Gates adds that it is also in line with how they were both raised, and how they are now raising their children, which is to try and leave the world better than they found it. She also notes that these values – the desire to live a meaningful life, to honour the values with which they were was raised and to set a good example for their children, are not unique but shared by most donors and volunteers (Gates & Gates 2018).

Awareness that giving money away makes the donor feel good is a factor that is shared by both rich and non-rich donors. Extensive studies into the "science of generosity" show that giving is associated with a wide range of benefits for the giver, including better health and well-being, self-reported quality of life, greater vitality and self-esteem (Allen 2018; Smith & Davidson 2014). The Harvard Study of Adult Development has tracked the lives of over 700 men from diverse income levels for nearly eight decades and reaches the clear conclusion that the key to a good life is having good relationships, rather than a lot of money (Waldinger 2015). The enjoyment that comes from building relationships with people as a result of being a donor, such as interacting with charity founders, front-line staff, trustees and (where appropriate) beneficiaries, as well as getting to know fellow donors who are passionate about the same cause, is a key driver, as one wealthy donor explains:

> If you give away large amounts of money … it gets you much more access, whether it's to actors in the theatre or to aid workers or to researchers in a facility, and you can get under the skin of it. People find huge satisfaction in feeling "not only have I made a difference to research into this disease but also in having interesting conversations with doctors about the nature of that disease", and that's all part of a set of stimuli and values that are interesting.
>
> (Quoted in Breeze & Lloyd 2013: 92)

Populist critics are troubled by the notion that donors benefit at the same time as their beneficiaries, but "win-win" is simply an updated version of Tocqueville's formulation of "self-interest properly understood". This can take many forms, including versions in which the philanthropist acknowledges the benefit with a side-eye, puncturing the populist image of rich donors as pompous egos-on-stilts. For example, when the Rockefeller Foundation provided $400,000 to fund the ground-breaking Kinsey Reports into human sexual behaviour during the 1940s, John D. Rockefeller Jr offered this self-deprecating explanation: "I have five sons to bring up and a man ought to know something about the subject, but no one can know less than I do" (Whitaker 1974a: 192). Scottish businessman and philanthropist Isaac Wolfson offered a similarly knowing comment about the recognitions he received in the form of numerous awards and honorary degrees. When asked where the degrees had come from he replied, "from writing". When asked what he had written he declared: "Cheques" (Gribben 2006). Despite being agnostic, Andrew Carnegie spent millions of dollars donating almost 8,000 organs to churches in order, he explained, "To lessen the pain of the sermons" (cited in Krass 2002: 423). In my experience big donors can be pretty funny and perfectly likeable. Another line that my students enjoy is Warren Buffett's observation that "holding onto cash is a bit like saving up sex for old age – at some point you've got to use it" (cited in Clark 2008).

Anonymous giving and the caricature of conspicuous consumption

Anonymous giving is an issue that vexes many observers of philanthropy and prompts strong opinions as to whether anonymity constitutes a "better" way to give. It is a matter of some frustration for donors that they get criticized either way – anonymous giving is called out for being secretive, opaque and not transparent, while donors who give publicly are decried for seeking applause and personal benefits.

For obvious reasons it is extremely difficult to count how many donations are given anonymously or to quantify their collective value, which makes rebuttal of the "show off" critique trickier. My research finds that most rich UK donors (69 per cent) have made anonymous donations at some point in their lives, and decide whether to "go public" or not depending on what is appropriate in any given context (Breeze & Lloyd 2013: 126). The provenance of some anonymous gifts become known over time. In addition to Rockefeller's gifts between 1892 and 1910 to found the University of Chicago, George Eastman, the founder of the Kodak company, gave $20 million to the Massachusetts Institute of Technology between 1909 and 1916 under the pseudonym "Mr Smith" (Brayer 1996: 344). More recently, the Irish American founder of Duty Free Shoppers, Chuck Feeney, maintained anonymity for most of the lifetime of his Atlantic Philanthropies foundations as he gave away almost his entire wealth of $8 billion (O'Clery 2007).

Desire to engage with the work being funded and become involved in the cause being supported is one reason that some philanthropy is not conducted anonymously, and becomes susceptible to accusations that donors' true intention is to flaunt their wealth and be conspicuous about their philanthropic acts. Another common circumstance when donors are willing to "go public" is when they believe – or have been told by fundraisers – that doing so will encourage other donors to step forward. Most big donors are involved in helping to raise funds for their favoured causes and therefore understand the mechanics of fundraising, as this philanthropist explains: "I once asked another donor to please go public about his donation so that others would give. He agreed reluctantly and guess what? Others did give! It got covered in the *Evening Standard* and the next thing somebody phoned me and the money quadrupled" (quoted in Breeze & Lloyd 2013: 126).

Gloria Jollymore, vice-president for advancement at Mount Allison University in Canada, relates a similar story:

> We knew that an alumna was planning to leave us a significant, multi-million dollar gift and persuaded her to let us run a feature about her pledge in the university alumni newsletter in 2019. It was a really nice piece telling her story and explaining why legacy donations are so important to the university. In Autumn 2020 we got a phone call from a solicitor letting us know that his client, another of our alumni, had sadly died and left us CAN$900K, which she wrote into her will after seeing that article!

In a historic example, the Johns Hopkins University would not exist if his friend George Peabody had not talked about his philanthropic interests, which were focused on building affordable housing in London. After that conversation, in which Peabody enthused about the pleasures of giving away money, John S. Hopkins decided to leave $7 million in his will for a university and a hospital (Whitaker 1974a: 57).

This is why it is a mistake to assume that anonymity is intrinsically the more virtuous approach, because talking publicly about gifts can create greater impact and benefit for the cause (Esposito 2010: 20). The head of fundraising at Canterbury Cathedral told me why they chose to shout loudly about receiving a £3 million gift in the early days of a major campaign: "A gift of that size does more than bring us closer to our appeal target of £50 million, it helps to open doors to other high-value donors that we need to reach. In particular, it sends out a reassuring message to potential donors that our governance is good, and that they can have confidence in our trustees to manage their money well."

Donors also have pragmatic reasons for giving anonymously. They may not wish other people, including loved ones, to be aware of the extent of the wealth they hold – this is often the case for parents who shield their children until they are old enough to understand the family's financial situation. The fear of drawing attention to wealth holding that is related to concerns for personal safety was realized for one unfortunate California-based philanthropist in 2007 when Ernest Rady and his family were attacked and held hostage in their home shortly after making several large, public gifts, including $60 million to the Children's Hospital and Health Center in San Diego (Beatty 2008).

Some anonymous giving is an attempt to avoid attracting approaches from fund-seeking organizations, especially if donors already have a clear plan in mind for their philanthropic distribution and wish to avoid both the stress of oversolicitation and the costs incurred by fundraisers. Other donors give below the radar in order to be able to engage with charity staff, volunteers and beneficiaries without being viewed as "the big donor", which feels more comfortable and enables them to get an "unobstructed view" of the charity. Other reasons for giving anonymously include a desire not to be associated publicly with causes that might cause controversy in their personal lives – such as a Jewish donor who contributed a significant sum towards the restoration of a Christian church in her village, or a Catholic donor supporting birth control.

These examples are open to interpretation. Is it understandable or sneaky to meet recipients without "outing" yourself as the donor? Is it a sign of care or of obstruction to deflect fundraising attention? As with most elements of the populist critique, the interpretation is in the eye of the beholder. As Paul Schervish argues, anonymous giving has the potential to be both the more caring or the more manipulative option depending on the context (Schervish 1994b, 2018).

Recognizing donors: the graffiti of government

Implicit in the populist critique is an assumption that big donors are uniquely demanding in terms of expecting to be recognized, honoured and celebrated for their gifts. As noted above, public recognition is sometimes a strategy to benefit the cause by helping to attract additional support, rather than trumpeting the donor's name for its own sake. Clearly everyday donors also get some recognition for their giving, such as stickers, pins, poppies or wristbands as a public display of their support for a charity, and it also worth noting that other kinds of funding can come with even more explicit "recognition demands" attached. For example, projects that have received financial support from the European Union must display the EU logo of yellow stars on a blue background, along with the name of the funding programme that provided the money. In 2020, when the UK government awarded £257 million of emergency funding in "Culture Recovery Awards" to arts organizations affected by the Covid-19 pandemic, the money came with a stipulation that recipients must publicly welcome the funding on their social media accounts and in their newsletters, as a condition of receiving it. Recipients were instructed to use a government-designed logo and hashtag (#HereforCulture) to acknowledge and express thanks for the award, and were "required" to alert local media outlets of the news. Grantees were also encouraged to use quotes from the relevant politician, Culture Minister Oliver Dowden, that were sent to grantees along with their funding (Hill & Redmond 2020). If individual donors made this sort of request – supplying the wording of the thanks they expected, and making it a condition of the grant that such thanking be undertaken – there would be an understandably negative reaction. Yet opprobrium is directed at "ostentatious" individual rich donors and not at other types of funder.

Challenging the "reputation-washing" caricature

The caricature that the badly behaved rich use public generosity in order to make amends for past wrongs faces at least three challenges. First, that most donors make at least some donations anonymously, as noted above, which undermines any PR strategy. Second, that not all big donors have, or accept that they have, bad behaviour that requires reputation washing. Third, that many big donors started being philanthropic long before they had time to accumulate either sins or a fortune.

The "Road to Damascus" hypothesis, which views donations as a necessary final step in the narrative arc of a rags-to-riches story, from exploitation to redemption through philanthropy, obscures the reality of fortunes made through non-exploitative and non-extractive careers in the arts, sport, music and ethical businesses. The examples of people such as Harry Potter author J. K. Rowling, tennis star Andre Agassi, musicals supremo Andrew Lloyd Webber and environmental businesswoman Anita Roddick are all testament to the feasibility of a different way of accumulating and philanthropically distributing large fortunes. Populist critics focus on the opposite scenarios, such as the immorality behind the Sackler family fortune created by aggressively marketing the prescription opiod OxyContin, which is responsible for thousands of overdose deaths. Generalizing from this terrible but extreme example to tar all big donors with the same brush is clearly unfair and unhelpful but is routinely left unchallenged. As is the presumption of a radical conversion from greed to philanthropy when the wealthy feel the need "to cool public anger". The imposition of the redemption narrative arc is easily countered by evidence that giving often predates becoming rich. John D. Rockefeller started donating a percentage of his income from his very first pay packet, and Andrew Carnegie was committed to "benevolence" before he had significant wealth to defend or an image to polish (Karl & Katz 1987: 14; Krass 2002: 97). David Harding, who made the largest single donation yet given by a British philanthropist with a £100 million gift to the University of Cambridge in 2019, explicitly rejects the "reputation-washing" caricature: "I like philanthropy, and I have plenty of money to do it, but I don't like the idea that I am some socially useless entity trying to redeem myself", he says. "I don't like that because it implies I have sinned in some way."

Many contemporary philanthropists point to a family tradition of generosity, even when there was little to spare, which they chose to maintain from their first pay cheques. Rather than philanthropy being a necessary corrective to prior immoral behaviour, the causal relationship may run in the other direction with wealth creation being understood as the necessary prelude to become a big donor. This strategy is advocated by the Effective Altruism movement, which advises young people to choose a high-paying career in order to maximize their later philanthropic capacity. For others, the realization of wealth and a greatly enhanced philanthropic capacity occurs in closer proximity, with the latter representing a pre-existing goal. For example, Lisa Greer and her husband Josh became rich "overnight" as a result of developing the technology that enables 3D movies. In her book detailing their entry to the world of wealth and philanthropy, Lisa Greer writes: "Of all the freedoms I anticipated having when our lives were so dramatically altered, the one that excited me the most was the freedom to give. Specifically to give of our money" (Greer 2020: 11).

Not only did the Greers immediately start funding a range of causes that connected with their life experiences, they also chose to buy a family home because its layout was suitable for hosting charity events. Greer's book is an appropriate bridge into the second element of this defence as she wrote it to help improve philanthropy practice.

Populist critiques overlook ongoing efforts to improve philanthropic practice

Despite secularization removing the ultimate donor benefit of eternal salvation, philanthropy nonetheless grew in popularity over the twentieth century. The fact that philanthropists were not deterred when the promise of paradise was replaced with the mundanity of a free lunch or naming rights (at an agreed height for a set period of time) suggests that donor benefit is overblown as the driver of big giving. Yet the populist critique remains frozen in time and impervious to evidence of change. While charges of hidden interests, hypocrisy and material benefits probably contain some truth in relation to specific donors and to dominant past practices, this critical heat has been turned up at the same time that broader social changes and heightened philanthropic introspection make them less salient. A key argument of this book is that critiques fail to take account of changes over time in the meaning and practice of philanthropy, and the variety of forms it takes in different eras and in different countries. We cannot assume that the contemporary manifestation of private giving for the public good is the exact same as was practised in ancient Rome, Victorian Britain or even the recent turn of the millennium. Nor can we assume it is the same in London, Lima, Lagos and Los Angeles. Any study of philanthropy must take account of the context in which it occurs, because "each culture develops a distinctive philanthropic tradition that reflects other aspects of that society ... To understand philanthropy in any culture, we have to understand the sources of the philanthropic tradition, both ancient and modern, and how these influenced philanthropic actions and meaning over time" (Payton & Moody 2008: 131).

Generalizations about philanthropy leave it denuded of its socially and culturally embedded context which, in these early decades of the twenty-first century, involves philanthropy becoming more reflective and introspective and focused on improvement. Since the millennium there has been a steady flow of books exploring the role and ethics of private giving and advising donors how to give better and more smartly, the establishment of dozens of philanthropy education and support organizations that enable donors to learn, network and share good practice, plus hundreds of conferences, seminars and webinars designed to reflect on the challenges facing the philanthropy sector (including those set out in the three critiques discussed in this book) with the goal of finding new and better ways to undertake philanthropy. Populists view this as hot air and cheap talk because they believe that the rich, including the philanthropic rich, will never undermine their advantaged position at the apex of society by supporting fundamental social, economic or political change: "that's exactly what rich philanthropists will never do. They work on the symptoms but not the causes. If we rely on the philanthropy of the rich, we will have to rely on it forever, because rich philanthropists will never fund work that addresses the cause of our problems, because addressing the cause would mean building a society in which there are no poor people and no rich philanthropists" (Darby 2020).

This commonly expressed position, which believes philanthropy will only ever administer self-interested sticking plasters, overlooks the existence of a range of successful efforts by rich donors that are not aligned with maximizing their own interests. Contrary to populist expectations, there are philanthropically funded efforts to find viable alternatives to capitalism, and there are philanthropists on public record recognizing that the current economic system is not serving society well, as the following examples show.

Pierre Omidyar, the founder of eBay, points to the "increasingly harmful and untenable inequities across economic, racial and geographic lines" that have been fostered by free market ideology, and states: "We are capitalists who know that the current form of capitalism is fundamentally broken" (Omidyar Network n.d.). The Omidyar Network's initiative to "Reimagine Capitalism" is investing $35 million to tackle structural economic challenges, with a focus on advancing workers rights – a theme also present in MacKenzie Scott's first grant-making in 2020 which featured a number of labour organizations.

The Ford Foundation's prioritization of funding social and racial justice includes alignment with the concept of "inclusive capitalism" to create "an equitable, sustainable future … that works for everyone", according to the foundation's president Darren Walker (Walker, n.d.). This includes pushing corporations to look beyond shareholder returns to focus on the welfare of employees and local communities (Daniels 2020).

Australian philanthropists Andrew and Nicola Forrest are tackling a particularly unacceptable aspect of current global capitalism in which many businesses are implicated: modern slavery (Seibert 2017). The Forrests' funding of the Global Slavery Index and the Global Freedom Network, which seeks to highlight and remove forced labour from supply chains, has uncovered slavery in a dozen suppliers to their own business interests. Andrew Forrest is using this knowledge to force change through personal and social pressure, claiming, "Not only will you be cut from our supply chain, we'll make sure you're cut from everyone we speak to" (quoted in Farrell 2017), and also through funding research and advocacy to encourage legislative change, which resulted in the Australian government's Modern Slavery Act 2018.

The William and Flora Hewlett Foundation goes further in seeking not to improve but to "replace" the status quo. Announcing a $50 million initiative to develop new ideas in economic and political thought, the foundation's president, Larry Kramer, expresses sentiments that align with those articulated by many critics of philanthropy:

> Neoliberalism's emphasis on free market absolutism has outlived its usefulness, as evidenced by the fact that it's worsening some of our biggest problems, like skyrocketing wealth inequality and the unfolding climate crisis. But addressing problems like these requires more than one-off policy ideas, activist pressure, and incremental change. We need a new way of thinking about policy, law, and the proper role of government to shift the underlying terms of debate and open up space for solutions that neoliberalism is currently choking off.
>
> (Hewlett Foundation 2020)

Other grant-makers and donors whose efforts may surprise populist critics include the Anti-Monopoly Fund launched by Facebook co-founder Chris Hughes, which is a $10 million programme to support policy advocacy and grassroots groups fighting antitrust matters, and academic research into market power and monopolies (Economic Security Project, n.d.). Tech philanthropist Nick Hanauer, whose Civic Ventures project explicitly rejects "trickle down economics" and seeks to "create systemic disruptive change" (Civic Ventures n.d.), and the Surdna Foundation, led by Don Chen, whose focus on "Inclusive Economics" involves investing in businesses led by people of colour and collaborating with other private funders, shares the view that: "the economic system isn't serving society very well" (quoted in Daniels 2020).

It is not difficult to find examples of philanthropy invested in challenging, or even seeking to replace, the status quo, as well as plentiful evidence of private donors striving to make their giving more thoughtful and impactful.

Philanthropists get it and change is happening. Maybe not enough of them, or not fast enough, but changes are evident: "there seems to be a significant surge in interest in checking inequality, in supporting grassroots social justice organizations, in empowering beneficiaries, and in attending to class and racial privilege ... Each of these approaches entertains the possibility of real sacrifice on the part of the elite" (Soskis 2018).

Yet the caricature of *Homo economicus* persists, especially in relation to the rich who, it is assumed, will only ever act on the basis of self-interested calculation. This is despite decades of sociological, psychological and even economic research confirming that people do not simply pursue self-interest and that there are always other, often more highly regarded, values involved (Beattie 1964: 199). People do have the inclination and capacity for other-directed, altruistic behaviour; are influenced by internalized values, habits and social norms; and constantly face ambiguous situations in which the "best" outcome for a self-maximizing strategy is unclear (see, e.g., Batson & Shaw 1991).

The refusal to believe that people can act in any way that does not directly benefit themselves is not only contradicted by examples of philanthropists funding projects that ultimately "harm" their own class interests, it is also inconsistent with the general acceptance that the non-rich can and do often behave altruistically, as explored in the final plank of the defence against the populist critique.

Cultural approval of philanthropy is related to donors' wealth

When France's richest families were criticized for their donations in response to the 2019 Notre Dame Cathedral fire (as discussed in Chapter 2) there was an addendum relevant to the populist critique. It was not only the prosperous and the powerful who donated; many "ordinary" or "everyday" people also sent contributions to help restore this beloved religious and cultural landmark. One of them was a nine-year-old British girl whose letter accompanying a few euros was published on the BBC News website. "I heard about the Notre Dame fire and wanted to help", she wrote, "I know it's not much but every bit helps". The news article is illustrated with a photograph of her envelope and its contents, showing the postage cost £1.60 to send nine coins which add up to about the same amount. The gift is a nice gesture and children need time and encouragement to grow into effective givers, but it is curious to celebrate her financially illogical gift while denigrating those giving millions. The populist critique is evident in the journalists' decision to write approvingly about "modest amounts" contributed by ordinary donors, while describing rich donors as "trumping up" and "stumping up" their offering (Cuddy & Boelpaep 2019).

The time-worn debate of egoism versus altruism has gained a curious new dimension in contemporary populist critiques as only the rich are understood to be subject to universal egoism, while ordinary people are exempt. Media reporting of charity and philanthropy routinely holds up ordinary people and lower-level donors for applause while probing the motivations of richer donors. There is little evidence to show that the population of philanthropists has any greater or lesser quantities of positive or negative characteristics than the rest of the population, and it is unclear how this mechanism can work in practice. At precisely what size bank balance does the capacity to be altruistic cease? If someone becomes rich overnight, by coming into an inheritance or winning the lottery, does their desire to benefit others vanish at the same moment that their numbers come up?

The defence against this aspect of the populist critique is so simple that it is hard to believe it needs spelling out: rich people are people too. Being cast as essentially unlikeable and driven by egotistical motives will not help make philanthropy an attractive option. Normally we nudge desired behaviours through positive encouragements. It is also unfair to cast aspersions on one type of donor as both wealthy and non-wealthy people can give well or badly, with humility or hubristically. Hidden interests, hypocrisy and material benefits can accrue at all points on the income and donation scale. In my work on a university campus, I applaud the vigorous volunteering and fundraising of our students, while knowing it is helping them to create memorable experiences and improving their CVs so they can secure better jobs in the future. These are accepted and largely unproblematic benefits of charitable activity by young people. The reasons why larger gifts are routinely misrecognized as being self-interested while the acts of ordinary donors receive cultural approval are discussed in Chapter 6. The relevant point for a defence against the populist critique is that the charges laid against rich donors are selectively applied, with consequences that are set out in the final section of this chapter.

The problematic consequences of the populist critique

When I drop a £1 coin into a charity collecting box, I get a warm smile from the person shaking the tin, an expression of gratitude and often a sticker that I can wear to display my support. The average household income in the UK is about £30,000 – no fundraiser has ever berated me for "only" giving the equivalent of 0.00003 per cent of my available resources, nor questioned why I should expect thanks, nor mocked me for wearing the sticker "to look good". Street fundraising collections would cease succeeding immediately if contempt was shown for those who responded, yet these complaints are routinely directed at those making larger gifts.

"Who made us the philanthropy police?" asks Ian MacQuillin, noting that the opprobrium heaped on rich givers regarding their motivations and the proportionate size of their gifts undermines all the precepts of good practice in fundraising (MacQuillin 2020). Critics of "show off" philanthropy seem unaware that the main proponents against anonymous giving are fundraisers and charities, who know that public evidence of giving helps them to raise more funds by setting an example for others to be generous and specifically appealing to those who admire, or are linked to, donors who "go public". To then be judged and found wanting, the subject of a contemptuous eye roll in a viral video watched by millions, is the exact opposite of the encouragement shown to "ordinary" donors who are told that "every little helps". Philanthropists are not unaware of the populist critique – some have told me they worry about their children hearing them being criticized, and are delaying their giving to avoid such playground taunts. As John Arnold, the donor mocked for being "jug eared", notes: "Personal attacks such as those that I have experienced have the clear objective of intimidating me into standing down" (Arnold 2014).

Deterring the rich from giving not only results in less funding for good causes, it involves treating people differently on the basis of their wealth, which is unfair. All donors receive some return from their gifts, and a philosophical investigation of philanthropy deems the presence of mixed benefits, "morally acceptable, even desirable insofar as it strengthens the overall pursuit of good ends" (Martin 1994: 123).

A curious outcome of the populist critique is virtue hoarding: denying the rich the right to be, and enjoy being, philanthropic, or to be given credit when they are. Philanthropic virtue need not be rationed, it is an infinite property, yet populist attitudes deny some types of donors the opportunity to feel good about engaging in philanthropy. Who gets to frame how those acts are construed? The philanthropy sector is fundamentally voluntary in nature – no one has to give – yet still there are bouncers on the door passing comment on who should and should not be free to take part. If social disapproval follows a philanthropic donation but not the purchase of luxuries, that is good news for companies selling private yachts and bad news for cash-strapped charities.

Conclusion

The populist critique encourages a simplistic understanding of the complex role and varied practice of philanthropy. It encourages an unhelpful and unfair "othering" of rich donors whose giving is assumed to be qualitatively different and of lesser social value than giving by ordinary donors. Ad hominem attacks and unfair generalizations about rich donors impede the promotion of philanthropy as an aspirational identity among those with the greatest capacity to give, which makes fundraising harder and ultimately affects those organizations and people most reliant on philanthropically funded goods and services.

The criticisms discussed in this chapter encourage dislike of, and distancing from, rich donors, constituting the third and final trick up the sleeve of those intent on derogating do-gooders. Chapter 6 explains how our understanding of do-gooder derogation can be applied to make sense of the three critiques of philanthropy.

6

WHY DO ATTACKS ON PHILANTHROPY STICK AND WHAT CAN BE DONE ABOUT IT?

Every fan of the murder mystery genre, among whom I count myself, knows that the satisfactory conclusion of a case requires assembling all the potential culprits to identify three elements that reveal the guilty party among them: the means, the motive and the opportunity for the crime. In our case, is philanthropy guilty of being a plutocratic power grab that promotes donors' hidden agendas and causes more harm than good? Do philanthropists have the means, motive and opportunity to be revealed as the villains among us?

Do big donors have the *means* to cause harm?

Clearly the richest philanthropists possess unimaginably vast fortunes, but even the $195 billion wealth of the world's richest individual in early 2021, Jeff Bezos, is a fraction of the annual expenditure of governments such as the US, China, Germany, Japan and France which count their annual expenditure in trillions. Bezos could cover the annual running costs of Denmark or Indonesia for one year, or Ecuador for five years, or one smaller Pacific island for a generation, which is still a startling fact, but easily disproves the possibility of plutocracy. The biggest philanthropic spending in 2020 by an individual was MacKenzie Scott's $5.8 billion distribution. Even if we look only at one area of spending, such as health or education, philanthropists lack the means to compete with either national or state spending (Scott's 2020 giving could just about cover healthcare costs for one year in one small US state such as Wyoming or Hawaii), or global institutions of governance such as the World Health Organization (annual budget in 2020–21 *c*.$6 billion) or the World Food Programme (total income in 2019 $8 billion). Private donors can and do make substantial contributions to the success of those programmes but are in no position to take them over or become anywhere near "majority shareholders". Nor do big donors have anything like the means to outspend and overpower the wishes of "ordinary" donors.

To take the biggest philanthropy that has existed to date: the Bill and Melinda Gates Foundation has distributed $55 billion in the 20 years since its founding in 2000. That two-decade total is worth less than a quarter of the one-year total of all annual giving in the US, which was $450 billion in 2019 (Giving USA 2020). There is no concentration of philanthropic power that would enable any private donor to exert untoward influence on anything but the narrowest of issues and for the briefest of time periods, never mind be a realistic alternative to either democratically elected governments or the collective will of the people beyond the ballot box. We know from success stories of philanthropy that private donors can have the means to make a disproportionate impact in a focused area, so the case for the prosecution still requires them to have a motive to spend it in a way that causes "more harm than good".

Do big donors have the *motive* to cause harm?

Philanthropic motives, like all motives, cannot be examined directly, they can only be explained by actors and interpreted by observers. There is a chasm between the self-reported accounts of donors and the critical interpretations of some observers which is ultimately unbridgeable. Self-reported motivations by donors, as detailed in examples across this book, include empathy, compassion, sympathy, anger, solidarity, belief in equality and personal fulfilment. Only the latter overlaps with assumptions that donors are driven by self-advancement, but in practice philanthropists' ideas of how giving enhances their own lives is more aligned with the Aristotelian contention that one's own happiness and human flourishing depend on living a virtuous and generous life, than with an attempt to be philanthropic in pursuit of power or pecuniary advantage. The manner in which philanthropic motives are enacted – hubristically or with humility – is also in the eye of the beholder rather than an observable quantity, although it is worth noting that people who work closely with big donors describe them reporting feelings of anxiety, lack of confidence and awareness of their "awesome responsibility" (Buchanan 2019a: 1), while the most widely cited example of hubris – that philanthrocapitalists believe they can or should "save the world" – are words written by a journalist and an economist (Bishop & Green 2008) rather than uttered by philanthropists. Of course, donors may be lying to themselves and to other people, or unaware of their own hidden motivations, but for the most cynical critics to be correct, every big donor is either a liar or suffering from false consciousness. Furthermore, the case made by critics in relation to donor motivation is contradictory because accusations simultaneously state that philanthropists are engaged in highly visible reputation laundering to secure public approval while also undertaking secretive efforts to promote advantageous policies or practices. Whatever can or cannot be said about philanthropic motivation, there is also the final element of the case against big donors, which relies on them having the opportunity to use their private resources to cause harm.

Do big donors have the *opportunity* to cause harm?

If rich people could be shown to have both sufficient resources and reasons to cause problems through their philanthropy, they also need the help of others to be able to put those self-interested plans into practice. Money only has a latent value, it is not sufficient to achieve the intentions – problematic or otherwise – of philanthropists. We know that nonprofits need donors, but rarely acknowledge that the reverse is also true: donors need nonprofits because money cannot achieve anything until it is spent. Harmful donors – whether by design or default – require the cooperation of other people and organizations willing to commit their operational capacity and access to stakeholders (beneficiaries, community leaders, scientists, policymakers, etc.) in order to spend donors' funds in ways that run counter to their individual and institutional expertise. Criticism of philanthropy overlooks the agency of recipients: it is simply not the case that donors have all the power and recipients are passive dupes. Major funding decisions typically emerge from long, ongoing, in-depth conversations between donors and doers who share a passion for an issue or cause. For example, Dr Christof Koch, a neuroscientist at the Allen Institute in Seattle, set up by the late Paul Allen, co-founder of Microsoft, explains how his philanthropic funding works in practice:

> Paul [Allen] never pretended he was an expert. He was interested in it, he was fascinated by the vast complexity of biology. Fundamentally he was a nerd, he wanted to understand how it works. It wasn't that he said "I have an intuition, I think this is where you should look, I think you should do this particular technique in this particular type of brain and then I will fund you for that." It wasn't at all like that. The most interesting research that's funded by people such as Paul is where they go to the community and say, "I'm in general interested in this field but you have to tell me what are your challenges, what are your pain points, where can we make a difference?"
>
> (Speaking on the BBC World Service, 14 May 2020)

Dr Koch's comments reflect a truth well understood by fundraisers: that donors can only make things happen in collaboration with people and organizations who share their goals and can spend the money well to achieve the desired outcomes. This situation was noted three decades ago by philanthropy scholars Susan Ostrander and Paul Schervish, who explained that "donors have needs to be fulfilled as well as resources to grant, and recipients have resources to give as well as needs to be met. In other words, *donors and recipients both give and get in the social relation that is philanthropy*" (Ostrander & Schervish 1990: 93, italics in original).

A social relations framework understands philanthropy as a collaboration between donors and recipients such that philanthropy can only be realized when a donor is willing to give and a recipient is willing to seek and accept philanthropic support: "Unless and until both parties agree, there is no philanthropic relationship" (Ostrander 2007: 380). Carrie Morgridge, a donor giving through her Colorado-based family foundation, explains how the social relations theory works in practice: "To me, giving is definitely a group activity. I look to others to tell me what a prospective grantee is like, to tell me what they need, to spend the money wisely and to share the joy and burden of getting the job done" (Morgridge 2015: 149).

As it is in the realms of conspiracy theory to speculate that nonprofit grantees are systematically acting as willing dupes of big donors, both theory and practice refute the notion that big donors have the opportunity to cause the harm of which they stand accused.

Given the absence of means, motive and opportunity for wealthy philanthropists to realize the worst fears of their critics, why do these attacks not only seem plausible but have landed successfully with public, practitioner and policy audiences who are repeating, amplifying and acting on these concerns?

Reasons why attacks on philanthropy and philanthropists stick

This chapter explains the stickiness of attacks on philanthropy and philanthropists as owing to a broader context that is conducive to such criticism, as well as drawing on explanations from sociology and social psychology including the selective misrecognition of egoistic and altruistic gifts, the consequences of unfavourable upward social comparisons and reactions to positive deviance. Particular attention is paid to the phenomenon of "do-gooder derogation", which is a jargonistic way of saying that morally motivated people, such as environmentalists, vegans and generous people, are often disliked and rejected rather than admired and appreciated because of pre-emptive concerns that their behaviour makes other people look bad in comparison (Monin 2007; Minson & Monin 2012; MacInnis & Hodson 2017). The concept of do-gooder derogation and its applicability to philanthropy and philanthropists is explained in more detail below, after noting three contextual factors that create conducive conditions for criticism of private giving: that there is some accuracy in criticisms, that there is almost no pushback when criticisms are expressed and that criticisms reflect dominant concerns about wealth and inequality which leads to the acts of rich donors being routinely interpreted in a more negative light than the acts of non-rich donors.

There is some truth in the criticisms. The first reason that attacks on philanthropy land successfully is because they are sometimes reasonable. Thinking of the academic, insider and populist critiques in turn: some big donors do enjoy some degree of undue power and influence, some giving is inefficient and misdirected, and some donors are hypocritical and unlikeable. It would be astonishing for that to not be the case: to find an activity that is entirely devoid of power dynamics, that is run with total efficiency and effectiveness, and that involves a subset of people containing no bad apples. The issue is whether it is fair to generalize from problematic instances to damn the whole orchard. Philanthropy is complex, messy and imperfect because it is an all too human response to enduring and intractable problems. As Cath Dovey, co-founder of the Beacon Collaborative – a philanthropist-led UK initiative to encourage more, and more effective, giving – says:

> The reason philanthropy is fallible is because people are fallible. Private individuals have a responsibility to make the best decisions they can possibly make but sometimes they will fall short of what they, and observers, hope for in terms of choosing the right ideas to back and achieving the most successful impact. If critics fail to take account of the often ambiguous and uncertain contexts in which philanthropists are working, they risk turning human fallibility into a conspiracy theory.

There is almost no pushback on criticism from donors, practitioners or scholars. The second reason that attacks on philanthropy stick is because of the lack of counterarguments. It used to be the case that books on philanthropy were either "self-congratulatory, mostly boring, insider accounts [or] … shrill denunciations by outsiders" (Prewitt 2009: vii), but the balance has clearly tipped in favour of the latter since that remark was made. Not only are there more books that are broadly critical of philanthropy, these books sell more copies than those offering a neutral-to-positive perspective, and their authors have much larger followings on social media, resulting in a very one-sided debate. The only significant philanthropist on record disputing the validity of critiques is Melinda Gates who gave this rather muted response, considering the charges she and her husband frequently face: "I'm not sure that the attack has been on philanthropy. I think the attack has been on wealth" (cited in Ho 2019). In the absence of an alternative, substantive articulation of a more positive take on the value of philanthropy, from any quarter of society, the detractors have had the floor to themselves.

Criticism of philanthropy reflects dominant concerns about wealth and inequality. The third factor creating favourable conditions for critics of philanthropy is that their narrative fits well with dominant concerns about wealth and inequality. Philanthropists are often caught in the crossfire of these wider debates, which results in the curious situation where big donations spark a debate about the merits of capitalism whereas buying a private jet or super-yacht does not. When Dutch historian Rutger Bregman expressed anger at "stupid philanthropy schemes" during his now famous appearance at Davos in 2019, those words were part of a much broader point conveying frustration at the damage being done by unrestrained capitalism, the merits of higher taxation, the need to clamp down on tax avoidance, questioning of business practices that prioritize profits over people, and all of the ills of extractive and exploitative capitalism. Yet the spotlight, and the viral memes, shone solely on the practice, and the assumed problematic of philanthropy, rather than on those wider issues.

Why have philanthropists rather than the non-giving rich become emblematic of economic injustice? It is largely the visibility factor: philanthropists are more easily identifiable because their charitable actions occur in the public sphere, whereas the non-giving rich can live entirely sequestered in a private bubble of wealth and privilege, remaining unnoticed and out of the firing line. Wealth accumulation is clearly more problematic than wealth distribution, but by virtue of identifiability the giving rich are held in greater contempt than the non-giving rich. There is also some evidence that trying to do good and not meeting public expectations that donations should be entirely devoid of donor benefit is viewed more negatively than not trying at all. The "tainted altruism" hypothesis states that: "people rate individuals who do good for self-interested reasons as less moral than individuals who are selfish and do no good at all" (Newman & Cain 2014: 652).

Relatedly, the charitable acts of the giving rich are routinely interpreted in a more negative light than donations made by non-wealthy people, such that the former are assumed to be acting egoistically and the latter more altruistically. Criticisms of big philanthropy come in many guises, but what almost all have in common is some variation on a big reveal of the "shocking" truth that elite donors gain some kind of benefits from their giving. The gift's intrinsic and paradoxical combination of interestedness and disinterestedness lies behind many critiques of philanthropy, yet the exposé is moot because most big donors "readily admit" and emphasize the rewarding effects of giving (Silber 1998). The "return" is an inescapable feature of all gifting practices, and it has long been understood that private benefits created by gift-giving are enjoyed by all types of givers (Mauss 1950). Nonetheless, critics distinguish elite philanthropy – which is viewed as "contaminated" by its connection to money, power and privilege – from the ordinary humanitarian impulse, which is assumed to be "free of this taint" (Jeffreys 2016). Sustaining this distinction involves making assumptions en masse about the "better" motives of non-rich donors, which is not supported by research showing that all donors, rich and non-rich, have mixed motives. It is a false dichotomy to attribute altruistic and egoistic motives on the basis of donors' wealth because they always coexist, regardless of the donors' bank balance, such that "motivational multiplicity is the usual pattern" (Batson & Shaw 1991; Van Til 1988: 25). Why then, to take the example of the philanthropic reaction to the 2019 Notre Dame Cathedral fire (discussed in Chapter 5), did the billionaire donors receive so much criticism while the little girl's donation, which did not cover the cost of its postage, attract praise?

Appropriately, given the latter example, the explanation of why giving by the rich is critiqued while giving by the non-rich is celebrated draws on the work of French sociologist and twentieth-century public intellectual Pierre Bourdieu. In Bourdieu's writing on gift-giving he notes the collective decision to "misrecognize" the reality of exchange that underlies gifting practices. We prefer to pretend that we give and get "free" gifts, despite gift-giving occurring in the context of established relationships where we can realistically expect a return. As we unwrap our gifts on occasions such as Christmas or Valentine's Day, it is accepted practice to say, "Oh thank you so much, you shouldn't have!", but of course they should have. Reciprocity is one of the rare universal norms: without return gifts, social relationships become irreparably damaged. And when we get in a round of drinks at the pub, our friends will express pleasure and gratitude: "Cheers!" Even though everyone knows it was that person's *turn* to get a round in, we choose to be silent about the truth of the exchange. Bourdieu explains that we repress the "structural truth" about exchange in order to enjoy the feeling of giving and getting gifts: "No one is really unaware of the logic of exchange ... but no one fails to comply with the rule of the game which is to act as if one did not know the rule" (Bourdieu 1997: 232).

In the charity context, ordinary donors are allowed to enjoy feeling generous and can expect their donations to generate thanks and praise from the recipient nonprofit organization, to be given stickers, pins and wristbands to publicly signal their generosity, and to be encouraged to highlight their giving on social media to help raise awareness of the cause.

Every gift involves an exchange, even if we largely pretend it does not, but we are increasingly resistant to maintaining collective silence about the truth of exchanges that involve richer donors. We are happy to misrecognize and cele-brate smaller donations made by "ordinary" donors, overlooking the returns they receive, but we choose not to misrecognize the much bigger gifts made by richer donors, assuming they have a self-interested agenda. Thus the charge of hypocrisy is selectively applied.

The compulsion to expose the underlying self-interested logic of exchanges involving richer people is partly because, as noted above, these donors have become emblematic of wider concerns about inequality and it also derives from a desire to conform to modern notions of sophisticated realism. In modernity there is a fear of being considered naïve and unaware of hidden meanings. To be a modern realist means to "know" that certain gifts are motivated by material interests rather than by altruism, just as it means "knowing" that politics is always motivated by power and never by ideals. As Osteen notes: "modernity prides itself on a ferocious individualism that mistrusts selflessness" (Osteen 2002: 22) or, as the philosopher Michael Martin puts it, "cynicism about philanthropy is a fashionable sign of sophistication" (1994: xi).

The need to be more sceptical about scepticism relates to the final explanation discussed in this chapter for the success of attacks on philanthropy: that derogation of big givers is a defensive reaction on the part of those sceptics.

Do-gooder derogation: the preference for Goldilocks givers

Do-gooder derogation is a concept developed in the psychology literature that explains when, why and how the behaviour of morally motivated people is sometimes disparaged rather than applauded (Monin 2007; Minson & Monin 2012). Studies show that both children and adults can find generosity off-putting and unappealing, resulting in the rejection of generous individuals (Parks & Stone 2010; Tasimi *et al.* 2015: 5; Pleasant & Barclay 2018). Comparative studies in multiple countries find that dislike of do-gooders is universal, although the extent to which overcontributors are viewed negatively varies in different societies (Herrmann *et al.* 2008).

As the title of one paper on the subject asks: "Why hate the good guy?" (Pleasant & Barclay 2018). The authors' answer is that punishing overly generous people "is a social strategy that low co-operators use to avoid looking bad when high co-operators escalate co-operation" (Pleasant & Barclay 2018: 868). A plain-speaking version of the same hypothesis was offered by Ben Whitaker after surveying the arguments for and against philanthropic foundations back in the 1970s: "Hypercriticism of philanthropy from comfortably-off armchair revolutionaries or others, can often be attempts to rationalize their own meanness" (Whitaker 1974b).

Undergiving as a result of free riding is a known and significant problem in the philanthropy sector. In the absence of the compulsion to pay tax, or the compelling attraction of owning all that you pay for, the generation of income in the philanthropy sector, which relies on the voluntary contribution of private resources to fund public goods, is a much tougher call than raising funds in either the government or the business sectors. It might be assumed that hostility would be reserved for free riders, those who take without contributing, but antipathy extends to those who freely give. The preference for neither undergiving nor overgiving remains constant even when it is known that some members of the group have sufficient resources to give more, and even if that levelling down of generosity results in suboptimal outcomes for the group (Parks & Stone 2010). This is because the objective benefit of a greater quantity of resources being made available for the whole group is outweighed by the subjective cost to the self of a negative comparison, as "worrying about how a benevolent person hurts me instead of how he or she helps the group fits nicely within the structure of a social dilemma" (Parks & Stone 2010: 309).

Social dilemmas, also known as "collective action problems", are situations where there is a conflict between individual interests and the collective interest. These dilemmas are prevalent in the philanthropy sector, which requires self-interested individuals to participate in achieving outcomes that are available to everyone, regardless of whether or not they made a contribution (Olson 1965).

The preference for Goldilocks givers (those giving neither too little nor too much) is explained by social comparison theory, which notes that people evaluate themselves by comparing their attributes and achievements with those of others (Festinger 1954; Fiske 2011). Fiske's extensive study of the processes by which people compare themselves to others shows how such comparisons lead to feelings of anger and bitterness at those we "envy" for being above us, and adversely affects our sense of self, with damaging effects for social cohesion. Upward social comparison in the moral domain is an especially "stinging threat" (Monin 2007), so we punish generous individuals even when their behaviour benefits the group, and even more than we punish free riders (Irwin & Horne 2013). Upward comparisons can make us feel, and be, hostile. But when our self-image is secure there is no threat to our sense of self. Praise for small donations occurs because they constitute no threat to the observer's self-worth: such gifts can be applauded without the potential for an unfavourable comparison or any implicit or anticipated moral reproach.

Those willing to give more than the average to the public good are viewed as "rule breaking" and "establishing an undesirable behaviour standard" because they constitute an unwanted and undesirable standard for comparison. This results in the rather curiously named phenomenon of "antisocial punishment", which means punishing people for doing the right thing. Howard Becker's deviance theory (1963) is helpful for understanding the social processes at play in rejecting seemingly useful group members. Becker notes that deviance includes both negative and positive outliers, with "moral rebels" (those who are more moral than the norm) falling into the latter category. We generally prefer people who fit in with social expectations rather than act beyond the norm, and who present in a similar way to us, including in their charitable behaviour. In-group deviance may lead to derogation because it violates social norms. This preference for normative conformity leads to the sanctioning of atypically generous deviants (Irwin & Horne 2013).

People care a lot about being viewed as moral, and are therefore sensitive to any criticism about their moral standing, even if it is implicit or anticipated, rather than explicitly articulated. Individuals respond to self-threat by attacking the source of that threat (Monin *et al.* 2008). Writing in relation to the do-gooder derogation experienced by vegans and vegetarians, "This uncomfortable feeling of being morally judged motivates, even if just tacitly, [people] to take measures to protect the positive view they hold about themselves and their sense of morality. One way of doing so is derogating the source of the perceived threat to one's positive self-image" (Dhont & Stoeber 2020).

How does this happen in practice? Derogation of "do-gooding" is found to follow a normative tripartite pattern of *denying* the virtue in an ostensibly moral act, *trivializing* the efforts made by morally motivated others and *disliking* those morally motivated actors (Monin 2007). These three elements can be seen to be the outcome, respectively, of the academic, insider and populist critiques:

1. *The academic critique denies virtue* by favouring alternative self-interested explanations for philanthropy, such that it is understand as being "really" about the pursuit of power, influence and acquiring other personal benefits.
2. *The insider critique trivializes donors' actions* as being well intentioned but naïve, undertaken with a lack of awareness of the realities of the "real world", such that donors' contributions are shown to be negligible or resulting in unintended negative consequences.
3. *The populist critique encourages dislike of donors* by showing them to be annoying and worthy of scorn and derision, allowing observers (including those giving smaller amounts and non-donors) to distance themselves from big donors.

The cumulative impact of the three critiques is to portray philanthropy and philanthropists as illegitimate, ineffective and unlikeable. "Do-gooding" is also known in different countries by names such as the Tall Poppy syndrome, Pollyanna and Goody Two Shoes, but the mechanism and the end result are the same: to deny the legitimacy of the intended virtue, to trivialize the actions of those seeking to do good and to depict "do-gooders" (or Tall Poppies, or Pollyannas) as unlikeable.

A nuanced response to critiques of philanthropy

I have described, and offered a defence against, three bodies of critique that collectively result in delegitimizing, demoralizing and demeaning philanthropy. That end result does not mean that every aspect of these critiques is wrong or ought not to be articulated, rather it is their cumulative impact and the absence of any substantive pushback that is my concern. The value of critical scholarship is accepted, as is the need to root out and expose bad behaviour, but there is also a need to recognize the consequences of a persistently one-sided debate in which atypical and extreme examples of problematic philanthropy are presented as commonplace, aggravated by psycho-social mechanisms that provoke negative reactions to the charitable acts of rich givers.

The known problems of philanthropy are evident, longstanding and worth attention. But the question I have tackled asks whether the problematic aspects of philanthropy make it an illegitimate or an improvable activity. I hold the latter view, which raises the next question of how we can more carefully draw attention to the paradoxes and problems with philanthropy in a manner that avoids harming, however unintentionally, the overall greater good. With that end in mind, I offer a simple three-point plan to respond to and engage with the different types of critique:

1. *End* ahistorical, unnuanced and ad hominem attacks on philanthropists.
2. *Disentangle* critiques of philanthropy from critiques of wealth and inequality.
3. *Improve* the practice of philanthropy so that it produces greater social and environmental benefits, and encourages more, and better, giving.

This three-pronged proposal enables a nuanced response to the generalized depictions of philanthropy as illegitimate and ineffective that are conveyed in some scholarly and insider accounts, while giving short shrift to populists attacks on big giving, and offers a way forward that enables the positive potential of philanthropy to flourish.

End ahistorical, unnuanced and ad hominem attacks on philanthropists

This first element – ending ahistorical, unnuanced and ad hominem attacks on philanthropists – relates primarily to the populist critique and is the most straightforward.

Clearly it is best to pay attention to historical precedents in order to avoid mistaken assumptions that there is something distinctively and newly problematic about contemporary philanthropy which needs to be called out and rectified. In particular, the mistaken assumption that today's big givers have distorted a previously disinterested practice and have remoulded philanthropy so that it primarily serves their own interests is not supported by historical evidence. A historically attuned approach also reminds us of the longstanding presence of mixed motives driving all kinds of philanthropic acts, the unavoidable benefits created for both donors and for wider society, and the instances of philanthropic success in saving and improving lives over the centuries which can helpfully rebut the proposition that philanthropy does more harm than good.

Striving for a more nuanced approach to philanthropy helps to avoid the danger of assuming that private voluntary giving is a constant phenomenon across time and place, when in reality it is a complex, dynamic and multifaceted aspect of human life and behaviour. We would do well to remember that "the enormous range of 'varieties of philanthropy' practised across the world" (Rymer 2018) do not lend themselves to homogenous critique.

Finally, ad hominem attacks, which are directed at someone personally rather than focused on their position or actions, have no place in grown-up debates and need to end. As detailed in Chapter 5, the appearance, likeability or personal travails of individual donors are irrelevant and should not be factored into an assessment of the rights and wrongs of their philanthropic acts or of philanthropy per se.

Disentangle critiques of philanthropy from critiques of wealth and inequality

The second element, which is to disentangle critiques of philanthropy from those of wealth and inequality, appears in different guises in all three types of critique so is particularly useful to address.

There is a crucial distinction between the problems that arise from excessive and unfair wealth accumulation, and the problems of philanthropic distribution, yet these have become unhelpfully elided, leading to a number of confusing positions including an unfortunate and illogical critical focus on the wealthy who give, rather than on the wealthy who do not give.

One root of this confusion is the unfounded assumption that the purpose of philanthropy is to tackle poverty and inequality, despite there being neither historical precedent nor legal obligation for any type of donor to make this their exclusive philanthropic goal. Nonetheless, the fact that philanthropy cannot undo inequality nor serve as a meaningful substitute for robust and fair tax and spend policies is held up as proof of philanthropy's ultimate inadequacy. The unfairness of this position is barely captured by noting this is a "straw man argument".

Pointing out the existence of false and simplistic binaries is a start, such as the supposition that those in favour of philanthropy are therefore opposed to a generous, tax-funded welfare state. Outside the US many big donors live in jurisdictions that have national, publicly funded health services and a more robust welfare safety net, and yet still see plenty of opportunities to use their private wealth to promote public goods. Within the US, the case for higher taxation of the rich has been made repeatedly by many of today's most high-profile donors, including Bill Gates and Warren Buffett, the "Millionaires for Humanity" who call for a "permanent tax increase" (Millionaires for Humanity 2020), and the "Patriotic Millionaires" movement in the US which seeks a fairer tax system and also a guaranteed living wage for all, affordable housing and equitable access to higher education.

Concerns about inequality are not restricted to any one part of society. The abundance of evidence demonstrating that an unequal society is harmful at the global, societal and individual level (as shown, for example, by Thomas Piketty 2014), is available to the rich, non-rich, givers and non-givers alike. As a result, many philanthropists prioritize supporting causes to advance many different types of equality, from a focus on the financially disadvantaged, to those suffering from health inequalities, to those experiencing unequal treatment at the hands of the law. Other donors choose to focus on issues that have no direct connection to tackling poverty and inequality, such as supporting excellence in education and the arts, animal welfare or medical research, although these efforts may indirectly help to mitigate some individual and structural inequalities.

While philanthropy cannot, and has never claimed to be able to, undo inequality, it does involve the diversion of money from private pockets to public goods. Piketty's central concern with patrimonial capital, whereby cascades of inherited wealth result in ever-increasing concentrations of wealth and inexorable inequality, can be tempered by giving away money, either as charitable donations or endowed in a philanthropic foundation, that would otherwise have passed on to descendants to perpetuate inequality and confound social mobility. It is worth noting that Piketty shows no substantive concern with philanthropy's role in either creating or remedying inequality; his recommendations are focused on governmental solutions, notably a global wealth tax and a greater focus on domestic public policy to tackle inequality. Yet critiques of philanthropy continue to hold private giving accountable for problems it has no capacity to solve, and assume big donors wish to sustain inequality in order to secure undue influence, while overlooking the potential of private donors to make small but helpful contributions. As US philanthropy commentator David Callahan notes:

> a simple narrative about plutocratic power is the wrong way to understand big philanthropy. Things are more complicated, given the flow of new money to empower people working on issues like climate change, poverty, and criminal justice. Even if you worry about inequality, it's

> hard not to feel hope as super-empowered, high-minded givers look to
> solve problems in ways that get around partisan gridlock or dated ideas
> or entrenched interest groups. (Callahan 2017: 8)

Callahan points to philanthropy's role in going beyond the deficient status quo,
which is why being in favour of philanthropy and also in favour of thriving, well-
funded public services are in no way incompatible. Every fundraiser knows that
donors are not motivated by plugging gaps in public spending, indeed that is a
deeply off-putting proposition. What donors want is to use their resources to
achieve something additional, to have a transformative impact that would not
otherwise have happened, which is the exact opposite of becoming a substitute
for public spending. As Bermuda-based global philanthropy adviser Gina Pereira
told me:

> Philanthropy is far from perfect and there's too much expected of it,
> if you look at the scope of what's available philanthropically versus
> what the needs are. Until we get into a mindset where we stop looking
> at philanthropy as being the solution to addressing inequities and
> all the challenges that we're facing in the world, it's going to keep
> falling short. Philanthropy has its place. But we also need public
> sector funding, we need private sector funding, and we need to work
> together.

There is also no basis for conflating concerns about the wealthy being taxed too
lightly with beliefs that philanthropy occurs to distract observers from noticing,
or caring about, the amount of tax paid by rich donors. There is no evidence to
support the view that those seeking to evade their fiscal responsibilities by not
paying their fair share of tax are the same set of people or organizations that are
enthusiastic philanthropists. Indeed, I knew of a philanthropist who proudly
wore a badge proclaiming "I Am Not a Tax Dodger" when attending events
where she anticipated bumping into politicians, policymakers and journalists.
People can – and many do – simultaneously believe that philanthropy has
positive value while also supporting arguments in favour of higher levels of
progressive taxation and the urgent need to close tax loopholes.

Although some big donors are keen to be taxed more heavily in the future,
some are also focused on the need to rectify historic wrongs in the accumulation of wealth. Peter Buffett (son of Warren) and his wife Jennifer, who together
fund and run the NoVo philanthropic foundation, wrote the foreword for Edgar
Villanueva's powerful analysis of philanthropy's role in sustaining long-term,
structural oppression in settler-colonial societies such as the US, Canada and
Australia. Villanueva argues that philanthropy is "money that's been twice

stolen" and should therefore be focused on funding reparations and decolonization (Villanueva 2018: 80). Peter Buffett supports that view and sets out his personal opposition to capitalist domination and exploitation, and the harm that lies behind many family fortunes, arguing that philanthropic money should "be spent trying out concepts that shatter current structures and systems that have turned much of the world into one vast market" rather than on donors' "conscience laundering" (Buffett 2013). This example highlights the variety of positions within big giving about the right use of money, and the readiness to critique fellow donors, further undermining the assumption of problematic uniformity among philanthropists.

In Chapter 3 I cited Rob Reich's comment that "wealthy elites can cause problems for democratic politics" (Reich 2018: 64). This statement is true, whether these wealthy elites give or not. It is the accumulation, possession and passing on of wealth that is the problem, rather than solely wealth that is channelled into philanthropic giving, which may to some extent mitigate the problem of intergenerational transfers of wealth. It is the spending power of the wealthy in the for-profit sector, not the nonprofit sector, that is the real issue: the ability of the wealthy to distort the housing marking, to opt out of publicly provided education and health services, and to cause disproportionate environmental damage because of their lifestyles, including greater use of air travel and conspicuous consumption, all attest to the problem of wealth, rather than the problem of philanthropy. We therefore need to disentangle concerns about philanthropy from concerns about wealth and inequality, because reducing or removing the former will not lead to a better world, it will simply remove a key channel that the giving wealthy have for minimizing their negative impact and potentially making a positive contribution to the world.

The likelihood of realizing that positive potential is the focus of the third and final element of this plan.

Improve the practice of philanthropy

The third element – improving the practice of philanthropy – also relates to all three critiques and ought to be an easy sell because I have never met, or heard of, a big donor who believes that their giving is perfect and cannot be improved.

There is a deep disjuncture between the worrying about philanthropy that regularly pops up in the media and in public discussions as if no one – including donors – has ever noticed a problem before, and the longstanding, deep commitment of many donors and people working in the philanthropy sector to understand, address and improve their practice. As a philanthropy scholar,

I am bombarded with invitations to attend conferences, panel discussions and working groups to dissect and address every conceivable challenge facing philanthropy including (in just the past month) events focused on improving legitimacy, better collaboration, decolonizing philanthropy, trust-based philanthropy, ethical investment, good governance, achieving equity and sustainability. I am also frequently asked to participate in reviews and commissions that involve a research-led effort to generate new knowledge and recommendations to improve philanthropic practice. These efforts almost always involve the contributions of individual and institutional philanthropists, at a minimum as funders (because that is the business model of the philanthropy sector) and frequently as participants and contributors on the platform and in the audience, as commissioners and consumers of commission findings. I have got to know many philanthropists as a result of our joint participation in efforts to improve the sector. In short: donors are on board with helping to improve the practice of philanthropy.

The quest for improvement also occurs at the personal level. In my last job before I moved from working in the nonprofit sector to working at a university, the charity that I worked for ran a donor education programme called the Philanthropy Workshop. This programme has recruited hundreds of donors from over 20 countries who each pay many thousands of pounds to join a cohort following a curriculum of structured learning to become more effective givers. Fran Perrin is a member of the Sainsbury family, a multi-generational philanthropic family who over the decades have established 17 different grant-making foundations in the UK. She told me that she decided to participate in the Philanthropy Workshop after becoming frustrated with her initial grant-making efforts: "I realized that in my professional life I'd always trained or studied for every job I'd ever done and that's what I needed to do to become a strategic philanthropist. I also realized I needed to understand the grantee perspective, so I volunteered with several charities who have to fight a constant fundraising battle – it is very important that philanthropists see the other side of giving".

After completing the programme, Fran not only had a clearer plan for her philanthropic focus and strategy, she had also gained a network of fellow donors who continue to support and learn from each other, and has developed an approach for running her foundation based on trust and flexibility:

> We build our relationships by working closely with grantees on their proposals. We have a discussion with them to find out what it is that they most need, how best we can support them, what's new and what's exciting, so hopefully by the time the proposal comes in we have a pretty

good idea of whether it's going to get funded or not ... We often find that it takes time to get through an "honesty barrier" because people who need funding often think they have to sell us an all-singing, all-dancing proposal, but after a while they understand that's not what we're about ... Once they know they can just tell us what they need, then we try to keep that level of honesty, so a grantee can come back to us and say "we realized we needed to spend that money on something else" or "we've lost a key member of staff so can we hold the money until next year?" – and that's fine. So long as they tell us, we can be really flexible and reallocate the money as needed.

Three ways to improve philanthropic practice

Most people make charitable donations throughout their lives, but the decision to become a thoughtful, proactive philanthropist rather than an ad hoc, reactive giver, involves a long and involved process of getting organized, choosing a cause area to focus on, learning about the issues, researching what others are doing and who to collaborate with, clarifying what contribution you are best placed to make, deciding what specific philanthropic goals to pursue, making a plan to achieve those goals, evaluating progress and monitoring the changing context to make course corrections as needed. As this open-ended "to do" list indicates, being consciously philanthropic and striving to give well involves a considerable investment of time and energy and potentially a lifelong learning curve. There is little comparable nonprofit equivalent of the support offered in the for-profit sector for those seeking advice and support and maximizing the return on their private investment decisions, yet supporting donors to improve their giving would generate far more meaningful returns for wider society.

The injunction to "improve" has many dimensions but the most important in the context of the criticisms being discussed are: more ethical and effective philanthropy, and more trust between donors and doers, in order to address the "doing more harm than good" and "money misspent" critiques. The real question is not how to eliminate big givers but how to educate them to give better (Callahan 2020).

So what can and should be done? Based on 15 years of conversations with big donors those working in the philanthropy sector, and participation in numerous events, discussions and commissions focused on improving philanthropic practice, here are three sets of ways in which the philanthropy sector could, and is, striving to improve. This list relates to the three sets of critiques discussed in this book, and draws on ideas presented in Andrews *et al.* (2020), Beeston (2020), Dale (2020), Keidan (2021), Levere and Nissenbaum (2021) and the Trust-Based Philanthropy project (2021).

1. More ethical philanthropy, responding to the academic critique:
   - Incorporate social justice, racial justice and environmental justice into grant-making processes and practices.
   - Ensure that investments of philanthropic capital are mission-aligned.
   - Be aware of power dynamics – be transparent and responsive, proactively seek feedback from grantees.
   - Collaborate where possible, with other donors as well as with nonprofits, community leaders and those affected by the issue.
2. More effective philanthropy, responding to the insider critique:
   - Take donor education seriously by seeking – and taking – expert advice.
   - Be open to learning about problems that haven't yet touched your life, solutions you haven't yet thought of and ways of funding you haven't yet tried.
   - Take evaluation seriously and in proportion to the size of the donation, and undertake course corrections openly and willingly.
   - Champion representation in all aspects of your giving (including diversity on grant-making boards and among the advisers you hire) and in your grantees – seek out organizations led by people with lived experience of the cause.
3. More trust-based philanthropy, responding to the populist critique:
   - Simplify and streamline grant-making processes and make quick funding decisions so that the burden of the application process falls on donors' shoulders, not the applicants.
   - Make multi-year, unrestricted "core" funding the default option.
   - Be flexible, only asking for necessary reporting, and always being respectful of front-line experience and expertise.
   - Leverage contributions by offering non-financial support but do not demand that recipients accept it as a condition of their grant.

The criticisms have been set out, have been heard and are being worked on. Perhaps not fast enough or by enough philanthropists, but the direction of travel is moving towards more effective, ethical and trust-based philanthropy. If we wish to keep the wheels moving in that direction, and avoid derailment under the weight of disproportionate critique, it is now time for a different conversation about the positive role of philanthropy in society. If we wish to encourage more people to give, and to give more thoughtfully, then we need to balance out the critiques with acknowledgement of, and even praise for, the positive potential of philanthropy.

CONCLUSION: IN PRAISE OF PHILANTHROPY

Having shared stories of a range of philanthropists from across the centuries and across the world, this concluding chapter starts with three men from the second half of the nineteenth century – an English constitutional expert, a Swedish chemist and a Swiss businessman – mentions 14 cows and a princess, and ends with a namecheck for Noah (of the Ark) and the Roman god Janus. All will become clear.

Writing about the need for the British monarchy to avoid public and parliamentary scrutiny, Walter Bagehot declared, "We must not let in daylight upon magic" (Bagehot 1867). While an air of mystery may have proved useful for the Crown in maintaining support for its role and relevance in modern society, this is clearly not the case for philanthropy. Reticence to engaging with the growing chorus of concerns about the legitimacy and impact of private giving, and the absence of counterarguments to academic, insider and populist critiques, has left philanthropy looking distinctly dodgy rather than helped it to maintain an air of advantageous mystique. All those involved in the philanthropy sector – whether as donors, doers or part of the mediating infrastructure – need to get better at explaining the positive value and contribution of philanthropy. Letting a little daylight in on how and why philanthropy happens in practice – every day, in every community, with everyone involved as givers and takers – might help to slow, or even reverse, the tide of unfavourable and unhelpful narratives.

Twenty-one years after Bagehot's declaration, a Swedish man, Ludvig Nobel, died in France unexpectedly and prematurely from a heart attack. After a journalistic mix-up where the deceased man was confused with his brother, Alfred Nobel found himself in the unusual position of being able to read his own obituary. What he read horrified him: he was described as a chemist whose invention of dynamite had made it possible to kill more people more quickly than anyone else who had ever lived. Unsurprisingly, Alfred became obsessed with improving his posthumous reputation and in 1895 signed his last will and testament in which he bequeathed his substantial fortune to create the Nobel Prizes for outstanding achievements in literature, peace, economics, medicine and the sciences. Rewarding those who have most benefited humanity was, he believed, "a cause upon which no future obituary writer would be able to cast aspersion" (Fant 2014: 207; Andrews 2016).

The inaugural winner of the Nobel Peace Prize, first awarded in 1901, was Henry Dunant, the Swiss founder of the International Committee of the Red Cross. Dunant was inspired to create a neutral humanitarian organization to provide medical care for wounded combatants after inadvertently witnessing mass suffering in the aftermath of the Battle of Solferino in 1859 in northern Italy, where he had travelled to lobby Napoleon for assistance with his business interests. From its inception to its existence today in almost every country in the world, the work of the Red Cross and Red Crescent movement has been funded by private donors, large and small. Many other philanthropically supported organizations have been awarded the Nobel Peace Prize over the years, including Amnesty International (1977), the International Campaign to Ban Landmines (1997) and Médecins Sans Frontières (1999). Australian donors Eve Kantor and Mark Wooton were the initial and continuing core funders of the International Campaign to Abolish Nuclear Weapons, which won the Nobel Peace Prize in 2017 for its work which led to the UN adopting the Treaty on the Prohibition of Nuclear Weapons (Richards 2017). Private donors collectively contributed a sixth of all funds to the World Food Programme, which was awarded the Nobel Peace Prize in 2020; in that year philanthropy was the eleventh biggest donor to that organization, higher than the contributions of 84 countries (World Food Programme n.d.).

When nonprofit organizations are awarded a Nobel Prize and achieve this highest of global accolades for their work, that unfortunately does not prevent aspersions being cast on the philanthropic element of their funding streams, despite the mutual interdependence of doers and donors. By the standards of the critiques discussed in this book, philanthropic support for these eventual Nobel Peace Prize winners is problematic because they were not democratically taken decisions, nor were all of those organizations focused solely on poverty and inequality, nor did the donors avoid reputational and associational benefits. How heavily do these criteria weigh against the aspiration – and ultimate benefits – of a world without hunger, political prisoners and nuclear weapons, and where medical care reaches people in conflict and disaster zones? Of course, philanthropy cannot solve any of these problems alone, but it can play a key role by working with other sectors if its legitimacy remains intact. That feels like an increasingly big "if", which will take a concerted effort to achieve and involve tackling how we think and talk about philanthropy, and how we feel about donors, especially the biggest givers. As Ruth Williams, a leader in the Austrian philanthropy sector explains: "We need to teach philanthropy literacy in order to find ways to work together on the most pressing issues of our time, such as the climate crisis or the growing gap between the rich and the poor. We need to find a new way to explain philanthropy, we need to change the story we tell" (Williams 2020).

Three main elements of the new story that needs to be told about philanthropy will help to rebut key concerns expressed in the critiques discussed in this book: that philanthropy is not perfect but has value distinct from that of government and the market that is worth defending and celebrating; that there is a need for nuance, avoidance of generalizations and awareness of American exceptionalism in relation to specific concerns about philanthropy; and that we need more, not less, philanthropists.

Philanthropy is not perfect but it has distinct value that is worth defending and celebrating

For many critics, scholars and populists alike, the solution to their concerns is less – or no – philanthropy and far more tax-funded government action. The false binary involved in counterposing private generosity with state-organized welfare has been exposed throughout this book. Philanthropy is a "third space" that is different to the public and private sectors, and should neither be judged by their criteria nor compelled to emulate their modus operandi. The philanthropy sector is distinctive and useful in its own right and deserves to be judged on its own merits (Brody & Tyler 2010). A further point underlining the distinct value of philanthropy is worth emphasizing here.

The values associated with philanthropy are worth encouraging and celebrating. Funding does not just pay for things to happen, it is also an expression of validation, solidarity and consolation. The financial element monopolizes the attention of critics but in practice philanthropy is about much more than money. Donors are using their resources to offer practical help *and* to demonstrate personal concern that certain things, people and issues matter: enslaved people matter, women's right to vote matters, education of poor children matters, ending child labour matters, autistic peoples' environments matter, the need for car parking when visiting loved ones in hospitals matters, the right to see relevant role models celebrated in statues matters, the lives of people living in poor countries without decent health systems matters and so on. As the recipient of Peter Lampl's funding for gun control advocacy, mentioned in the Introduction, noted: "It was a statement of support that he was behind us, which was just as important as the money."

Private donors have funded civic infrastructure, welfare provision and scientific and medical advances, and contemporary philanthropy continues to support a vast and diverse array of activities from the arts to zoos and every alphabetic cause in between. But philanthropy's distinct value includes practical allyship, and sometimes being the only outlet available when bad things happen.

After the horror of the terrorist attacks on New York and the Pentagon on 11 September 2001, among the donations of money, blood and goods that poured in from all over the world came the gift of 14 cows from the Masai tribespeople in Kenya. In that culture, the cow is a sacred and significant asset, indicating both wealth and status. The gift, therefore, indicated the "highest expression of regard and sympathy" according to the then US ambassador to Kenya, William Brencick, who received the gift, which has since been used to set up an education fund through sales of the offspring of the original 14 cows, which were branded with a symbol resembling the twin towers. An elder in the village that organized the gift, Mzee ole Yiamboi, explained: "We did what we knew best. The handkerchief we give to people to wipe their tears with is a cow" (Evon 2017). This evocative phrase beautifully sums up the driver and value of many philanthropic acts: when things go wrong and we wish to express solidarity and compassion, much giving is simply the best handkerchief that the donor is able to give at that time. The insider critique, discussed in Chapter 4, urges donors to better align their response with the needs they encounter, which of course makes sense. But sometimes compassion and consolation are a valuable response, and on occasion may be the only response that is available.

Further examples of generosity as solidarity across time and place include donations made in 1847 by enslaved Africans in Virginia to the Irish famine relief effort (Freeman 2020), and financial help from Indigenous Americans in the same year to help starving Irish families. The latter gift was reciprocated over 170 years later when Irish people enthusiastically donated to the Navajo and Hopi Families Covid-19 Relief Fund, which has raised over $7 million at the time of writing. "We have become kindred spirits with the Irish in the years since the Irish potato famine", explained Gary Batton, chief of the Choctaw Nation of Oklahoma. Irish historian Diarmaid Ferriter said that the gifts illustrate how suffering resonates with others who have also experienced terrible deprivation: "it has made Irish people more likely to make common cause with other marginalized people" (O'Loughlin & Zaveri 2020).

In August 1997, a champion of marginalized people and the then most famous woman in the world, Diana, Princess of Wales, died in a car crash in Paris. No financial needs arose from this sad incident, as clearly her children would be well provided for, but nonetheless over £30 million was donated by almost three million people in response to her death, and that number was doubled by other fundraising efforts including sales of Elton John's reworking of his song "Candle in the Wind". At the time, I was working as a fundraiser at a homeless charity that had a loose association with the princess. In the days after her death I opened envelopes containing cheques and cash from people who wanted "to do something" and had no other outlet for that urge, other than to leave bouquets of flowers to wither in the sun outside Kensington Palace. The monies were used to set up the Diana, Princess of Wales Memorial Fund, a grant-making foundation that distributed all the money by the end of 2012 to causes aligned with its namesake, including clearing landmines and supporting marginalized people such as child refugees and women in prison.

When philanthropy is depicted as a sham act to mask previous bad behaviour or an attempt to secure future advantages, as discussed in Chapter 5, it is hard to square this perspective with gifts that are spurred by solidarity, compassion and a sense of "what else can I do?". In his reflection on humanitarians, Michael Barnett writes: "They tried to make the world a better place, and in many cases they succeeded, and even when they failed (which was often), they offered a living reminder that it is possible to answer suffering with something more than mourning" (Barnett 2011: 9).

The desire "to answer suffering with something more than mourning" is applicable to much philanthropy. "Solidarity" is not a word that is commonly discussed or celebrated in the US (perhaps because of connotations with socialism), but in my experience solidarity – or if you prefer, allyship, fellowship or togetherness – is an overlooked yet key driver and explanation of much private action for the public good.

Need for nuance, avoidance of generalizations and awareness of American exceptionalism

The second element of the story that needs to be told about philanthropy is relevant to the reductionist element of the insider critique, which suggests there is one "best" way to be philanthropic. The problems with this approach were explored in Chapter 4, and one further dimension of taking a very narrow view of the role and purpose of philanthropy is that it privileges the perspective of critics, most of whom are based in the US, which may well not be universal.

While some Americans seem genuinely concerned about the impact of too much big giving, for the rest of the world the opposite problem looms far larger: there is not enough philanthropy, which results in a chronically underfunded and subsequently underpowered nonprofit sector. The gap between the US and the rest is abundantly evident in David Callahan's description of private money "crowding into" science, medicine, arts and higher education in the US when he describes scenarios that do not exist outside of that country:

> Pick nearly any disease, and you'll find a deep-pocketed donor who's hot on the trail of a research breakthrough. Name a leading cultural

institution, and chances are its lately received new infusions of cash from billionaire backers. Get lost in a top hospital, and you'll find yourself wandering from one named wing to another. Visit any major university, and it will be hard to find a big building on campus that doesn't bear the name of a mega-donor.   (Callahan 2017: 239)

Meanwhile, on the other side of the Atlantic the financial viability of equivalent institutions is reliant on government funding and the collective contribution of millions of small donors. For example, the UK's largest funder of cancer research is a nonprofit charity where, according to Cancer Research UK's director of philanthropy, Chris Gethin, "90 per cent of the donations we receive are worth less than £10. So in the field of cancer research in the UK it is not billionaire philanthropists that are driving the greatest discoveries and significant breakthroughs in our field, it's the generosity of the general public."

It is the same story in the arts, where government funding and large volumes of small donations are key to the financial viability of organizations such as London's Royal Opera House and National Theatre. When the leader of a US woman's fund is reported as saying, "I can count all my million dollar-donors on one hand" (cited in Callahan 2017: 194), her intention is to make the point that gender-related issues struggle to secure the same level of support as other issues, but readers outside the US probably take away a different message. In the UK I cannot think of many charity leaders in any cause area that need more than one digit, never mind one hand, to count their seven-figure donors, and having one such major supporter would be a cause for celebration not comparative woe.

Of course, in the UK some medical research nonprofits, major arts institutions, hospitals and universities do receive the occasional, much-appreciated major donation from an individual, foundation or corporate donor. But an overview of philanthropy in 26 countries shows that big giving is very much the exception, not the norm for most of the world (Wiepking & Handy 2015). The US contains 4 per cent of the global population yet dominates 99 per cent of debates about the merits and problems of philanthropy, which cannot be assumed to be the same everywhere.

The role that money plays in politics and the subsequent outsized influence of the rich on wider society is another key example of American exceptionalism. In the US, more so than in other countries, wealthy donors can pay to amplify their views by funding research organizations to get their issues onto the agenda, supporting policy development and financing campaigns (Goss 2016: 442). In many countries, such as the UK, there are laws prohibiting "charitable" activity that might unduly influence the political process, avoiding the growth of policy-oriented philanthropy which is a "peculiarly American problem" (Karl & Katz 1981). This situation is the result of the longstanding preference of US voters for small government and local control over social issues, combined with growing awareness, backed by scientific knowledge, of the need to intervene at the national, and sometimes international, level to innovate and implement solutions for issues as diverse as raising educational standards, improving working conditions and tackling climate change. The clash between localist ideals and the necessity of national and supranational solutions has created a gap in the US that has been filled by powerful generalist foundations. The decision to prioritize private solutions over public solutions, and to choose welfare capitalism over a welfare state, means that US-based critics are writing about a very different, and exceptional, situation (Karl & Katz 1981: 269, 243).

For much of the world, philanthropy has not been the "preferred partner" for tackling major social problems since the nineteenth century, and there is no meaningful prospect of a return to philanthropic primacy, or of philanthropic influence surpassing that of elected officials, as some suggest is on the cards in the US (Callahan 2017: 7). While the problem of too many donors with too much influence may well be a legitimate concern in the US, it is reasonable to depict many current critiques of philanthropy as a universal hammer to crack on American nut.

We need more, not fewer, philanthropists: the billion dollar – or 2.5 trillion dollar – question

One thing that is universal is the business model of charity being reliant on voluntary donations, so the third element of the story that needs to be told in relation to the burgeoning critique of philanthropy is the billion dollar question. Across the world at least $1 billion a day is made available by private individuals and organizations to fund a very wide range of nonprofit activity.[2] If philanthropy is inherently problematic and deserving of attack, and if over time that problematizing makes private giving a less attractive option for those with money to spare, how will that $1 billion-plus gap be plugged?

Of course, that figure assumes we are currently in an equilibrium state where all necessary nonprofit work is in receipt of sufficient funding, which is far from the truth. To take the most obvious example of unfunded good work, in 2015 all member states of the United Nations signed up to the Sustainable Development Goals (SDGs): 17 specific targets to be reached by 2030 including an end to poverty and hunger, free education for all children, universal access

---

2. There are no global data on total philanthropy, but Giving USA regularly records annual totals of $400 billion or more, so the $1 billion a day is a very conservative minimum, excluding all donations made outside of the US.

to clean water and significant advances in global health outcomes. The cost for achieving all 17 goals is estimated at between $5 and $7 trillion per year, and the current funding gap is $2.5 trillion (Voriseck & Yu 2020; SDG Philanthropy Platform, n.d.). Many philanthropic donors and the organizations they support are aligned with the SDGs, because the goals cover issues that are also longstanding philanthropic concerns, such as ending poverty and promoting education. The SDGs have been agreed by democratically elected governments, and it is indisputable that they need philanthropic funding to help make them happen. Given the ambition inherent in these goals and the huge resources required to reach them, we clearly need far more, not fewer, philanthropists.

Would that outcome inevitably exacerbate the problem of "top-heavy philanthropy"? This concept, which highlights the greater influence of big donors over declining small-dollar donors, appears to blame bigger donors for the disproportionate value of their gifts and resulting "outsized" voice. But there are two ways to dilute the influence of rich donors: either by having fewer of them (which would create significant funding gaps) or by increasing the propensity to give and the donation size across a broader slice of the population. To anyone involved in the practice of philanthropy, the latter is the more sensible and appealing approach. The latent philanthropic power of the mass affluent is immense and, given the known benefits that accrue to givers, could be an effective two-pronged policy to increase the health and happiness of the global population while also generating more funding for nonprofit action. A rising tide of more philanthropic funds would lift all boats – malaria nets as well as modern art galleries – with no need to play one type of "good" off against another. Shifting the focus from attacking elite givers to enabling and celebrating all kinds of philanthropy would enable a multitude of different types of causes to flourish, increase the viability of non-government and non-market action, and strengthen global civil society with all its known positive outcomes for both democracy and social cohesion.

There are two preconditions for moving forward in this way: changes in the norms that result in the disparagement of giving and do-gooder derogation, and greater investment in fundraising so that all those with surplus funds receive appropriate and ideally enjoyable invitations to support the causes they care about. There is a reason that fundraisers currently focus on, and long for more, major donors: because having a big giver is the most efficient way to raise the largest amount of money. If we want more democratic giving, we need more democratic asking, and that means fundraising will cost more (at least initially) in order to communicate with, and build relationships with, a much broader mass affluent donor base. That will be more time-consuming and costly than focusing on a handful of major donors, but if the latter is unacceptable to our democratic sensibilities or results in suboptimal outcomes then one key solution to the problem of philanthropy is more, and more professional, fundraising.

Noah's principle: credit only for building arks

Unfortunately, solutions are sorely lacking among many of the critics. Reviewing the leading texts setting forth the critique of philanthropy, veteran philanthropy expert Gara LaMarche notes that, "in general, these books are heavy on diagnosis, and light on remedy" (LaMarche 2020). To take the most egregious example of being marched to the top of a hill by a critic and then offered no clue as to how to get back down, Giridharadas' scathing critique of philanthropy concludes: "the inescapable answer to the overwhelming question – Where do we go from here? – is: somewhere other than where we have been going, led by people other than the people who have been leading us" (Giridharadas 2018a: 246).

This clearly leaves many questions unanswered, as do all those critics who detail the problems of philanthropy without offering the scantest denouement to their argument. Do we ban private voluntary giving? Or just outlaw gifts over a certain size? If so, what size? Why is virtue hoarding better than virtue signalling? Is philanthropy the best scapegoat for all the ills of capitalism? Do we want all nonprofits not serving the poor to shut down? Can nonprofits serving minority interests ever pass the democracy test? Ditto for advocacy and policy-related activities? How then do we ever challenge the state? Or bring down capitalism, if that is the critics' true concern?

Those of us who prefer analyses to be accompanied by solutions might usefully cite Noah's principle: "No more credit for predicting rain. Credit only for building arks" (Levy 2009: 7). The primary purpose of this book is to offer a defence against attacks on philanthropy, but in the spirit of Noah's principle Chapter 6 offers a three-point plan to move past the current impasse, including top-line ideas on how to improve philanthropic practice. Many excellent books written by experienced philanthropy advisers are available for those seeking more detailed suggestions.

Ideas and solutions matter because the story of philanthropy that needs to be told and heard is not that it is perfect but that it is improvable and legitimate, with inherent value that is worth supporting and – when it advances the public good – celebrating.

Philanthropy is flawed because it is Janus faced, having sharply contrasting characteristics that can generate both positive and negative outcomes. Philanthropists can be careful and compassionate as well as careless and controlling (Schervish 2006: 175). This is why philanthropy "fits one set of views of the world as a progressive and valuable force, while it is seen from another perspective as retrograde, inegalitarian, and deceptive" (Van Til 1990: 24). In other words, this is why philanthropy is so easy to either demonize or sentimentalize. Both are viable positions to take, yet those taking the critical stance are shouting far louder with no indication that they intend to yield the floor. Those of us who have witnessed and believe in the transformative power of philanthropy need to offer an alternative perspective and speak up for its positive potential. An argument facing no pushback wins by default: the other side needs to show up to this debate.

Conclusion

I began this book by explaining that my inspiration was Bernard Crick's masterly *In Defence of Politics*. Crick's defence is not based on a belief that democratic politics always gets everything right and produces the best decisions, but rather that it is the only viable option that enables order while protecting freedom. He shows that defending the realm and activity of politics is not the same as defending any particular type of political ideology. So too, we can defend and celebrate philanthropy with full awareness that not every philanthropic approach or decision will be "right", always bearing in mind how subjective that judgement can be. Rather, we can defend the philanthropic impulse, and advance the position that philanthropy is often a better, although unlikely to be perfect, option than excessive personal consumption.

Like voters, donors can make poor choices, and sometimes those choices produce poor outcomes, but these are ineluctable features of any system comprising fallible human beings. Overall both democracy and philanthropy have proven resilient and a far better alternative to the absence of democratic systems and the banning of private action for the public good, as has only ever been attempted in totalitarian states.

Like politics, philanthropy is imperfect, messy and complex, but it is better than a world without philanthropy. Those attacking philanthropy should be careful what they wish for. What kind of society would prohibit individuals from doing more than paying tax and buying things for themselves? Who truly thinks that only elected politicians have all the answers to the problems of our time? Even if we do not advocate legislating philanthropy out of existence, the populist backlash could result in those with money to spare deciding that it is not worth the price of sticking their head above the philanthropic parapet.

I wrote this book because I believe that the current waves of mutually reinforcing critiques are overstating the nature of the threat posed by private giving and understating the positive benefits of philanthropy. I believe a defence against the delegitimization of philanthropy is needed to avoid deterring future donors, demoralizing those currently funding and working in the philanthropy sector, and – most crucially – to avoid harming beneficiaries who rely on philanthropically funded nonprofit action.

Philanthropy is not perfect but nor is it inherently problematic. It is improvable but not illegitimate, and it has value that urgently needs articulating and defending.

REFERENCES

ACNC 2020. *Bushfire Response 2019–20: Reviews of Three Australian Charities*. Australian Charities and Not for Profits Commission, October 2020. https://www.acnc.gov.au/tools/reports/bushfire-response-2019–20-reviews-three-australian-charities.

Adams, G. 2006. "Celebrity and the new philanthropy". *The Independent*, 26 September.

Agerholm, H., E. Simpson & D. Palumbo 2020. "The multimillionaire's plan to reinvent a town". *BBC News*, 4 March. https://www.bbc.co.uk/news/business-51648556.

Alexander, S. 2019. "Against against billionaire philanthropy". Blogpost on Slate Star Codex. https://slatestarcodex.com/2019/07/29/against-against-billionaire-philanthropy/.

Allen, M. 2015. "Bloomberg: philanthropy should 'embolden government'". *Politico*, 6 April.

Allen, S. 2018. *The Science of Generosity*. Greater Good Science Center, UC Berkeley, prepared for the John Templeton Foundation.

Andreoni, J. 1990. "Impure altruism as donations to public goods: a theory of warm-glow giving". *Economic Journal* 100(401): 464–77.

Andrews, E. 2016. "Did a premature obituary inspire the Nobel Prize?" *History*, 9 December. https://www.history.com/news/did-a-premature-obituary-inspire-the-nobel-prize.

Andrews, E., L. Bartczak, P. Brest, R. Shamash & P. Tantia 2020. *Community-Based Organizations and High-Capacity Donors: Relationships, Perceptions, and Behaviors*. Stanford, CA: Stanford Center on Philanthropy and Civil Society.

Andrews, F. 1950. *Philanthropic Giving*. New York: Russell Sage Foundation.

Arnold, J. 2014. "Attacks and vitriol will not deter me from supporting fixes to public policy". *The Chronicle of Philanthropy*, 31 March.

Arnove, R. (ed.) 1980. *Philanthropy and Cultural Imperialism: The Foundations at Home and Abroad*. Bloomington: Indiana University Press.

Bagehot, W. 1867. "The English constitution". Originally published in *The Fortnightly Review* from 1865 to 1867.

Barnett, M. 2011. *Empire of Humanity: A History of Humanitarianism*. Ithaca, NY: Cornell University Press.

Batson, C. & L. Shaw 1991. "Evidence for altruism: toward a pluralism of prosocial motives". *Psychological Inquiry* 2(2): 107–22.

Beattie, J. 1964. *Other Cultures: Aims, Methods and Achievements in Social Anthropology*. London: Routledge & Kegan Paul.

Beatty, S. 2008. "Why donating millions is hard to keep secret". *Wall Street Journal*, 9 January.

Becker, H. 1963. *Outsiders: Studies in the Sociology of Deviance*. New York: The Free Press.

Beeston, E. 2020. *The Brighter Side of 2020*. Blogpost, 18 December. http://www.emmabeeston.co.uk/insight/2020/12/18/the-brighter-side-of-2020.

Bekkers, R. & P. Wiepking 2011. "A literature review of empirical studies: eight mechanisms that drive charitable giving". *Nonprofit and Voluntary Sector Quarterly* 40(5): 924–73.

Bella, T. 2020. "Dolly Parton helped fund Moderna's vaccine: it began with a car crash and an unlikely friendship". *Washington Post*, 18 November.

Ben-Ner, A. 2002. "The shifting boundaries of the mixed economy and the future of the nonprofit sector". *Annals of Public and Cooperative Economics* 73(1): 5–40.

Berger, K. & R. Penna 2013. "The elitist philanthropy of so-called effective altruism". *Stanford Social Innovation Review*, 25 November.

Berman, J., A. Barasch, E. Levine & D. Small 2018. "Impediments to effective altruism: the role of subjective preferences in charitable giving". *Psychological Science* 29(5): 834–44.

Bernholz, L. 2020. "Confronting philanthropy's uncomfortable truths". *Chronicle of Philanthropy*, 25 August.

Bernholz, L., C. Cordelli & R. Reich 2016. "Introduction: philanthropy in democratic societies". In R. Reich, C. Cordelli & L. Bernholz (eds), *Philanthropy in Democratic Societies: History, Institutions, Values*. Chicago: University of Chicago Press.

Berresford, S. 2010. "What's the problem with strategic philanthropy?" *Chronicle of Philanthropy*, 3 October. https://www.philanthropy.com/article/whats-the-problem-with-strategic-philanthropy/.

Billis, D. & H. Glennerster 1998. "Human services and the voluntary sector: towards a theory of comparative advantage". *Journal of Social Policy* 27(1): 79–98.

Bishop, M. & M. Green 2008. *Philanthrocapitalism*. New York: Bloomsbury.

Black, R. 2015. *Scandal, Salvation and Suffrage: The Amazing Women of the Temperance Movement*. Leicester: Matador.

Body, A., K. Holman & E. Hogg 2017. "To bridge the gap? Voluntary action in primary schools". *Voluntary Sector Review* 8(3): 251–71.

Bourdieu, P. 1997. "Marginalia: some additional notes on the gift". In A. Schrift (ed.) *The Logic of the Gift: Towards an Ethic of Generosity*. New York: Routledge.

Bowman, A. 2012. "The flip side to Bill Gates' charity billions". *New Internationalist*, 1 April. https://newint.org/features/2012/04/01/bill-gates-charitable-giving-ethics/.

Bradbury, S. 2015. "Former Folio editorial director Sue Bradbury remembers Bob Gavron". The Folio Society, 30 March. https://www.foliosociety.com/uk/blog/former-folio-editorial-director-sue-bradbury-remembers-bob-gavron/.

Brayer, E. 1996. *George Eastman: A Biography*. Baltimore, MD: Johns Hopkins University Press.

Breeze, B. 2011. *More than Money: The Social Meaning of Philanthropy in Contemporary UK Society*. PhD thesis, University of Kent.

Breeze, B. 2013. "How donors choose charities". *Voluntary Sector Review* 4(2): 165–83.

Breeze, B. 2017. *The New Fundraisers: Who Organises Charitable Giving in Contemporary Society?* Bristol: Policy Press.

Breeze, B. 2020. *The Philanthropy Paradox: Public Attitudes and Future Prospects for Planned Giving*. London: Prism the Gift Fund.

Breeze, B. & T. Lloyd 2013. *Richer Lives: Why Rich People Give*. London: Director of Social Change.

Breeze, B. & P. Ramsbottom 2020. "Don't dismiss philanthropy: it's crucial during the coronavirus crisis". *The Guardian*, 28 April.

Bremner, R. 1960. *American Philanthropy*. Chicago: University of Chicago Press.

Brody, E. & J. Tyler 2010. "Respecting foundation and charity autonomy: how public is private philanthropy?" *Chicago-Kent Law Review* 85(2): 571–618.

Brooks, C. 2015. "'The ignorance of the uneducated': Ford Foundation philanthropy, the IIE, and the geographies of educational exchange". *Journal of Historical Geography* 48: 36–46.

Bryant, K. 2020. "MacKenzie Scott redefines F-ck-You Money". *Vanity Fair*, 16 December.

Buchanan, P. 2019a. *Giving Done Right: Effective Philanthropy and Making Every Dollar Count*. New York: Public Affairs.

Buchanan, P. 2019b. "Philanthropy's blighted reputation threatens global giving". *Financial Times*, 15 April.

Buffett, P. 2013. "The charitable-industrial complex". *New York Times*, 26 July.

Caesar, E. 2006. "Meet Britain's most generous tycoon". *The Independent*, 17 July.

Callahan, D. 2017. *The Givers: Wealth, Power, and Philanthropy in a New Gilded Age*. New York: Knopf.

Callahan, D. 2020. "Stronger government is a must: but billionaire donors are here to stay – and can do good". *Inside Philanthropy*, 21 April.

Capgemini 2021. *World Wealth Report 2021*. https://worldwealthreport.com/resources/world-wealth-report-2021/.

Charity Tax Commission 2019. *Reforming Charity Taxation: Towards a Stronger Civil Society*. London: NCVO.

Chesterton, G. 1909. "Gifts of the millionaire". *Illustrated London News*, 29 May.

Christianson, F. 2007. *Philanthropy in British and American Fiction: Dickens, Hawthorne, Eliot and Howells*. Edinburgh: Edinburgh University Press.

Church, M. 2005. "Banker with a baton". *The Independent*, 7 March. https://www.independent.co.uk/arts-entertainment/music/features/banker-baton-5002.html.

Civic Ventures, n.d. "Values, missions, and goals". http://civic-ventures.com.

Clark, A. 2008. "Banking crisis: Warren Buffett sees US bailout as a golden opportunity". *The Guardian*, 24 September.

Clarke, J. 1964. "Turgot's critique of perpetual endowments". *French Historical Studies* 3(4): 495–506.

Collins, C. & H. Flannery 2020. *Gilded Giving 2020: How Wealth Inequality Distorts Philanthropy and Imperils Democracy*. Washington, DC: Institute for Policy Studies.

Connolly, P. 2011. "The best of the humanistic and technocratic: why the most effective work in philanthropy requires a balance". *The Foundation Review* 3(1–2): 120–36.

Credit Suisse 2016. *Global Wealth Databook 2016*. https://www.investerum.se/dokument/broschyrer/global-wealth-databook-2016.pdf.

Crick, B. 2000. *In Defence of Politics*, 5th edition. London: Continuum.

CRS 2020. *Tax Issues Relating to Charitable Contributions and Organizations*. Congressional Research Services, 4 August. https://fas.org/sgp/crs/misc/R45922.pdf.

CSP, n.d. Centre for Strategic Philanthropy website. https://www.jbs.cam.ac.uk/faculty-research/centres/strategic-philanthropy/.

Cuddy, A. & B. Boelpaep 2019. "Notre-Dame fire: has too much money been given to rebuild it?" *BBC News*, 24 April. https://www.bbc.co.uk/news/world-europe-48039770.

Cunningham, H. 2016. "The multi-layered history of Western philanthropy". In T. Jung, S. Phillips & J. Harrow (eds), *The Routledge Companion to Philanthropy*. Abingdon: Routledge.

Cunningham, H. 2020. *The Reputation of Philanthropy Since 1750: Britain and Beyond*. Manchester: Manchester University Press.

Dale, E. 2020. "5 ways MacKenzie Scott's $5.8 billion commitment to social and economic justices is a model for other donors". *The Conversation*, 16 December. https://theconversation.com/5-ways-mackenzie-scotts-5–8-billion-commitment-to-social-and-economic-justice-is-a-model-for-other-donors-152206.

Daniels, A. 2020. "Hewlett commits $50 million to new effort to rethink how capitalism should work". *Chronicle of Philanthropy*, 8 December.

Darby, D. 2020. "What's wrong with billionaires?" Lowimpact blogpost, 15 March. https://www.lowimpact.org/whats-wrong-with-billionaires/.

Davies, R. 2015. *Public Good by Private Means: How Philanthropy Shapes Britain*. London: Charities Aid Foundation.

Davies, R. 2016. *Lights, Camera, Altruism: Philanthropy at the Movies*. Giving Thought blogpost. https://www.cafonline.org/about-us/blog-home/giving-thought/the-role-of-giving/lights-camera-altruism-philanthropy-at-the-movies.

Davis, S. 1996. "Philanthropy as a virtue in late antiquity and the middle ages". In J. Schneewind (ed.), *Giving: Western Ideas of Philanthropy*. Bloomington: Indiana University Press.

DfE 2020. "Pupil premium". Department for Education policy paper, 17 December. https://www.gov.uk/government/publications/pupil-premium/pupil-premium.

Dhont, K. & S. Stoeber 2020. "The vegan resistance". *The Psychologist*, 6 August.

Donovan, D. 2014. "Hewlett ends effort to get donors to make dispassionate choices on giving". *Chronicle of Philanthropy*, 3 April.

Duquette, N. 2019. "Founders' fortunes and philanthropy: a history of the U.S. charitable-contribution deduction". *Business History Review* 93(3): 553–84.

Ealy, L. 2014. "The intellectual crisis in philanthropy". *Society* 51(1): 87–96.

Economic Security Project, n.d. "We're in the midst of a historic consolidation of corporate power". https://www.economicsecurityproject.org/antimonopoly/.

Eikenberry, A. & R. Mirabella 2017. "Extrem ephilanthropy: philanthrocapitalism, effective altruism, and the discourse of neoliberalism". *PS: Political Science & Politics* 51(1): 43–7.

Esposito, V. 2010. *The Power to Produce Wonders: The Value of Family in Philanthropy*. Washington, DC: National Center for Family Philanthropy.

Evers-Hillstrom, K. 2019. "Big Pharma continues to top lobbying spending". *OpenSecrets*, 25 October. https://www.opensecrets.org/news/2019/10/big-pharma-continues-to-top-lobbying-spending/.

Evon, D. 2017. "Did Masai tribespeople donate 14 cows to the United States after 9/11?" *Snopes*, 23 May. https://www.snopes.com/fact-check/masai-cows-911-donate/.

Fant, K. 2014. *Alfred Nobel: A Biography*. New York: Arcade Publishing.

Farrell, P. 2017. "We had slavery in our supply chains, says Andrew Forrest". *The Guardian*, 6 April.

Festinger, L. 1954. "A theory of social comparison processes". *Human Relations* 7(2): 117–40.

Finchum-Mason, E., K. Husted & D. Suárez 2020. "Philanthropic foundation responses to COVID-19". *Nonprofit and Voluntary Sector Quarterly* 49(6): 1129–41.

Fisher, D. 1980. "American philanthropy and the social sciences: the reproduction of a Conservative ideology". In R. Arnove (ed.), *Philanthropy and Cultural Imperialism: The Foundations at Home and Abroad*. Bloomington: Indiana University Press.

Fisher, D. 1983. "The role of philanthropic foundations in the reproduction and production of hegemony: Rockefeller foundations and the social sciences". *Sociology* 17(2): 206–33.

Fiske, S. 2011. *Envy Up, Scorn Down: How Status Divides Us*. New York: Russell Sage Foundation.

Fraser, G. 2017. "It's called effective altruism but is it really the best way to do good?" *The Guardian*, 23 November.

Freeman, T. 2020. "400 years of black giving: from the days of slavery to the 2018 Morehouse graduation". Generocity blog, 13 January. https://generocity.org/philly/2020/01/13/400-years-of-black-giving-from-the-days-of-slavery-to-the-2019-morehouse-graduation/.

Freeman, D., F. Waite, L. Rosebrock, A. Petit, C. Causier, A. East, L. Jenner, A.-L. Teale, L. Carr, S. Mulhall, E. Bold & S. Lambe 2020. "Coronavirus conspiracy beliefs, mistrust, and compliance with government guidelines in England". *Psychological Medicine* 1–13. https://doi.org/10.1017/S0033291720001890.

Frumkin, P. 2006. *Strategic Giving: The Art and Science of Philanthropy*. Chicago: University of Chicago Press.

Fulton, K. 2018. "The predicament of strategic philanthropy". Center for Effective Philanthropy website, 22 February. https://cep.org/predicament-strategic-philanthropy/.

Garthwaite, K. 2016. *Hunger Pains: Life Inside Food Bank Britain*. Bristol: Policy Press.

Gates, B. 2015. "A big bet for 2030". Annual letter 2015. GatesNotes: The Blog of Bill Gates. http://www.gatesnotes.com/2015-annual-letter?page=0&lang=en&WT.mc_id=01_21_2015_AL2015-GF_GFO_domain_Top_21.

Gates, B. & M. Gates 2018. "10 tough questions we get asked". Annual letter 2018. GatesNotes: The Blog of Bill Gates. https://www.gatesnotes.com/2018-annual-letter.

Gates, B. & M. Gates 2020. "Reflecting on the first two decades of our foundation". Annual letter 2020. GatesNotes: The Blog of Bill Gates. https://www.gatesnotes.com/2020-Annual-Letter?WT.mc_id=20200210000000_AL2020_BG-COM_&WT.tsrc=BGCOM.

Gates, B. & M. Gates 2021. "The year global health went local". Annual letter 2021. GatesNotes: The Blog of Bill Gates. https://www.gatesnotes.com/2021-Annual-Letter.

Gates, B. & M. Gates, n.d. Giving Pledge signatory letter. https://givingpledge.org/Pledger. aspx?id=199.

Gharabaghi, K. & B. Anderson-Nathe 2017. "The need for critical scholarship". *Child & Youth Services* 38(2): 95–7.

Gilding, M. 2010. "Motives of the rich and powerful in doing interviews with social scientists". *International Sociology* 25(6): 755–77.

Giridharadas, A. 2018a. *Winners Take All: The Elite Charade of Changing the World*. New York: Knopf.

Giridharadas, A. 2018b. "Beware rich people who say they want to change the world". *New York Times*, 24 August. https://www.nytimes.com/2018/08/24/opinion/sunday/ wealth-philanthropy-fake-change.html?login=email&auth=login-email.

Giving, USA 2020. *Giving USA 2020*. Chicago: Giving USA Foundation.

Global Polio Eradication Initiative, n.d. "The virus". Global Polio Eradication Initiative. http:// polioeradication.org/polio-today/polio-prevention/the-virus/.

Goldberg, S. 2009. *Billions of Drops in Millions of Buckets: Why Philanthropy Doesn't Advance Social Progress*. Hoboken, NJ: Wiley.

Goodman, C. 2006. "Charity's rich legacy". *Sunday Express*, 1 October.

Goss, K. 2016. "Policy plutocrats: how America's wealthy seek to influence governance". *PS: Political Science & Politics* 49(3): 442–8.

Gray, B. 1905. *A History of English Philanthropy: From the Dissolution of the Monasteries to the Taking of the First Census*. London: Frank Cass.

Gray, B. 1908. *Philanthropy and the State, or Social Politics*. London: P. S. King & Son.

Greer, L. 2020. *Philanthropy Revolution: How to Inspire Donors, Build Relationships, and Make a Difference*. London: Harper Collins.

Greer, L. & L. Kostoff 2020. *Philanthropy Revolution: How to Inspire Donors, Build Relationships, and Make a Difference*. London: Harper Collins.

Gregory, A. & D. Howard 2009. "The nonprofit starvation cycle". *Stanford Social Innovation Review*, Fall 2009: 49–53.

Gribben, R. 2006. "Clock stops for GUS, the empire started by a legend". *Daily Telegraph*, 7 October.

Guardian, The 2018. "Buzzwords and tortuous impact studies won't fix a broken aid system". Letters to the Editor, 16 July. https://www.theguardian.com/global-development/2018/jul/ 16/buzzwords-crazes-broken-aid-system-poverty.

Handy, C. 2006. *The New Philanthropists*. London: Heinemann.

Hansmann, H. 1986. "The role of non-profit enterprise". In S. Rose-Ackerman (ed.), *The Economics of Nonprofit Institutions: Studies in Structure and Policy*. Oxford: Oxford University Press.

Hansmann, H. 1987. "Economic theories of nonprofit organization". In W. Powell (ed.), *The Nonprofit Sector: A Research Handbook*. New Haven, CT: Yale University Press.

Harambam, J. 2020. "Why we should not treat all conspiracy theories the same". *The Conversation*, 12 June.

Harris, K. 2019. *The Truths We Hold: An American Journey*. London: Penguin.

Harris, M. 2020. "A controversial TikTok visually illustrates Mark Zuckerberg's coronavirus donation in comparison to his total wealth". *Insider*, 30 March. https://www.insider.com/ mark-zuckerbergs-coronavirus-donation-as-percentage-of-wealth-tiktok-2020-3.

Havens, J. & P. Schervish 2014. *A Golden Age of Philanthropy Still Beckons: National Wealth Transfer and Potential for Philanthropy*. Boston, MA: Center on Wealth and Philanthropy, Boston College.

Herrmann, B., C. Thöni & S. Gächter 2008. "Antisocial punishment across societies". *Science* 319, 7 March: 1362–7.

Herro, A. & F. Obeng-Odoom 2019. "Foundations of radical philanthropy". *Voluntas* 30: 881–90.

Hewlett Foundation 2020. "Hewlett Foundation announces new, five-year $50 million Economy and Society Initiative to support growing movement to replace neoliberalism". William and Flora Hewlett Foundation, 8 December. https://hewlett.org/newsroom/hewlett-foundation-announces-new-five-year-50-million-economy-and-society-initiative-to-support-growing-movement-to-replace-neoliberalism/.

Heydemann, S. & S. Toepler 2006. "Foundations and the challenge of legitimacy in comparative perspective". In K. Prewitt, M. Dogan, S. Heydemann & S. Toepler (eds), *The Legitimacy of Philanthropic Foundations*. New York: Russell Sage.

Higgins, A. 2018. "Inside the self-serving world of wealthy do-gooders". *Bright Magazine*, 31 August.

Hill, L. & A. Redmond 2020. "Hundreds of arts organisations rejected for emergency funding". Arts Professional, 13 October. https://www.artsprofessional.co.uk/news/hundreds-arts-organisations-rejected-emergency-funding.

Himmelfarb, G. 1995. *The Demoralization of Society: From Victorian Virtues to Modern Values*. New York: Vintage.

Hirsch, J. 2011. "The Rockefeller University Hospital 1910–2010: creating the science of medicine". *Perspectives in Biology and Medicine* 54(3): 273–303.

HMRC 2019. *UK Charity Tax Relief Statistics 1990–91 to 2018–2019*. London: HM Revenue & Customs. https://assets.publishing.service.gov.uk/government/uploads/system/uploads/attachment_data/file/811710/UK_Charity_Tax_Relief_Statistics_Commentary.pdf.

Ho, S. 2019. "Bill, Melinda Gates unfazed by criticism of wealthy giving." *Associated Press*, 12 February. https://apnews.com/article/melinda-gates-north-america-bill-and-melinda-gates-foundation-us-news-ap-top-news-b1279711ee234b3ab3916d292d262643.

Hobbes, M. 2014. "Stop trying to save the world". *New Republic*, 17 November.

Hobhouse, A. 1880. *The Dead Hand: Addresses on the Subject of Endowments and Settlements of Property*. London: Spottiswoode.

Horvath, A. & W. Powell 2016. "Contributary or disruptive? Do new forms of philanthropy erode democracy?" In R. Reich, C. Cordelli & L. Bernholz (eds), *Philanthropy in Democratic Societies: History, Institutions, Values*. Chicago: University of Chicago Press.

IFS 2019. *2019 Annual Report on Education Spending in England*. Institute for Fiscal Studies. https://www.ifs.org.uk/publications/14369.

Ilchman, W., S. Katz & W. Queen III (eds) 1998. *Philanthropy in the World's Traditions*. Bloomington: Indiana University Press.

Inside Philanthropy 2020. *Philanthropy Awards 2020*. https://www.insidephilanthropy.com/home/2020/philanthropy-awards.

Irwin, K. & C. Horne 2013. "A normative explanation of antisocial punishment". *Social Science Research* 42: 562–70.

Jeffreys, E. 2016. "Elite philanthropy in China and America: the disciplining and self-discipline of wealth". In D. Bray & E. Jeffreys (eds), *New Mentalities of Government in China*. Abingdon: Routledge.

Jenkins, S. 2020. "We can't leave it to billionaires like Bezos and Bloomberg to solve the world's problems". *The Guardian*, 21 February.

Johnson, J. 2017. *Funding Feminism: Monied Women, Philanthropy and the Women's Movement 1870–1967*. Chapel Hill: University of North Carolina Press.

Jordan, W. 1959. *Philanthropy in England 1480–1660: A Study of the Changing Pattern of English Social Aspirations*. London: George Allen & Unwin.

Karl, B. & S. Katz 1981. "The American private philanthropic foundation and the public sphere 1890–1930". *Minerva* 19(2): 236–69.

Karl, B. & S. Katz 1987. "Foundations and ruling class elites". *Daedalus* 116(1): 1–40.

Karlan, D. & J. List 2007. "Does price matter in charitable giving? Evidence from a large-scale natural field experiment". *American Economic Review* 97(5): 174–9.

Karlan, D. & D. Wood 2017. "The effect of effectiveness: donor response to aid effectiveness in a direct mail fundraising experiment". *Journal of Public Economics* 66: 1–8.

Keidan, C. 2021. "A mirror to our field: my five-point plan for the future of philanthropy". *Alliance Magazine*, 21 January. https://www.alliancemagazine.org/blog/a-mirror-to-our-field-my-five-point-plan-for-the-future-of-philanthropy/.

Kendall, J. and M. Knapp 1996. *The Voluntary Sector in the UK*. Manchester: Manchester University Press.

Kings Court Trust 2017. *Passing on the Pounds: The Rise of the UK's Inheritance Economy*. Bristol: Centre for Economics and Business Research.

Kozol, J. 2012. *Savage Inequalities: Children in America's Schools*. New York: HarperPerennial.

Krass, P. 2002. *Carnegie*. Hoboken, NJ: Wiley.

Kulish, N. 2020. "Giving billions fast, MacKenzie Scott upends philanthropy". *New York Times*, 20 December. https://www.nytimes.com/2020/12/20/business/mackenzie-scott-philanthropy.html.

Lafortune, J., J. Rothstein & D. Schanzenbach 2018. "School finance reform and the distribution of student achievement". *American Economic Journal: Applied Economics* 10(2): 1–26.

Lagemann, E. & J. de Forest 2007. "What might Andrew Carnegie want to tell Bill Gates?" In R. Bacchetti & T. Ehrlich (eds), *Reconnecting Education and Foundations: Turning Good Intentions into Educational Capital*. San Francisco: Jossey Bass.

LaMarche, G. 2020. "Big philanthropy faces a reckoning, too." *The Nation*, 30 April. https://www.thenation.com/article/politics/philanthropy-politics-billionaires/.

Lansley, S. 2006. *Rich Britain: The Rise and Rise of the New Super-Wealthy*. London: Politicos.

Layton, M. 2015. "The influence of fiscal incentives on philanthropy across nations". In P. Wiepking & F. Handy (eds), *The Palgrave Handbook of Global Philanthropy*. London: Palgrave Macmillan.

Lenkowsky, L. 2009. "Lights, camera, generosity". *Chronicle of Philanthropy*, 18 June. https://www.philanthropy.com/article/lights-camera-generosity.

Lenkowsky, L. 2012. "Realistic film on philanthropy doesn't get box office appeal". *Chronicle of Philanthropy*, 28 October. https://www.philanthropy.com/article/realistic-story-of-philanthropy-is-ho-hum-to-americans.

Lenkowsky, L. 2020. "'Philanthropy' review: thanks to the givers". *Wall Street Journal*, 24 November.

Leonhard, D. 2008. "What makes people give?" *New York Times*, 9 March. https://www.nytimes.com/2008/03/09/magazine/09Psychology-t.html.

Levere, A. & D. Nissenbaum 2021. "Investors trust the companies they support: here's how grant makers can do the same". *Chronicle of Philanthropy*, 12 January. https://www.philanthropy.com/article/investors-trust-the-companies-they-support-heres-how-grant-makers-can-do-the-same?cid2=gen_login_refresh&cid=gen_sign_in.

Levy, R. 2009. *Yours for the Asking: An Indispensable Guide to Fundraising and Management*. Hoboken, NJ: John Wiley and Sons.

Lewis, N. 2006. "Joan Weill's support of dance company marked by a personal touch". *Chronicle of Philanthropy*, 10 December.

Lewis, P. 2019. "Exploring the rise of populism: 'It pops up in unexpected places'". *The Guardian*, 22 June.

Lloyd, S. 2002. "Pleasing spectacles and elegant dinners: conviviality, benevolence, and charity anniversaries in eighteenth-century London". *The Journal of British Studies* 41(1): 23–57.

Low, J. 2012. "Rising to the challenges of philanthropy". *Huffington Post* blog, 22 August. https://www.huffingtonpost.co.uk/john-low/philanthropy-rising-to-the-challenges.

Luks, A. 1988. "Doing good: helpers high". *Psychology Today* 22(10): 39–42.

MacAskill, W. 2015. *Doing Good Better: Effective Altruism and a Radical New Way to Make a Difference*. London: Guardian/Faber.

MacInnis, C. & G. Hodson 2017. "It ain't easy eating greens: evidence of bias toward vegetarians and vegans from both source and target". *Group Processes & Intergroup Relations* 20: 721–44.

MacQuillin, I. 2020. "Who made us the philanthropy police?" *Third Sector*, 5 May. https://www.thirdsector.co.uk/ian-macquillin-made-us-philanthropy-police/fundraising/article/1682309.

Malins, J. 1895. *The Ambulance Down in the Valley*. https://tonycooke.org/stories-and-illustrations/ambulance-valley/.

Mandeville, B. 1714. *The Fable of the Bees*. London: J. Tonson.

Martin, M. 1994. *Virtuous Giving: Philanthropy, Voluntary Service and Caring*. Bloomington: Indiana University Press.

Mathiason, N. 2006. "Big game hunter aims for pot luck at the garden centre". *The Observer*, 5 March.

Matthews, D. 2019. "Philanthropy is undergoing a massive backlash: a new book argues it's gone too far". *Vox*, 27 May.

Mauss, M. [1950] 2002. *The Gift*. London: Routledge.

McCully, G. 2012. "What is – and is not – philanthropy?" Conversations on Philanthropy discussion paper, *Academia*. https://www.academia.edu/36978441/What_Is_and_Is_Not_Philanthropy_docx?email_work_card=view-paper.

McGoey, L. 2015. *No Such Thing as a Free Gift: The Gates Foundation and the Price of Philanthropy*. London: Verso.

Metcalf, T. 2020. "Jeff Bezos donating $10 billion barely dents his surging fortune". *Bloomberg*, 18 February. https://www.bloomberg.com/news/articles/2020–02–18/jeff-bezos-donating-10-billion-barely-dents-his-surging-fortune.

Mill, J. 1848. *Principles of Political Economy*. https://www.econlib.org/library/Mill/mlP.html.

Millionaires for Humanity 2020. "Millionaires for Humanity sign on letter". https://www.millionairesforhumanity.com.

Minson, J. & B. Monin 2012. "Do-gooder derogation: disparaging morally motivated minorities to defuse anticipated reproach". *Social Psychological and Personality Science* 3(2): 200–7.

Monin, B. 2007. "Holier than me? Threatening social comparison in the moral domain". *Revue Internationale de Psychologie Sociale* 20(1): 53–68.

Monin, B., P. Sawyer & M. Marquez 2008. "The rejection of moral rebels: resenting those who do the right thing". *Journal of Personality and Social Psychology* 95: 76–93.

Moody, M. & B. Breeze (eds) 2016. *The Philanthropy Reader*. Abingdon: Routledge.

Moody, M. & T. Martin 2020. "Increasing critiques of (big) philanthropy". In *11 Trends in Philanthropy for 2020*. Grand Rapids, MI: Dorothy A. Johnson Center for Philanthropy, Grand Valley State University.

Moore, J. 2020. "MacKenzie Scott's billionaire philanthropy proves we need a proper taxation system". *Independent*, 17 December. https://www.independent.co.uk/voices/mackenzie-scott-philanthropy-taxation-b1775572.html.

Morgridge, C. 2015. *Every Gift Matters: How Your Passion Can Change the World*. Austin, TX: Greenleaf.

Moyo, D. 2010. *Dead Aid: Why Aid Is Not Working and How There Is Another Way for Africa*. London: Penguin.

Murphy, E. 2018. *The Politics of Compassion: The Challenge to Care for the Stranger*. London: Rowman & Littlefield.

Nasaw, D. 2016. "Looking the Carnegie gift horse in the mouth: the 19th-century critique of big philanthropy". *Slate*, 10 November. https://slate.com/news-and-politics/2006/11/the-19th-century-critique-of-big-philanthropy.html.

Newman, G. & D. Cain 2014. "Tainted altruism: when doing some good is evaluated as worse than doing no good at all". *Psychological Science* 25(3): 648–55.

Nightingale, B. 1973. *Charities*. London: Allen Lane.

O'Clery, C. 2007. *The Billionaire Who Wasn't: How Chuck Feeney Secretly Made and Gave Away a Fortune*. New York: PublicAffairs.

Odendahl, T. 1990. *Charity Begins at Home: Generosity and Self-interest among the Philanthropic Elite*. New York: Basic Books.

O'Loughlin, E. & M. Zaveri 2020. "Irish return an old favor: helping native Americans battling the virus". *New York Times*, 5 May.

Olson, M. 1965. *The Logic of Collective Action: Public Goods and the Theory of Groups*. Cambridge, MA: Harvard University Press.

Omidyar Network, n.d. "Reimagining capitalism". Omidyar Network. https://omidyar.com/reimagining-capitalism/.

Osteen, M. 2002. (ed.) *The Question of the Gift: Essays Across Disciplines*. New York: Routledge.

Ostrander, S. 2007. "Ostrander's response to Schervish". *Nonprofit and Voluntary Sector Quarterly* 36(2): 380–89.

Ostrander, S. & P. Schervish 1990. "Giving and getting: philanthropy as a social relation". In J. Til (ed.), *Critical Issues in American Philanthropy*. San Francisco: Jossey-Bass.

Ostrower, F. 1995. *Why the Wealthy Give: The Culture of Elite Philanthropy*. Princeton, NJ: Princeton University Press.

Owen, D. 1964. *English Philanthropy 1660–1960*. Cambridge, MA: Harvard University Press.

Oxfam 2017. "An economy for the 99%". Oxfam briefing paper, January.

Parks, C. & A. Stone 2010. "The desire to expel unselfish members from the group". *Journal of Personality and Social Psychology* 99(2): 303–10.

Parnell, S. 2019. "Plutocrats or pluralists?" *Philanthropy*, Spring. https://www.philanthropyroundtable.org/philanthropy-magazine/article/plutocrats-or-pluralists.

Parnell, S. & D. Callahan 2017. "Does big philanthropy threaten democracy?" *Inside Philanthropy*, 11 September.

Participant, n.d. Participant website. https://participant.com/about-us.

Payton, R. & M. Moody 2008. *Understanding Philanthropy: Its Meaning and Mission*. Bloomington: Indiana University Press.

Pearce, A., n.d. "Determining the number: Norman Borlaug – the green revolution". *Scienceheroes*. http://www.scienceheroes.com/index.php?option=com_content&view=article&id=68&Itemid=116.

Pegram, G. 2017. "NSPCC's Full Stop campaign – a fundraising triumph". Showcase of Fundraising Innovation and Inspiration, 29 November. https://sofii.org/article/nspccs-full-stop-campaign-part-two.

Pevnick, R. 2016. "Philanthropy and democratic ideals". In R. Reich, C. Cordelli & L. Bernholz (eds), *Philanthropy in Democratic Societies: History, Institutions, Values*. Chicago: University of Chicago Press.

Pickering, A. 2016. "Philanthropic power: the awkward consequence of pluralism". *Alliance Magazine*, 6 September. https://www.alliancemagazine.org/feature/philanthropic-power-the-awkward-consequence-of-pluralism/.

Piketty, T. 2014. *Capital in the Twenty-First Century*. Cambridge, MA: Harvard University Press.

Piketty, T., E. Saez & G. Zucman 2016. "Distributional national accounts: methods and estimates for the United States". National Bureau of Economic Research Working Paper series. Cambridge, MA: NBER.

Piper, K. 2019. "The charitable deduction is mostly for the rich: a new study argues that's by design". *Vox*, 3 September. https://www.vox.com/future-perfect/2019/9/3/20840955/charitable-deduction-tax-rich-billionaire-philanthropy.

Pleasant, A. & P. Barclay 2018. "Why hate the good guy? Antisocial punishment of high cooperators is greater when people compete to be chosen". *Psychological Science* 29(6): 868–76.

Porter, M. & M. Kramer 2002. "The competitive advantage of corporate philanthropy". *Harvard Business Review* 80: 56–69.

Prewitt, K. 2009. "Foreword: social science and philanthropic studies". In D. Hammack & S. Heydemann (eds), *Globalization, Philanthropy and Civil Society: Projecting Institutional Logics Abroad*. Bloomington: Indiana University Press.

Prochaska, F. 1990. "Philanthropy". In F. Thompson (ed.), *The Cambridge Social History of Britain 1750–1950*. Cambridge: Cambridge University Press.

Prochaska, F. 2002. *Schools of Citizenship: Charity and Civic Virtue*. London: Civitas.

Prochaska, F. 2014. "The state of charity". Charity Commission Lecture 2014. https://assets. publishing.service.gov.uk/government/uploads/system/uploads/attachment_data/file/ 356191/Lecture_-_Dr_Frank_Prochaska.pdf.

Putnam, R. 1993. *Making Democracy Work: Civic Traditions in Modern Italy*. Princeton, NJ: Princeton University Press.

Putnam, R. 2000. *Bowling Alone: The Collapse and Revival of American Community*. New York: Simon & Schuster.

Putnam-Walkerly, K. 2020. *Delusional Altruism: Why Philanthropists Fail to Achieve Change and What They Can Do to Transform Giving*. Hoboken, NJ: Wiley.

Reich, R. 2005. "A failure of philanthropy". *Stanford Social Innovation Review* 2: 24–33.

Reich, R. 2013. "Philanthropy and caring for the needs of strangers". *Social Research: An International Quarterly* 80(2): 517–38.

Reich, R. 2014. "Gift giving and philanthropy in market democracy". *Critical Review* 26(3–4): 408–22.

Reich, R. 2016. "Repugnant to the whole idea of democracy? On the role of foundations in democratic societies". *PS: Political Science & Politics* 49(3): 466–71.

Reich, R. 2018. *Just Giving: Why Philanthropy Is Failing Democracy and How It Can Do Better*. Princeton, NJ: Princeton University Press.

Reich, R., C. Cordelli & L. Bernholz 2016. *Philanthropy in Democratic Societies: History, Institutions, Values*. Chicago: University of Chicago Press.

Rhodes, C. & P. Bloom 2018. "The trouble with charitable billionaires". *The Guardian*, 24 May.

Richards, N. 2017. "Big bets and spending down: the Poola Foundation". *Philanthropy Australia*, October. https://www.philanthropy.org.au/stories-poola-foundation.

Robinson, S. 1892. *Yarns, Being Sundry Reminiscences*. London: London Printing Alliance.

Rockefeller, J. [1908] 2016. "The difficult art of giving". In M. Moody & B. Breeze (eds), *The Philanthropy Reader*. London: Routledge.

Rockefeller University, n.d. "Our history". https://www.rockefeller.edu/about/history/.

Rodgers, B. 1949. *Cloak of Charity: Studies in Eighteenth-Century Philanthropy*. London: Methuen.

Rogers, R. 2012. "The hidden dangers of million-dollar donations". *Washington Post*, 1 January.

Rooney, P. 2018. "The growth in total household giving is camouflaging a decline in giving by small and medium donors: what can we do about it?" *Nonprofit Quarterly*, Fall edition.

Rooney, P. 2019. "Where have all the donors gone? The continued decline of the small donor and the growth of megadonors". *Nonprofit Quarterly*, Winter edition.

Rosenthal, J. 1972. *The Purchase of Paradise: Gift Giving and the Aristocracy 1307–1485*. London: Routledge & Kegan Paul.

Rowntree, J. 1904. The Founder's Memorandum. https://www.jrrt.org.uk/wp-content/ uploads/2019/08/The-Founders-1904-Memorandum.pdf.

RPA 2020. "Strategic time horizons: a global snapshot of foundation approaches". Rockefeller Philanthropy Advisors and NORC at the University of Chicago; https://www.rockpa. org/wp-content/uploads/2020/01/Strategic-Time-Horizons-a-Global-Snapshot-of-Foundation-Approaches_FNL.pdf.

Rymer, B. 2018. "The radical who wasn't: a review of *Winners Take All: The Elite Charade of Changing the World*". FundraisingVoices blog. https://fundraisingvoices.wordpress.com/ 2018/10/16/the-radical-who-wasnt-a-review-of-winners-take-all-the-elite-charade-of-changing-the-world/.

Salamon, L. 1987. "Partners in public service: the scope and theory of government-nonprofit relations". In W. Powell (ed.) *The Nonprofit Sector: A Research Handbook*. New Haven, CT: Yale University Press.

Sanders, L. 2020. "The difference between what Republicans and Democrats believe to be true about COVID-19". YouGov, 26 May. https://today.yougov.com/topics/politics/articles-reports/2020/05/26/republicans-democrats-misinformation.

Schervish, P. 1994a. "The moral biographies of the wealthy and the cultural scripture of wealth". In P. Schervish (ed.), *Wealth in Western Thought: The Case For and Against Riches*. Westport, CT: Praeger.

Schervish, P. 1994b. "The sound of one hand clapping: the case for and against anonymous giving". *Voluntas* 5(1): 1–26.

Schervish, P. 2000. "The spiritual horizons of philanthropy: new directions for money and motives". *New Directions for Philanthropic Fundraising* 29: 17–31.

Schervish, P. 2006. "Philanthropy's Janus-faced potential: the dialectic of care and negligence donors face". In W. Damon & S. Verducci (eds), *Taking Philanthropy Seriously: Beyond Noble Intentions to Responsible Giving*. Bloomington: Indiana University Press.

Schervish, P. 2007. "Why the wealthy give: factors which mobilise philanthropy among high net-worth individuals". In A. Sargeant & W. Wymer Jr (eds), *The Routledge Companion to Nonprofit Marketing*. London: Routledge.

Schervish, P. 2018. "Revisiting 'Disciples or Demigods': the case for and against anonymous giving now and a quarter century ago". *HistPhil*, 11 September.

Schiller, A. 2015. "The end of 'Parks and Recreation' is sad for philanthropy". *Chronicle of Philanthropy*, 27 February.

Schindler, S. 2007a. "Pensions for America's educators: TIAA-CREF, one of the wealthiest pension funds in the world". In J. Fleishman, J. Kohler & S. Schindler (eds), *Casebook for the Foundation: A Great America Secret*. New York: PublicAffairs.

Schindler, S. 2007b. "Preventing crashes on America's highways". In J. Fleishman, J. Kohler & S. Schindler (eds), *Casebook for the Foundation: A Great America Secret*. New York: PublicAffairs.

SDG Philanthropy Platform, n.d. "Engaging philanthropy in response to COVID-19 and the SDGs". https://www.sdgphilanthropy.org.

Seibert, K. 2017. "Funding the challenge: the philanthropy issue". *The Australian*, 15 September.

Shaw, G. 1901. *Socialism for Millionaires*. London: Fabian Society.

Shirley, S. 2010. *Desert Island Discs*. First broadcast on BBC Radio 4, 23 May.

Sievers, B. 2004. "Philanthropy's blindspots". In P. Karoff (ed.), *Just Money: A Critique of Contemporary American Philanthropy*. Boston, MA: The Philanthropic Initiative, Inc.

Sievers, B. 2010. "Philanthropy's role in liberal democracy". *Journal of Speculative Philosophy* 24(4): 380–98.

Silber, I. 1998. "Modern philanthropy: reassessing the viability of a Maussian perspective". In W. James & N. Allen (eds), *Marcel Mauss: A Centenary Tribute*. Oxford: Berghahn.

Silber, I. 2001. "Philanthropy and civil society: the gift relationship in an era of 'loose' solidarities". In W. James & N. Allen (eds), *Marcel Mauss: A Centenary Tribute*. Oxford: Berghahn.

Singer, A. 2008. *Charity in Islamic Societies*. Cambridge: Cambridge University Press.

Singer, P. 2013. "Good charity, bad charity". *New York Times*, 10 August. https://www.nytimes.com/2013/08/11/opinion/sunday/good-charity-bad-charity.html.

Singer, P. 2015. *The Most Good You Can Do: How Effective Altruism Is Changing Ideas about Living Ethically*. New Haven, CT: Yale University Press.

Smith, C. & H. Davidson 2014. *The Paradox of Generosity: Giving We Receive, Grasping We Lose*. Oxford: Oxford University Press.

Smith, J. 2001. "The evolving role of American foundations". In C. Clotfelter & T. Ehrlick (eds), *Philanthropy and the Nonprofit Sector in a Changing America*. Bloomington: Indiana University Press.

Smith, J. 2006. "In search of an ethic of giving". In W. Damon & S. Verducci (eds), *Taking Philanthropy Seriously: Beyond Noble Intentions to Responsible Giving*. Bloomington: Indiana University Press.

Snapes, L. 2020. "Dolly Parton partly funded Moderna Covid vaccine research". *The Guardian*, 17 November. https://amp.theguardian.com/music/2020/nov/17/dolly-parton-partly-funded-moderna-covid-vaccine-research?CMP=share_btn_tw&__twitter_impression=true.

Soskis, B. 2014. "The importance of criticising philanthropy". *The Atlantic*, 12 May.

Soskis, B. 2018. "A new critique raises a question: can the rich learn how to save the world?" *Chronicle of Philanthropy*, 28 August.

Stiglitz, J. 2018. "Meet the 'change agents' who are enabling inequality". *New York Times*, 20 August.

Sulek, M. 2010a. "On the modern meaning of philanthropy". *Nonprofit and Voluntary Sector Quarterly* 39(2): 193–212.

Sulek, M. 2010b. "On the classical meaning of *philanthropia*". *Nonprofit and Voluntary Sector Quarterly* 39(3): 385–408.

Tasimi, A., A. Dominguez & K. Wynn 2015. "Do-gooder derogation in children: the social costs of generosity". *Frontiers in Psychology* 6, article 1036.

Tierney, T. & J. Fleishman 2011. *Give Smart: Philanthropy that Gets Results.* New York: Public Affairs.

Time 2005. "TIME names Bono, Bill and Melinda Gates Persons of Year". *Time Magazine*, 19 December.

Times, The. 1907. "Mr. Rockefeller's Gift for Education". *The Times*, 8 February.

Tocqueville, A. de. 1838. *Democracy in America*. New York: G. Dearborn & Co.

Tompkins-Stange, M. 2016. *Policy Patrons: Philanthropy, Education Reform, and the Politics of Influence*. Cambridge, MA: Harvard University Press.

Toynbee, P. & D. Walker 2008. *Unjust Rewards: Exposing Greed and Inequality in Britain Today*. London: Granta.

Trust-Based Philanthropy Project. 2021. "Trust-based philanthropy: an overview". https://trustbasedphilanthropy.org/resources-articles/tbp-overview.

Vallely, P. 2020. "How philanthropy benefits the super-rich". *The Guardian*, 8 September. https://www.theguardian.com/society/2020/sep/08/how-philanthropy-benefits-the-super-rich.

Van Til, J. 1988. *Mapping the Voluntary Sector: Volunteerism in a Changing Social Economy*. New York: Foundation Center.

Van Til, J. 1990. "Defining philanthropy". In J. Van Til *et al.* (eds), *Critical Issues in American Philanthropy: Strengthening Theory and Practice*. San Francisco: Jossey-Bass.

Veblen, T. 1994 [1899]. *The Theory of the Leisure Class*. New York: Dover.

Villanueva, E. 2018. *Decolonizing Wealth: Indigenous Wisdom to Heal Divides and Restore Balance*. San Francisco: Berrett-Koehler.

Villanueva, E. 2020. "MacKenzie Scott's philanthropy is admirable: but why is it possible?" *Washington Post*, 22 December. https://www.washingtonpost.com/opinions/2020/12/22/mackenzie-scott-philanthropy-wealth/.

Voriseck, D. & S. Yu 2020. "Understanding the cost of achieving the sustainable development goals". Policy Research Working Paper 9146. Equitable Growth, Finance and Institutions Practice Group, World Bank.

Wakabayashi, D., D. Alba & M. Tracy 2020. "Bill Gates, at odds with Trump on virus, becomes a right-wing target". *New York Times*, 17 April. https://www.nytimes.com/2020/04/17/technology/bill-gates-virus-conspiracy-theories.html.

Wakefield, J. 2020. "How Bill Gates became the voodoo doll of Covid conspiracies". *BBC News*, 7 June. https://www.bbc.co.uk/news/technology-52833706.

Waldinger, R. 2015. "What makes a good life?". *Daily Good*. https://ecole-commercer.com/IMG/pdf/80_years_study_hapiness_harvard.pdf.

Walker, D. 2020. "A lesson on philanthropy from Martin Luther King Jr". *Time Magazine*, 20 February. https://time.com/5786562/darren-walker-philanthropy-mlk-jr/.

Walker, D., n.d. "Profile of Darren Walker". Council for Inclusive Capitalism. https://www.inclusivecapitalism.com/member/darren-walker/.

Weale, A. 2018. *The Will of the People: A Modern Myth*. Cambridge: Polity.

Weisbrod, B. 1986. "Toward a theory of the voluntary sector in a three-sector economy". In S. Rose-Ackerman (ed.), *The Economics of Nonprofit Institutions: Studies in Structure and Policy*. Oxford: Oxford University Press.

Weisbrod, B. 1988. *The Nonprofit Economy*. Cambridge, MA: Harvard University Press.

Whitaker, B. 1974a. *The Foundations: An Anatomy of Philanthropy and Society*. London: Eyre Methuen.

Whitaker, B. 1974b. "One man's philanthropy is another man's tax burden". *The Times*, 12 March.

Wiepking, P. & F. Handy (eds) 2015. *The Palgrave Handbook of Global Philanthropy*. London: Palgrave Macmillan.

Williams, R. 2020. "It is time to act: together". *Alliance* blog, 27 January. https://www.alliancemagazine.org/blog/it-is-time-to-act-together/.

Williams, Z. 2011. "Be a real titan philanthropist: and close your hedge fund". *The Guardian*, 8 June.

Wolpert, J. 2006. "Redistributional effects of America's private foundations". In K. Prewitt, M. Dogan, S. Heydemann & S. Toepler (eds), *The Legitimacy of Philanthropic Foundations: United States and European Perspectives*. New York: Russell Sage Foundation.

Wood Foundation 2019. "Anniversary of Lady Helen Parking Centre". https://www.thewoodfoundation.org.uk/anniversary-of-lady-helen-parking-centre/.

World Food Programme, n.d. "Contributions to WFP in 2020". https://www.wfp.org/funding/2020.

Wyatt, E. 2006. "Los Angeles Opera is given $6 million for a 'Ring' Cycle". *New York Times*, 7 September.

Ylvisaker, P. 2008. "The spirit of philanthropy and the soul of those who manage it". In A. Kass (ed.), *Giving Well, Doing Good: Readings for Thoughtful Philanthropists*. Bloomington: Indiana University Press.

Zinsmeister, K. 2016. "12 common criticisms of philanthropy: and some answers". *Stanford Social Innovation Review*, 17 May.

Zitelman, R. 2020. "Are rich philanthropists like Bill Gates the real culprits?" *Forbes*, 11 May. https://www.forbes.com/sites/rainerzitelmann/2020/05/11/are-rich-philanthropists-like-bill-gates-the-real-culprits/#68d3dd6f16e0.

Zuckerberg, M. & P. Chan 2015. "Letter to Max". Chan Zuckerberg Initiative, 1 December. https://chanzuckerberg.com/about/letter-to-max/.

Zunz, O. 2011. *Philanthropy in America: A History*. Princeton, NJ: Princeton University Press.

INDEX